# the Two Burner Gourmet

by
Terry L. Searfoss

# The Cookbook for Cooking Far from Home

# Dedication

To my father, Ernest R., who built me my first sailboat so I could learn to appreciate the forces of nature...

To my mother, Doris, who taught me how to cook so I might share the bounty of this good earth with others...

To my parents, who have given me great joy and happiness all these years, I dedicate this book to you. And I hope that in some small way it conveys my love for you. Thank you for your support.

# Acknowledgments

If you think this book is really really great, I want you to know, I did it all by myself!

If you think this book really really stinks! I think you should know the names of all the people responsible...

Cause I's so bad with wurds I kneets lotts help from **Kathryn Reer, Sherry Ortman, Ann Schneider, Jan Nash, Roger Moiles,** and **Linda Grindahl** too mack sure I spell wright.

At the Review Magazine it was **Matt Kackmeister** and **Kerri Ramirez** who helped me come up with the final format and choose the type styles for this little project. And my thanks to **Bob Martin** who let me play around with all that expensive equipment.

Then there is **Lori Woodruff** at L.J. Graphics in Bridgeport. This poor innocent child had to put up with yours truly, while she checked and re-checked then type-set every single word in this book.

And there's **Gerd Veigel,** who stayed at home nights to do my German translations and **Irene Silva-Huerta** for the Spanish.

I'd like to thank **Bob Grindahl** for letting some of his vacation slides be seen in public with mine. And to **Harry Stuart** over at Spence and Associates, who had the skill & know how to pull them all together as one.

And finally, a play is only as good as its' actors. So as the curtain goes up, I'd like to introduce my little cast of characters...

On my old boat RESISTANCE, there was **Tony Asperger, Denny & Gail Moore,** and **Jim Castor.** On **Ed Kurth's** boat BAY MUSIC, **Dennis Maher, Doug Moiles, Craig Hodnet, Paul Markey, Roger Moiles, Larry Morley** and **John Kohut. Ron Tucker** and **Bill Schreiner** on DECADENCE. On **Mark Zaranski's** BONZAI DRAGON, **Lisa Zaranski, Bill Harper, Bill Jenkins, Eric Coffin,** and **Greg Bull.** On FANTASIA it was, and still is, **Les & Judy Schwab.** To **Doc, Phil, Nann,** and the whole **Noble clan** on the SARA-ANN...

Thanks mates, and take a bow, for one heck of a good show. (Too bad this is a book!)

# Table of Contents

ISBN 0-9643733-0-0

Photographic Credits
Wraparound Cover .... T.L. Searfoss
Back Insert ... Ed Kurth
Food, Sea and Landscape ... Bob Grindahl, Harry Stuart, & T.L. Searfoss

the Two Burner Gourmet
1800 Wilson Avenue
Saginaw, MI 48603

1-800-842-5539

Printed in the United States of America

First Edition / July 1991
Second Printing / August 1992
Third Printing / September 1994

# NOT JUST FOR BOATERS

This book is now in it's 3rd printing and since it's release in 1991, readers have mentioned that the techniques I use in this book for boaters, would also work for campers, hikers, and in RV's. Well, let the truth be known ... that's exactly where all the neat hints, tips, and tricks came from ... all my hiking and camping experiences. You see, I'm an old cub scout, boy scout, eagle scout, explorer, survival specialist, and camp counselor who taught outdoor cooking, backpacking, etc., etc..

Years later, when I got the opportunity to go sailing and took my vacations aboard a boat, I just applied all the stuff I did for provisioning and cooking while camping to boating.

I never ever thought I'd be writing a book about my experiences. I hated writing in school. I loathed English and composition classes so much that to further my education I went to a fine arts school and majored in painting. I'm one of those hippy dippy art students from the late 60's.

In fact, I really didn't even "write" this book. I just compiled some of the meal plans from those cruises, along with the shopping list and a few notes from my journals. The Two Burner Gourmet is just a well organized scrapbook.

Now, to keep all the hikers, campers, and all of you driving around in your RV's happy; Yes, I could have told stories and shown pictures about a bunch of geekie teenagers running around the backwoods in their cute little outfits, but I didn't think about it soon enough. The seeds for this book were planted, not back in my days of scouting, but when other boaters started asking me for copies of my recipes, meal plans, and my shopping list. Instead of running a copy machine into the ground, I decided to put it all in the form of a book. I just threw in my stories of high sea adventure as a little extra bonus.

Okay! I could have left out the stories and just given you a whole bunch of recipes, but you would never get to know and love the real me and to realize it doesn't take a genius or any special talent to cook some really great meals. I'm proof of that!

Like I remind people at my seminars, if I can prepare meals on a 25 foot sailboat, in a galley where I can't even stand up, you sure as hell can cook it at home, at a campsite, in a RV, at the cottage or for your hunting pals at the lodge.

Good Eating Wherever You Are ... Or Wherever You Go!

# Preface

*At last, the wind has finally subsided. The reef is out of the main. The storm jib has been replaced by the genoa, and the foul weather gear has been hung out to dry.*

*It's been one hell-of-a-night: caught out in the middle of the lake, sixty miles from nowhere, in 14 to 16 foot waves; battered by 30 to 50 knot winds; soaked to the bone by torrential rains. It was no Sunday picnic, to say the least. It was just one very cold, one very wet, one very uncomfortable evening. But now the nightmare is over. The sun's out and you're following a warm summer breeze over a gently rolling sea.*

*Exhausted from their ordeal, the crew is now basking in the warm afternoon sun, enjoying a well-deserved break. Everything may seem all "peaches and cream", but you're still faced with the formidable task of what to feed these champions of the sea.*

*Since the outbreak of the storm, the crew has only seen cold cereal and pop, if that, for breakfast, lunch and dinner. Now it's time for them to chow down. It's time to fill their bellies and lift their spirits with some dynamite vittles! Well, the last time I checked the charts, I didn't notice any McDonald's in these waters. And to my knowledge, the Coast Guard doesn't deliver pizza. Besides, the crew swears if you serve them one more tuna fish sandwich, they'll serve you to the sharks.*

Hopefully, you'll never have to survive such adverse weather conditions while sailing, but sooner or later, both novice and veteran yachtsmen alike will have to face the universal problem of what to feed a hungry crew after the first day of an extended cruise.

*Food, food, food! Who needs food? Boating is an adventure! A challenge! Man against the elements! It isn't a dinner party! If you want something to eat, open a can of sardines and throw them between a couple slices of stale, moldy bread. That'll tide you over until we reach port.*

Hey, I'm just as much of a gung-ho sailor as the next guy (if not more so), but I like to eat, and eat well! This isn't a two week survival course we're taking! It's our vacation! It's a time to relax and enjoy the pleasures of the open sea. To enjoy the serenity of remote and scenic anchorages. There's no reason on earth why we can't enjoy the delicate flavors of a plump chicken breast draped in a elegant lemon and wine sauce or feast on a thick, juicy sirloin steak, stuffed with oysters and Roquefort cheese, while we're on our boats. No reason at all! It just takes a little planning.

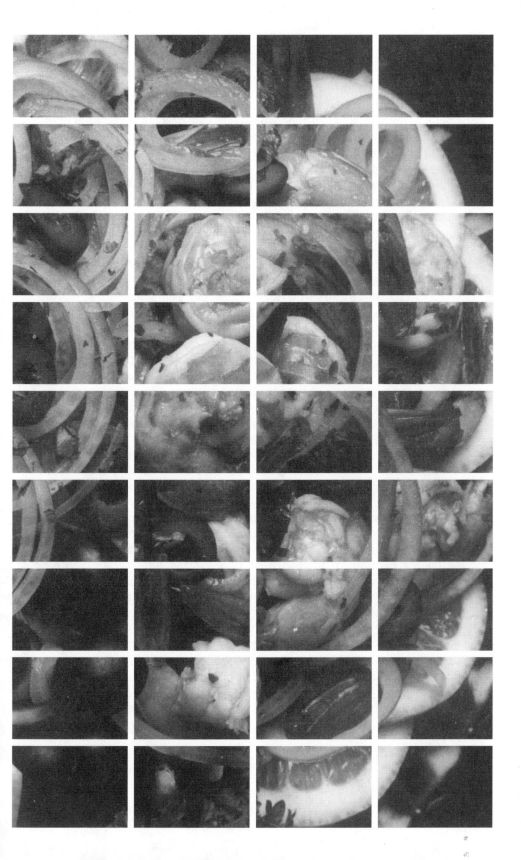

If you're like me and most of the other boaters around the Great Lakes, you can't wait until the waters are free of ice and the boat is in the water. Before THE final thaw, our crew spends every free moment of the winter months dreaming about and planning for the magical three weeks we'll spend, cruising the remote areas of the Lakes.

We study the charts and record possible ports of call. We plot tentative courses. We'll read all the periodicals and purchase the latest high-tech gizmos for fun and performance. We'll do everything humanly possible to prepare for our summer cruise, except one...plan our meals!

During the other forty-nine weeks of the year spent at home, most of us never have to worry about cooking a meal, let alone planning one. And for those of us who do, we generally aren't concerned about the technical aspects of preparing the food. Just look around your kitchen: a four burner stove with an oven and broiler, a microwave oven, food processor, blender, a 27-cubic-foot refrigerator, Mr. Coffee, toaster, garbage disposal, three cupboards filled with pots and pans, and an eighty-thousand-volume cookbook library. When you have to throw a meal together at the last minute, or you get the urge to play Julia Child for some dinner guests, no sweat! Everything is there!

Now picture yourself in the galley of a boat. What do you see? What's really there? A 9x9 inch stainless steel sink with NO running water. A 2-burner alcohol stove, that ISN'T gimballed. A sunken ICE chest. And that is it! Rather primitive, wouldn't you say? About the only thing you'd feel like creating in this environment is a peanut butter sandwich!

If you haven't already experienced it, you'll soon find out that there's a big difference between cooking at home and cooking at sea. But just because the facilities are limited, doesn't mean you have to settle for canned stews and tuna fish sandwiches for your entire vacation cruise. It just means that meals require a great deal of pre-planning and just a little understanding of what you can and cannot do with what's on board.

It's quite obvious that any boater in his right mind would prefer spending the off-season brushing up on the latest nautical advancements and techniques, rather than looking through a bunch of cookbooks, planning menus and compiling shopping lists for a three week cruise. I hate to break it to you, but if you want to eat, it has to be done by someone. *("Well great horny toads!")* Guess what? You're not in it alone! From now on, you'll be cruising with *the Two Burner* Gourmet.

# Forward

I'd like to make it perfectly clear, to all readers, right from the very start, that in no way do I subscribe to the philosophy that big boats are better than small boats or that small boats are more fun than big ones. That sailboats are more challenging than power or that power-boats are more exhilarating than sail. To me, all boats and boaters were and are created equal. And all can live and cruise in harmony.

I apologize to anyone who takes offense with the fact that most of the tales in this book are stories about sailing and that the techniques described here are designed to simplify and ease working conditions aboard a small vessel. It is not my intention to shun power-boaters or to exclude larger yachts.

In fact, the information revealed here is so basic that it can be applied to a variety of situations. There's guidance for a cook in a primitive cabin at a hunting camp; wisdom for a roamer out to see America in a RV; maybe you just need a efficient way to organize your weekly menus at home or you're looking for a few new and exciting recipes that are just easy to prepare. What this book is all about, is simply this: galley work in any restricted setting is hard work, a real challenge to the best of us, but it needn't take the wind out of anyone's sails.

In fact, in showing you how simple it can be to cook gourmet under such adverse conditions as cruising in a small sailboat, you'll find the underlying theme of this cookbook is enjoyment. So please, please, don't take anything I say too seriously. It could ruin all the fun.

## IT'S NOT FOR AN OCEAN CRUISE

If you're going on an ocean cruise and you're planning to take this book along, I hope it's for companionship and entertainment, and not as reference material. This book doesn't contain the latest tricks for turning the morning mist into milk for your cereal. Nor does it contain a section on the preparation of dried or pickled meats. This book was not written for those fortunate enough to actually fulfill the dream of every boater. . .to cruise around the world. That's a totally different ball game.

This cookbook is designed to help those of us who just want to drop out of the Old Rat Race for a relaxing few weeks' cruise. It's for families who just want to cruise up and down the coast for a little while. It's for adventurous friends who just want to do a little island hopping in search of quiet anchorages. In instances like these, the boat and her crew are never more than a few days' sail from a friendly port and fresh supplies. These are the boaters, the sailors, the yachters, this book was written for.

It was written to relieve the stress and the trauma; to remove the worry and the doubt; to vanquish the mental anxieties every person faces when saddled with the responsibility of planning, provisioning and cooking meals for a hungry crew aboard a boat far from home.

# Introduction

## I AM NOT A CHEF

To me, a chef is like one of those all-knowing, all-seeing, mystical figures we read about in children's fairy tale books. Someone, who, with the wave of a magical wand and the snap of the fingers, can transform an old tattered piece of shoe leather into a delicate entree, laced with a heavenly sauce.

I don't know how many of you believe that statement, but I do know that most of us have a great deal of respect for the skills and talents of the truly great chefs. And when we purchase a cookbook, we generally expect it to be written by a culinary wizard or someone equally qualified.

Well, before we go any further, let me tell you right here and now...I'm Not a Chef! Nor am I an assistant chef. In fact, I'm not even a short-order cook. I'm merely a loyal crew member, on one little old sailboat. It just happens that years ago, when nobody else would volunteer to do the cooking, instead of starving to death, I stepped forward to pitch in. That was back in 1974 and ever since then, I've been doing the cooking on just about every boat I've been on. Now, instead of being considered one of the best navigators around or one hell-of-a-helmsman or a top of the line sail trimmer, I'm renowned for my cooking.

## ANYBODY CAN COOK GOURMET

My previous description of a chef may have been a little more glamorous (or shall I say fictional) than it really is. But isn't that a part of the mystique that surrounds the great chefs of the world? That they can do what mere mortals can only dream about: Cook Gourmet!

I think I got that impression after looking at all those magnificent photos in all those fancy food magazines and expensive cookbooks. There it is, in full living color. Gourmet foods fit for a king. *Roast Quail with Sherry-Lime Sauce. Souffle'Benedetta. Oysters Tetrazzini. Pheasant Souvaroff. Torta Barozzi.* And all you have to do to recreate these masterpieces for your friends and family is follow the instructions. Instructions so elaborate, so complex, you had to be a rocket scientist to figure them out. When I finally did muster up enough courage to try something, I was devastated when the end product, my creation, didn't look anything like the mouth-watering temptation in the photo. After all the aggravation I went through; after all the time I spent preparing it and all the money I had invested in this meal, I couldn't just toss it in the garbage and order out for pizza. I had guests coming, and they'd be here in just twelve minutes. I had no choice. I had to serve what I had prepared. Then to my surprise, I discovered they loved it. Thought it was sensational. "Our compliments to the chef." To the Chef? I guess they didn't see the photo.

From this experience I learned a very important lesson. As bland as it may look, it's the taste, the full rounded flavors that satisfy the palate, not the presentation, the fine china and crystal (although that stuff is nice), that makes it Gourmet.

Just because we may not have the experience, the time or the facilities to prepare something gourmet like a Chicken Cannelloni Villa Cipriani or a Coq au Vin, doesn't mean we can't cook gourmet. A lot of the time, gourmet cooking is just a matter of knowing the right ingredients to add, that will transform the ordinary into the extraordinary. A couple drops of vanilla extract and a dash of nutmeg can really put a spark to mom's old French toast recipe. Try adding a touch of coffee liqueur to a creamy mushroom sauce. Sprinkle your pork chops with some garlic powder and a pinch of tarragon. And don't just grill a couple of steaks: create a memory by cutting a pocket in them and stuffing them with oysters, mushrooms, blue cheese and bacon, and then see what your guests have to say. Get the picture? You don't have to master a bunch of complicated techniques to create a masterpiece. Ya just gotta know what works with what and how much of it to use to Cook Gourmet!

And that's exactly the type of cooking you'll discover here in the world of _the Two Burner Gourmet._ We're not concerned with techniques, skills or equipment. Only the ingredients. The instructions are simple and straight to the point. Nothing fancy. In fact, the way I figure it, anybody who can use a measuring spoon, handle a little chopping and operate a can opener, can cook gourmet.

My philosophy and the motto for this book is simple:

**Chop-chop**
**Open a can**
**Throw it in a pan.**
**Sit back and relax**
**With a cocktail in hand.**

# FOOD FOR THOUGHT

Flip through a few pages of the book and you'll notice that *the Two Burner Gourmet* is more than just an assortment of recipes that can easily be prepared aboard a boat. It's a detailed, day-by-day, meal-by-meal, outline of exciting foods that you can prepare and serve while cruising and still enjoy the cruise.

In this book, I'm not trying to become the next Captain Bligh by telling you what you can and can't do, or when, or when not, to do it. What I am trying to do is show you the tried and true system I've used over the years to feed a bunch of hungry sailors. It's a seaworthy collection of fine vittles that can't be too bad, because I'm still around to tell the tales about it. Think about it like this, you're about to set sail on a difficult passage, through unfamiliar waters and I'm offering you the use of my charts and log. Of course, if you wish to chart another course, at least you'll know where the rocks and shoals are.

If you're going out for more than an overnight cruise, there are two very important facts to remember when planning meals. First, refrigeration on board a boat is not as good as it is at home. Foods will spoil faster. Secondly, some foods spoil faster than others. Therefore, plan to use easy spoilers like ground beef the first day, chicken and pork the second, and beef on the third day out. After that you can plan on using fully-cooked smoked meats, canned meats, pasta or freshly caught fish to sustain your diet. Even if you have an excellent refrigeration system on board, it's still a good idea to stay within the limits set forth here (unless you're fortunate enough to be on a large vessel with a large walk-in freezer).

# ORGANIZATION & PLANNING

A few years ago, I learned that organization and pre-planning are the key elements to keeping a crew well fed. I didn't pick this up because I was sailing with a very disciplined group of gentlemen. In fact they were quite the opposite. I learned it out of necessity. We were broke!

In the winter of 1980, a bunch of old sailing buddies and I got together and decided it was about time we went on our own, (guys only) two-week vacation cruise that summer. The only problem was, when it came around to the financial end of it, everybody was pretty well tapped-out. Before we could "really" start planning the trip, we needed a fairly good estimate of what it would cost.

Since we were ragbaggers and we weren't going to be in much of a hurry to get anywhere anyway, we could get by with a couple of tanks of gas at the max. There would also be dock and pump-out fees. These were standard charges; no problem figuring those out. Since each member of the cruise was responsible for his own liquid refreshments, there was nothing to figure there. That just left the cost of ice and food to calculate. The "bartender" of the group figured that to keep everything properly chilled to everyone's satisfaction, we'd require about 20 pounds of ice per day. Of course, he would be gracious enough to "donate" some for the meat and vegetable lockers. (I know what you're thinking and you're right. It was a continuous party.)

The final category, food, was left to me. "Thanks a lot, guys!" All the other calculations could be completed while everybody was looking over the charts, sipping beer and eating pretzels and popcorn! Two 12 gallon tanks of gas at $1.18 per gallon. Thirteen nights' dock fees at $12.50 each. Three pump-outs at $5.00. Twenty blocks of ice at a buck each. Those were the easy numbers to figure out. To estimate the food cost to any degree of accuracy, I had to figure out what we wanted to eat, establish some sort of menu, then add up the cost of all the ingredients.

*"Gollie gee willikers! We never had to do this before!"*

Well, we never had to start from scratch or pay full freight before either. It was always somebody else's boat.

We all agreed we weren't going to raid any home pantries for supplies. We might liberate a few teaspoons of spices along the way, but definitely no cans of ripe olives, jars of mustard, or bottles of soy sauce were to be requisitioned from any home. The cost of supplies for this trip was to be divided equally among all members of the cruise.

So, I started searching for recipes that I thought everybody would like. Since we would be tying up at public docks just about every night (and there's "always" a store within walking distance of a public dock), I really wasn't concerned about the spoilage factor on this particular cruise. So, after planning the menus, I arranged the meals in a palatable order to please the crew. Then I made up a shopping list of all the ingredients I needed: two 16-ounce cans of refried beans, one 4-pack of tapioca pudding, an 8-ounce package of elbow macaroni, ground turmeric, coffee, grapefruit juice, peanut butter. A quick trip to the grocery store to check the prices and I had a pretty good idea of what our food costs would be.

For the fresh food items we would purchase along the way, I simply figured the cost at about 25% more than they did at the highest-priced market in town. I would then record that figure next to the item on the final shopping list. If we discovered that, say the bananas, apples or filet mignon cost more than was originally estimated, we'd make the necessary adjustments to stay within our original budget.

All this figuring may seem like a lot of work, but rest assured it paid off quite handsomely for us later on, in both time and money. Look at it this way. There it was, the last week in February and we had a day-by-day outline of all our meals and a complete shopping list of all the food stocks we'd need for our two week cruise in July. Now all I had left to do was sit back and watch the newspapers for specials, use my coupons and guess what? By the first of June, I'd purchased all of our nonperishables and saved about $42 in the process. It may not sound like much now, but back then it represented two nights' dock fees, one pump-out, a case of beer, some ice, and three 1.7 ounce bottles of Captain Morgan.

Another advantage of planning meals and a shopping list ahead of time is you know exactly which spices to take along. There's nothing more frustrating than getting out there and discovering that the ground cumin you need for the Chicken Indienne is still back on the shelf at the grocery store. In my case, I found if I wanted to prepare the culinary masterpieces I had planned, I'd have to take along twelve different herbs and spices. There's no way I could justify carrying all those extra containers on board, when storage space was at such a premium.

The solution was simple enough. I'd take ONLY the amount I'd need. Not as individual spices, but *pre-packaged,* according to the dishes I'd be preparing. All the spices for ONE dish, in ONE package. I used to wrap them up in wax paper until I discovered those little zip lock plastic envelopes you find in hobby shops or office supply stores. I figure the only way *pre-packing* the spices could become a hassle was if I waited until the night before I was to leave on the cruise to do it.

In this particular situation, I had only eight or nine meals that required *pre-packaged* ingredients. So instead of doing them all at once, each morning while waiting to get into the shower, I'd get out the old measuring spoons and fill an envelope or two. If I found that I didn't have a particular spice, I'd ask around and borrow a teaspoon or two from a neighbor instead of running out and spending a buck-and-a-half on something I would never need again.

During the cruise I planned on purchasing our fresh foods daily. Regardless on how efficient the shipboard refrigeration and the cold storage units are, I still believe fresh is fresher straight from the market or butcher (you also get to meet some really neat people that way). When buying fresh supplies, I only get enough for us to reach the next port-of-call. It's a lot easier maintaining a fresh supply for a single day than it is for two or three days. Besides, if the crew wants to hit the local pizza joint or taco stand for dinner, I don't have to worry about anything spoiling. Just because we're organized, doesn't mean we can't be flexible!

It may seem like a lot of trouble to get organized, but it really isn't. The only things that involve a great deal of time are finding the appropriate recipes, assembling meal plans and then making out a shopping list. And if you happen to like what you see in *the Two Burner Gourmet,* then 80% of all that work has already been done for you.

# Chapter 1

## COOKWARE AND GALLEY EQUIPMENT

It doesn't matter whether it's a weeknight or weekend, when we head for the boat, we don't worry about who or what's cooking. We don't worry, because we don't cook. Of course we eat. We just don't cook. We'll either raid the refrigerators for leftovers, hit the nearest drive thru for burgers & fries, pitch in for a bucket of extra crispy, or just pig out on nacho chips and picante sauce. It may not be gourmet, but there's no cooking and no mess to clean up. Besides, we came out to sail, not feed our faces. If we want some real food, we can stop at the all night diner on our way home.

The point I'd like to make is, that unless you're actually living aboard a boat, there really isn't any reason to purchase a complete set of cookware and utensils just for the boat. And it doesn't make much sense to me to buy a bunch of stuff just for a two-week cruise, unless of course, you're filthy rich. Hey, call me Mr. Cheap Skate, but when we leave for our cruise, I shanghai everything I need from my kitchen. After all, who's going to be home to cook anyway?

But if you should decide to purchase a separate set of cookware for the boat (before some salesperson gets their hooks into you), let's take a look at what you'll actually need and use. Please excuse the appearance of some of the examples in the photos. They may not look pretty, but they've logged plenty of time at sea.

**#1) 6-quart Dutch Oven** - If I could have only one pot or pan on board a boat this would be it. (In fact many times it has been the only pan on board.) It can cook massive quantities of food for human consumption all at once, which fits so beautifully with my "chop chop, open a can, throw it all in the pan, sit back and relax with a cocktail in hand" style of cooking.

**#2 & #3) 10-inch Skillets** · I like to carry two skillets on board the boat. The one with the flared or sloped sides (#2) allows me to make omelets and flip foods while cooking. The second one with the straight sides (#3) prevents spills and overflows when cooking in deep oil or while preparing sauces.

**#4) 5-quart Saucepan or Pot** · For cooking soups, stew, pastas, or just for heating water. This one's an all-around utility pan. Don't even think about anything smaller. Big can do what little ones can, but little can't do what the big ones can. If you're under way and trying to cook with a smaller saucepan, you'll spend most of your time wiping up the spills.

**#5) Lids or Covers** · Lids are the most awkward little devils to store, so we don't want a whole bunch of them hanging around. If they weren't so valuable, I'd throw them all overboard. But we can't. So my best advice to you is to use pots and pans that can use the same size lids. In this example, I have 2 lids to cover 5 different pans.

**#6) 10" x 17" Griddle** · This will turn you into a short-order cook in no time: grilled sandwiches, flap jacks, eggs over easy, hash browns superb, French toast, double cheese burgers deluxe; in nothing flat. With such a large cooking area, not only can you prepare more food faster, but after you're done there's only one pan to clean. (Word of caution: refrain from cooking any hot dogs on the griddle while under way!)

Those are the basic pots and pans, I think, you'll need for any cruise. Now if you have additional storage available and you would like a few more modern conveniences on board, you might want to consider the following:

**#7) an Electric Tea Kettle** · This is the most fantastic appliance ever invented. It will boil 1½ quarts of water in just a couple of minutes. When we're in port I can fill all of our thermoses with hot water and have more than enough left over to do the dishes and clean up, all within 15 minutes, and never have to fire up the old stove.

**#8) an Electric Fry Pan** · When we're in port, I like doing the cooking out on the dock so I can do a little socializing with other boaters. Since most marinas now prohibit the use of small camp stoves and hibachis, I find my handy-dandy fry pan indispensable.

**#9) an Electric Toaster** · It's impossible to serve eggs for breakfast and not serve toast. It's just one of those things that will either make or break their day. And I, for one, am not going to stand around an open flame, toasting 8 pieces of bread all morning.

You will notice that I have not included a coffee pot amongst our boating cookware. The reason for this is the same reason I don't recommend cooking bacon on board a boat, it's an unnecessary pain in the butt. First of all, you only have two burners on which to prepare the meal and at some point, one of them has to boil water for clean up and whatever. If I boil clean water, I can use some of it to make tea, instant coffee, or hot cocoa and still have enough to use for clean up. If I brew a fresh pot of coffee, the only thing I can do with it is drink coffee. If your crew can function on something less than "REAL" coffee, you might want to try some of the coffee, tea and cocoa mixes on page 149. If they can not, by all means carry a coffee pot.

Although not normally classified as galley equipment, a couple of nice accessories to take along would be:

**A) a Pump Thermos** - These little gems are beautiful. They can hold hot water **HOT** for over 24 hours. Which means all I have to do is fill them with boiling water in the morning, then any time of day or night I need some hot hot water to make, say, a cup of hot cocoa, to make up a batch of instant rice or to revive a bunch of cooked pasta, it's there ready and waiting. (Tip: the ones with the thick glass insulated liners are the best.)

**B) Clip-On Fan** - You can call me anything you like to question my manhood or masculinity but I'll tell you this, a fan in the galley is the cat's behind. Not only does it keep the cook cool and refreshed but it helps ward off all those pesky flies that drive you crazy.

**C) Beverage Jug** - These are great for mixing up big batches of Kool-Aid, iced tea, lemonade and fruit punches for thirsty crews. I prefer the old steel-belted-style ($C^1$). Not only does it keep a big batch of 7-7's nice and cold, but if you use some polyurethane foam to insulate the top, it doubles nicely as a huge wide mouth thermos for soups and stews.

**D) 36-quart Ice Chest** - This is my trusted friend and companion. My Tonto. My Robin. My man Friday. It has traveled the length and breadth of the Great Lakes with me on 19-foot daysailors and 40-foot sloops. And it has never lost its cool. I trust it completely. My only regret is that it doesn't have a latch to secure the top. But the good Lord saw fit to create duct tape, so I can wrap it and wrap it and wrap it around and around to make a perfect seal.

**E) Metal Grills** - I love them! They're easy to handle and easy to store. When I want to barbecue, I simply take them ashore, dig a hole, build a fire and I'm in business. It's rock solid, nobody's in my way, and it works.

(No! Those aren't dirty seagulls sitting on top of the ice chest. Those are the "little two day bundles" I talked about in chapter 2, page 8, second paragraph.)

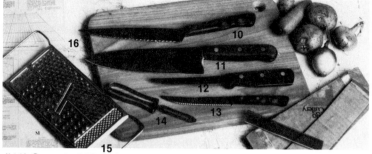

**#10) Serrated Knife** - Because of its versatility, it's my number one choice of kitchen cutlery for the boat. It will never win a gold medal in the chopping, dicing and mincing event; but when it comes to slicing onions, tomatoes and bread, it's the champ.

**#11) French Knife** - Besides being a superb cutting edge for meats and an excellent chopper and mincer, I find it invaluable when it comes to keeping the crew in line and settling disputes.

**#12) Boning Knife** - I like to carry this along because not only can I save us a few bucks by boning and prepping our meat myself, but it's also an extremely fine fillet knife.

**#13) Serrated Paring Knife** - Sometimes I'll need a little help in the galley and if you think I'm going to turn one of my big, sharp, not to mention expensive knives, over to an angry crew member who was just "volunteered" for K.P. duty, you're crazy. This little number is much easier to handle and a heck of a lot safer for me.

**#14) Vegetable Peeler** - This is by far the most intimidating utensil in the galley. One of these peelers and a bag of potatoes have been known to bring a grown man to his knees in a matter of minutes with tears in his eyes. But best of all, it's great for cutting zest of lemon for martinis.

**#15) Cheese Grater** - Sure, we can purchase shredded cheese at the store. But that's just one more thing to buy and worry about storing. It's also a convenience product, which means it costs twenty times more than just a regular old chunk of cheese. By shredding it ourselves, not only will we have a wider and fresher selection of cheeses to choose from at cooking time, but we'll also have the instrument to grate orange, lemon and lime rinds, shred the likes of carrots, zucchini, pickles and radishes for salads, and best of all, the tool necessary to make real hash browns and potato pancakes.

**#16) Cutting Board** - I know, a lot of boats already have one on board. But, it's either built into the counter or used as a cover for the stove. I prefer to take an extra one along anyhow. Not only does it allow me to take my chopping and dicing up on deck in the fresh air, but by putting a few little pegs on the bottom to keep it in place, I can put it over the sink and gain more counter space when I need it.

If you're taking along your good knives, you might want to consider making sheaths to protect them from damage. As you can see in the photo, they don't have to be anything elaborate. The ones I use are either a couple pieces of poster board taped together, a piece of thick cardboard, or just the plastic or paper cover they originally came in. Nothing fancy. Just something to protect them. Also keep in mind, to keep them sharp and in good condition, never, never wash or clean kitchen knives in salt water. In fact, whether you're cruising in fresh or salt water, it's a good idea to wipe them with a little vegetable oil after you're through using them.

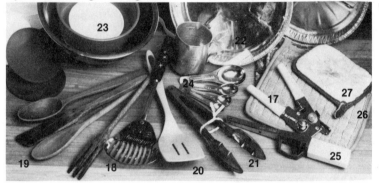

**#17) Can Opener** · To me it's the most important item on board, If you can't open it, you can't eat it. So take along two, just in case one decides to take a little swim.

**#18) Slotted Spoon** · I know! I know! It's not a slotted spoon. It's a "Kitchamajig" by EKCO. And it just happens to be a thousand times bigger and better and more useful than any old slotted spoon. So if you can find one, get it and use. If you can't, go with a standard, more traditional model.

**#19) Wooden Utensils** · I like to stay away from metal spoons and scrapers. Wood utensils don't nick or damage your pots and pans. Plus they don't get scorching hot if you happen to forget and leave them in the pot for a little while.

**#20) Spatula** · A heat resistant, plastic spatula (pancake turner) is great for fried eggs, flipping pancakes, and turning grilled sandwiches, but fritters have a tendency to slide off. So remember to hold the little buggers in place with a fork when turning them over.

**#21) Tongs** · You know those cute little metal rings that keep the tongs closed when not in use? Lose'em! There's nothing worse than having them slide down the stems, locking the tongs together, when you're trying to turn a thick piece of meat on a grill over a bed of hot coals (good-bye hair). Singe it into your memory to remove the rings and keep them closed with a wire twist tie instead.

**#22) Aluminum Pie Tin** · These come in handy when you're using batters that require a little dipping and dredging. And of course, in case a tired little sparrow drops in for a little rest, they make excellent bird baths.

**#23) Mixing Bowls** - Take along one large aluminum bowl and one or two small empty plastic butter tubs with covers. I rely primarily on the large bowl for ALL my mixing and mashing. It's got lots of room, so stuff doesn't end up all over the place when I get a little over-enthusiastic or P.O.'d. The smaller ones I like to keep around, just in case they're needed. Be prepared.

**#24) Measuring Spoons and Cups** - If you pre-package your herbs and spices and some of the other ingredients, you don't need this stuff. If you know your coffee mug holds, say twelve ounces, your plastic party glass holds sixteen and a dixie cup four, you don't need them. If you can tell when a spoon is half full, don't worry about them. But if you feel you must, then you should take along a few measuring tools.

**#25) Long Nose Butane Lighter** - They advertise these, "for those hard to reach areas". Granted, the burners on the boat are pretty accessible. You **can** easily light them with a paper match. It's just that I'm chicken. I like to have the extra 4-inches between my fingers and the ignition of the flame, no matter how safe it is.

**#26) Apron** - When you're cooking you need something to wipe your hands on quickly. There's no better place to do it than on an apron. But when hot oil starts to spit and splatter, or hot soup suddenly takes a spill, I'm very thankful that there's more between my baby soft skin and all that hot stuff than just my swim suit.

**#27) Hot Pads** - For more than just protecting hands from those so-called heat resistant handles, I use my hot pads to protect the counter, table or deck when I decide to serve dinner directly from a hot pan or skillet.

**#28) Tableware** - As you can see in the photo, when it comes to setting my table, I go all out. It may not look like "House Beautiful", but it's practical. The **plastic plates** are durable, inexpensive and easy to stack. A dab or two of a rubber silicon sealant on the bottom and they're non-skid. (Forget about using any form of paper plates; they take up too much room in the trash bin.)

You will notice that I do use matching **plastic bowls,** but I use them for serving salads and side dishes; never soups. I prefer to serve my hot soups in those freebee **coffee mugs** with spill-free tops.

For **utensils** we usually bypass the plastic and head for some inexpensive flatware. It has to be washed anyhow so we might just as well eat with the real thing. (Can't get too fancy though, sometimes the crew gets a little playful and rearranges their structural design.)

I like to serve drinks in these decorative **plastic party cups.** Not only are they versatile, durable and practical, but they stack nicely too.

For **napkins,** I simply use sheets of paper toweling. Whether the crew uses them or not, I can still use them to wipe off the plates, bowls, cups and clean out the pots and pans before they hit the dish water.

Putting rice in the salt shaker is a nice trick to keep it from clogging. But I like to take it one step further by using these **capped salt & pepper shakers** by Tupperware. This way, they don't even get a chance to think about clogging.

I know it isn't polite to use them at the table, but at some point I know the crew will need them, so I keep a supply of **toothpicks** around just in case.

And I know that we're supposed to be big, strong, macho sailors, but like Merlin Olson says, sometimes you need a little "pick-me-up", so I like to be ready with some **silk flowers, candles** and **matches** (for those special occassions).

Just because you've got lots and lots of room, don't get too carried away with all those fancy toys of the modern kitchen when you're trying to decide what to take on the cruise. All that extra stuff might be nice, but remember: at some point **you** have to carry everything aboard the boat and **you** are the one that has to carry everything off the boat. Personally, I like to travel light, so I stick to the basics. And to tell the truth, just about every meal in this book can be prepared with what you see here.

# Chapter 2

## STORAGE

Finding space to store dry goods and canned foods should be a snap. All you have to do is a little boat exploring. Look around, behind, above and under everything and you'll be amazed at all the empty space available to you. The only real problem will be keeping track of where you've put all the goodies. Some experts suggest that you draw a diagram of the boat and make a list of exactly where the cans of tomatoes, the pitted black olives, the tuna fish, the potato chips, etc., etc., etc., are hidden. It's a great idea and probably works for a lot of boaters, but I found it a pain in the behind. When I wanted to make my famous linguine with red clam sauce, I had to go to one area for the pasta, another for the can of clams, and still another to retrieve the tomato sauce and tomato paste. Not to mention the hassle of getting the bread sticks out from under the settee which was buried under the video camera, tape deck, power pack and oodles and oodles of loose cables. Why did I have so much trouble? Because that's how "they" recommended I store the stuff. Dry goods here. Canned fruits over there. Canned vegetables behind that. Crushables under here. The same products in the same area. That's great if you have a large pantry on board. But I didn't, I don't and I never will have one. So I decided to do something a little different; store them according to the meals, not the product.

Since I plan and schedule all our meals for the entire cruise well before we leave port, I've got a pretty good idea of what I'll be serving and when I'll be serving it. I know for instance, that on the 2nd or 3rd day of the second week of our trip, I'll be serving shrimp foo yong, calypso salad, carpetbagger steak, breakfast pie, tuna cakes, and chicken in lemon & wine sauce. So instead of storing the ingredients I'd need to prepare these meals all over the boat (like some suggest, I simply put them and any *'pre-packaged'* ingredients required, in a single brown paper bag. Tape the bag shut, as neatly as possible. Then, with a broad tipped marking pen, label it "2nd & 3rd day...WEEK II" for identification.

Now, if I use this system when we're on that two-week cruise, I only have to worry about storing and recovering six or seven of these little two-day bundles, instead of having to hunt down 40,000 individual cans, jars, and bottles hidden all over the boat. Not only that, but this way, when I retrieve the bundles, I know all the ingredients are there. I haven't misplaced, forgotten or lost anything.

There is one important thing to remember when making these little two-day bundles: if possible, transfer the contents of boxes to zip lock plastic storage bags. It not only saves space, but the smooth soft edges of plastic bags are less likely to tear through the paper bag.

Since the canned and dry ingredients for all our meals are all nicely bundled up and neatly tucked away in the hidden recesses of the boat, this means the only things I have to store in the area around the galley are the condiments and my basic cooking supplies (mayo, catsup, hot sauce, oil, vinegar, sugar, caviar, peanut butter, cornstarch, etc.). This leaves plenty of extra storage space close at hand. "Don't get all excited and start filling it up with lots of non-essential junk!" This empty area is where I stash the contents of those little two day bundles when they are needed. Now, for the next couple of days, instead of ransacking the boat looking for the supplies I need to prepare a fabulous meal for my hungry crew, everything is right here in the galley area, within an arm's reach.

This may seem like a lot of work, but I'd rather take my time and get organized ahead of time, than to get all bent out of shape trying to find everything when we're finally out on the water. All this **pre-packing** can be done days, weeks, even months in advance. I'll say it once again: the only time this can become a real pain is if you wait until the last minute to do everything.

## COLD STORAGE AREA

Anyone who doesn't have a 45 cubic foot refrigerator-freezer on board their boat, has to be, and should be, worried about keeping fresh foods fresh and cold foods cold while cruising the open water. The smaller the boat, the bigger the problem, and the more creative your solution may have to be.

I don't care how small your boat is, or how inadequate you think your cold storage area is, it's nothing compared with what I've had to, and do, deal with on our boat. And it isn't because we lack the space. It's because my "crew" chooses to allocate the majority of our cold storage space for their beer, booze, mix, and ice "cubes". And every time I come up with a way to reduce the space I need for food, they quickly lay claims to any extra territory I open up. I really can't blame them for their behavior, because if the truth be known, it was I and I alone who started them down this gluttonous path to the world of irresponsible, selfish use of precious cold storage space. Let me explain:

The first year we had the 28 footer, we discovered that the built in ice box was equipped with a refrigeration unit. The only problem was, that even if it were 20 below zero, with the refrigeration unit going full blast, a 10-pound block of ice would only last about 2 hours 27 minutes and 18 seconds. It became very apparent that the unit was not functioning the way it was supposed to. Instead of cooling the ice box off, it was heating it up! Since we didn't know how to fix it, and we couldn't afford to replace it, we just pulled the stupid thing out. Besides, it took up too much beer space. Then, I discovered that the ice box itself wasn't properly insulated to begin with. Therefore, if I wanted to keep things cold for a couple of days, I would have to look elsewhere. So I did. And I found out that for me, a 36-quart carry-on ice chest was just what the doctor ordered. Earlier, I had reached an agreement with the crew that food had top priority for cold storage areas, but if there was any extra room, they could use it. Well, since I no longer needed the built-in ice box for anything, they immediately jumped at the opportunity to fill it with six and one-half cases of beer five pints of butterscotch schnapps, three diet pops and then covered it with forty pounds of crushed ice!

A year later, I figured out that if I froze a lot of our meat and food for the trip before I put them in the 36-quart carry-on ice chest, I wouldn't need as much ice. Therefore, I would have some extra space if we needed it. And we did. . .And it wasn't for food.

Then there was the year our schedule placed us in a friendly port just about every night of our vacation. So I figured that instead of stocking the boat with three or four days worth of fresh foods, I'd just purchase what we'd need when we arrived in each port. This way I wouldn't need to take the 36-quart carry-on ice chest with us. Right? Wrong! The crew had other ideas. The arguments went something like this, "We're so used to it on board, it's like part of the boat." "Nobody spends any time down in the cabin, so it's not like it's in anybody's way." "It'd make a nice backgammon table for the cockpit." "Might just as well put it to good use." And you can imagine what they had in mind.

Well, once the pattern was established, there was no turning back. Now, instead of feeling like we're enthusiastic sailors on an exciting vacation cruise, I feel like we're a floating party store. All because I didn't realize or know, way back then, how to 1) properly insulate our built-in-ice-box, 2) the best and most efficient way to use ice, and 3) any of the tried and true tricks of the trade for storing fresh foods. But I do NOW!

## IMPROVING THE INSULATION

Contrary to popular belief, I didn't have to replace our old built-in-ice-box with a new and improved model to get that 10 pound block of ice to last longer than 2 hours 27 minutes and 18 seconds. Nor did I have to use any messy spray foam insulation or do any fancy fiberglass work. All I had to do to improve the insulation factor in our ice box was to take some scrap pieces of polyurethane foam and glue them to the inside walls with some liquid nails. It was as simple as that. Well, maybe not that simple. I did have to cut all those scrap pieces so that they all fit together nice and snug. Some say that this is a patchwork approach to the problem and maybe they're right. I wasn't able to cover 100% of the surface area and there were a few small gaps. But I came close and it didn't cost me anything.

There is one little trick I find quite helpful for maintaining a cold temperature in any built-in-ice-box or ice chest. After it's filled and ready to go, before I close it up or put on the top, I cover the contents with a couple of pieces of polyurethane foam. Not only does this help keep the cold air in and the warm air out, it also discourages fellow crew members from making frequent raids on our food supplies.

## ICE CHEST

If you should find it necessary to use a carry-on ice chest, make sure it has some type of latch to keep the top on and the lid closed. In order to keep things cold, a tight secure seal is very important. And be sure to use an ice chest that has a well insulated top or cover. Those "toy" coolers with the thin tops are OK if you're just heading to the beach or a back-yard barbeque, but they're almost worthless on a cruise, simply because their only purpose in life is to keep a six-pack cold long enough to drink. And for some crews that isn't very long.

A couple of things you might want to keep in mind when using a carry-on ice chest: first, keep it out of the sun. Obviously this means don't stow it on deck. But it also means, watch where you put it. At certain angles, the rays of the sun can shine down the old hatch or sneak through a companionway and spotlight Mr. Cooler. You may have to move or cover it, but things do stay cooler longer when they're in the shade and not in the sun. Second, it's extremely difficult to keep things cold when the ice chest is constantly being opened and closed. So try opening it as little as possible. **Open it once, before the meal, to get Everything out, and once after the meal, to put Everything back.** And make it very clear to everyone aboard, that **NOBODY** but **NOBODY** (except the cook) is allowed in the food cooler. If they don't abide by this rule, you might want to consider putting a chain and lock around it. This may not be popular with the crew the first day out, but by the end of the week, when the sour cream for the shrimp dip hasn't spoiled, and there's still some whipped topping left for dessert, all will be forgiven.

## ICE

"To drain or not to drain? That is the question!" It may not be the $64,000 question, but to many boaters without refrigeration units, it's a pretty important one. And everybody and his brother has a different theory. Aboard our boat, it's a major point of disagreement mainly because we have so many different ice chests in use. The ice water in one is good because it keeps the beer and pop cool longer. But you definitely don't want fresh foods and produce bobbing around, getting seasick in a cooler half-filled with melted ice. Ice cubes are a must for gin and tonics, but if they're in the cooler, they'll melt too fast. If you use a block of ice, then there isn't enough room for the Kahlua and milk. So what's a person to do? I can only tell you one thing. Ice melts faster when it's in water, and since you can't keep anything cold without ice, I say drain. Drain. Drain. Drain. If, for some reason, you chose not to drain, at least keep the ice out of the water.

Remember when you're purchasing ice, a small piece of ice will melt faster then a big piece of ice. So buy it by the block, it'll last longer. If you need cubes or crushed ice, you can always chip a few pieces from a block.

# WET OR DRY ICE?

At one time, I could never understand why any boater would ever consider, let alone actually use, dry ice. There's no question about it, dry ice is colder than wet ice. In fact, it's so cold, it doesn't just keep foods cold, it freezes them! But, a 10-pound block of dry ice will totally disintegrate within thirty hours after leaving the supplier, no matter how efficient your on-board refrigeration is, and could cost anywhere from 60 to 90 cents per pound. Where as, a well-kept 10-pound block of wet ice could last up to three days and only cost 10 to 15 cents per pound. Besides, can you imagine what it would be like making a Tom Collins with crushed dry ice?

Later on, I learned that it isn't a question of whether to use dry or wet ice, it's knowing how to use them. Since dry ice's greatest attribute is it's ability to freeze and keep things frozen, we have to think about what we want to keep frozen. "Milk? Sour cream? Lettuce? Steaks? TV Dinners? Frozen concentrates?" While it might be nice to keep some of these items frozen, what we really need to concern ourselves with is the wet ice. Wet ice is durable and versatile, and we'd like to keep it around as long as possible. The best way to do that is **keep it frozen.** And the best way to do that is with dry ice. If you place a block of dry ice on top of a block of wet, not only will it keep it frozen, but it will freeze it harder than it was when you first brought it from the store.

Using this technique, you can increase the cold storage life of your ice box or ice chest from under 30 hours (using a 10 pound block of dry ice) or from almost 3 days (using a 10 pound block of wet ice), to 5 good days using a combination of both. Of course that depends on weather conditions, the location of the box or ice chest, and whether or not you keep it under lock and key.

The important thing to remember is that dry ice starts to disintegrate as soon as it leaves the supplier and it doesn't matter if you store it in an ice box, ice chest or in a home freezer. Within 30 hours, that 10 pound block will be gone. So use it wisely. Or, buy more, if you can afford it.

# COLD FOOD STORAGE

When I told you all about losing my cold storage areas to beer, booze, pop and mixes, you might have thought I was spinning some sort of tall tale. But I wasn't. *"It's the truth. It's factual."* And now, " *"Everything is satisfactual, zip-piddy-do-da."* Because over the years, despite the inconvenience and hardships it caused, I learned one very important lesson: we really don't need as much cold storage area as we think we do. Granted, cold storage or refrigeration does slow down the spoilage rate of fresh foods, but a lot of what we keep in the refrigerator really doesn't have to be.

Put the book down for a minute and take a look at the contents of your refrigerator. What items in there would survive and what foods would perish if you pulled the plug?

Let's see: The beer, pop, wine, and that pitcher of Kool-Aid, would definitely manage without power. The catsup, jelly, pickles, olives and some of those salad dressings would survive without refrigeration. And if they had to, I bet the carrots, apples, onions, cucumbers and oranges are capable of hanging tough for a couple of days outside the crisper. It's only the fresh meats and some of the dairy products that we really have to be worried about.

If you've got the space, it's nice to keep everything, including the ground coffee and the popcorn, in the refrigerator. But on a boat, that is a luxury we can not afford. That's why, when allocating precious cold storage area for provisions for the cruise, it's nice to know that food stocks and supplies fall into four distinct categories of importance: 1) Absolute 2) Pursuant 3) Stand-By 4) Decadent.

**1) ABSOLUTE:** Foods that absolutely, without question need to be stored in the refrigerator, ice box or ice chest. Foods such as fresh meats and some, not all, dairy products.

## MEATS

Even at home fresh meats don't stay fresh forever, so on a boat, the best we can hope to accomplish, is to keep it from spoiling, for as long as we can. One of the best ways to do that (without drying, salting, marinating, pickling, canning, smoking, pre-cooking or freezing it) is to make sure that the meat is properly prepared for cold storage. To do that, remove the meat from its store packaging; dry the meat completely by patting it with a clean paper towel; rewrap the meat loosely with wax paper, then loosely with plastic wrap; finally, seal it in a zip lock plastic storage bag, but don't squeeze out all the air. We want a little air to circulate around the meat. Besides, if somebody forgets to drain the cooler, it'll keep the meat from drowning.

For poultry, it's an absolute must to thoroughly clean the meat before you even consider doing anything else. You must be absolutely certain that all that "gunky stuff" is rinsed out and wiped off and the meat is completely dry. Then you can loosely wrap it in wax paper and plastic wrap, seal it in a zip lock plastic storage bag and place it at the very bottom of the cooler, right next to the ice.

In fact, it's a pretty good idea to store all your meat at the bottom of the cooler, because that's the coldest part of any refrigerator, ice box or ice chest. Warm air rises. Cold air sinks and stays down. Down at the bottom of the cooler. The reason I stress this point is because many built-in-ice-boxes are equipped with trays that can be positioned at different levels to store food. This is great, except you have to remember that the air is warmer at the top than it is at the bottom. And many people have a tendency to put meat in the top tray, where it's easier to get at, instead of storing it at the bottom level where it's colder. Although the difference may seem insignificant to you now, after a couple of days at sea, this insignificance could mean the difference between having clean white healthy chicken breasts to serve the crew or the green sheen of tainted meat that you couldn't even serve to hungry sharks.

## DAIRY

When we go grocery shopping, we generally find dairy products displayed in the refrigeration section of the store. But not all dairy products fall into the category of foods that absolutely without question, need to be stored in the refrigerator, ice box or ice chest. Fresh eggs, for instance, can safely be stored for a couple of weeks in a cool, dry spot, if left in their original (paper fiber) cartons. This simply means keeping them stored somewhere below the water line and away from the bilge. Some old salts insist that if we coat the eggs with a layer of vaseline or margarine, they will last up to a month without refrigeration. We've never been away from port that long, so I've never had to grease my eggs. But, if you try this method, it's a good idea to remember, that when placed in a bowl of water, bad eggs float...fresh eggs sink.

The same method that applies to eggs also goes for all hard cheeses that are commercially packed in moisture resistant wrapping. No, no, not the vaseline and floating stuff. But storing it in a cool dry spot, instead of the refrigerator, ice box or ice chest. When dealing with cheeses like cheddar, Swiss, Gouda, provolone, etc., it's more important to keep the moist, bacteria infested, mold-forming air away from the chesse, than it is to keep it in the old fridge. That may be one of the reasons cheese has been a favorite source of protein in a sailor's diet for centuries. To keep it edible, all they had to do was wrap it in some vinegar-soaked muslin or seal it in a couple layers of wax, toss it down below and it would last for months.

While your hard cheeses can be stored in a cool, dry spot, soft cheeses such as creamed, cottage, camembert, Neufchatel, etc., must be placed in cold storage areas.

After opening any cheese, it's a good idea to remove any unused portions from the original package and rewrap it tightly in a clean piece of plastic wrap and seal it in a zip lock plastic storage bag. Squeezing out as much air as possible.

One nice thing to remember when dealing with hard cheese, if and when any mold does develop, you don't have to toss the whole thing out. Just cut off or remove the affected area and the rest of the cheese will retain its' flavor and will be perfectly safe.

While many of the dairy products that we use, such as sour cream, butter, and whipped topping, do require some sort of refrigeration, they are quite durable and don't occupy that much space in the cooler. Our biggest concern is the storage and handling of milk. Milk can spoil very, very fast and it takes up lots and lots of valuable space, no matter how large your cold storage area is. The easiest solution is simple, use dry, powdered or condensed milk. But the easiest solutions aren't always popular with the crew. I mean, have you ever had a White Russian made with powdered milk? Yuck!

If you must take milk along, there are a few things you should remember. 1) Check the expiration to make sure you're purchasing the freshest milk possible. 2) Buy the smallest units possible. If you need a gallon, for example, get four one-quart cartons. This way if one spoils, it doesn't destroy your whole supply. Besides, they're a lot easier to store and after one carton's empty, there's more room in the cooler for something else. 3) When you need milk, take it out of the cooler, pour it, then put it back in the cooler. Leaving it out, even for short periods, allows the milk in the container to warm, and that warming accelerates the spoiling process. 4) Never pour unused portions of milk back into the container. It's better to toss it over board than to have it contaminate the rest of the supply.

I've mentioned quite a few things that you might want to remember when dealing with foods that absolutely, without question, need to be stored in the refrigerator, ice box or ice chest. But when you're on a boat the most important thing to remember is that you are dealing with a refrigeration system that can be unreliable at times. If you have any questions about the quality of the food you've stored, **DO NOT USE IT!** Toss it over board and open a can of sardines. Break open the saltines, bring on the peanut butter, and mix up a pitcher of powdered milk. It may not be a culinary feast, but it's better to say "ick" than get sick.

**2) PURSUANT:** Food items that need to be stored in the refrigerator, ice box or ice chest only after or pursuant to their being opened. Until their seal is broken they can be stored anywhere, for any reasonable length of time. But once opened, items such as mayonnaise, processed cheese, spreads, salad dressings and sauces must be refrigerated.

One nice thing about this category is that there is no guesswork or misunderstanding about which products do or do not need to be kept in the cooler. Because right there on the label it will say "Refrigerate After Opening!".

I'd like to point out that a lot of the products in this category are accents and condiments for our foods, not the staples or our diet. In other words, we don't use or need them for every meal. At home, we've got a big old fridge with lots and lots of room, so there's no problem keeping them around. Unfortunately, aboard a boat, we're not that lucky. So I'd strongly suggest that you purchase these items in the smallest quantities (size) possible. Not only will they take up less space in the cooler, but if anything should go wrong and it does spoil, you'll only lose a couple of ounces instead of your whole supply. At times I've taken this "buying small" advice one step further by picking up a bunch of those little, single serving size packages of jams, jellies, taco sauce and salad dressings they use in some diners. I know this doesn't sound like we're the classiest act in town (or on the water) but it does allow me to carry a wide variety of these condiments to satisfy the individual tastes of the entire crew instead of just one or two of my favorite flavors. Besides, a few dozen of these little soft plastic packages takes up a heck of a lot less room than a couple of those large hard breakable jars.

**3) STAND-BY:** Foods that would prefer to travel in the refrigerator, ice box or ice chest, but because of the lack of space and over-booking they are forced to wait patiently in the cool, dark, dry recesses of the boat until more suitable accommodations open up. Unlike a hearty chunk of cheese or a carton of eggs, broccoli, grapes, celery, tomatoes, strawberries and avocados can tolerate these sub-standard conditions for only so long, before they start to spoil. Fortunately, they don't have to suffer the indignity very long. Because as time goes by, after each meal, after each snack, as you steadily devour it's original contents, more and more space will open up in the cooler for these fresh vegetables and fruits.

When dealing with vegetables and fruits, one thing to remember is that it is more important to keep vegetables in the cooler than it is fruits. Vegetables are picked at their peak. And as soon as they're harvested all their sugar starts turning to starches, their nutritional value diminishes and they start to spoil. Sticking them in the old fridge helps slow the process. Fruits, on the other hand, are picked before they're fully mature and still continue to ripen at room or cabin temperature. Refrigeration is only needed after they're totally ripened. (P.S. tomatoes ARE fruits but on the shopping list you'll find it in the vegetable column.)

**4) DECADENT:** Food items that could survive an eternity without being stored in the refrigerator, ice box or ice chest, yet we insist on keeping them in there because **we** couldn't survive if they weren't. Items such as beer, pop, mixes, wine, canned puddings, custards, fruit juices, apple sauce, and fruit cocktail. Other than the fact we just like them served cold, there's absolutely no reason to keep these items in the cooler.

I know the taste of a warm Coke or Pepsi isn't one of the most refreshing experiences in life. But I think you should know that it isn't necessary to keep your entire supply of drinks in the fridge to be cool.

In fact, a good way to keep all these Decadent items in a cool, comfortable range is to store them below the waterline next to the hull or in a dry area of the bilge. If you happen to be anchored, you might want to try placing them in a mesh bag or fish basket and putting them over the side and ten feet below where it's nice and cold. While these techniques will keep these "essential" supplies cool, it will not get them cold or "properly" chilled, they'll just be. . .cool. If the crew still demands cold, I'd suggest placing a few smaller "cool" items in the cooler instead of a lot of large warm (air temp.) ones. Not only will they chill quicker, but it won't put a big hurt on your supply of cold. And remember, once you're at sea, cold is an irreplaceable commodity and you have other **fresh** food supplies that are much more perishable.

# Chapter 3

**CLEAN-UP**
(Required reading for ALL crew members)

*"When everybody is sitting around the dock enjoying a few libations, who's down in the galley, all alone, preparing the hors d' oeuvres? And, during a storm in heavy seas, who's the one being bounced around the cabin like a pinball, while trying to fix his fellow shipmates a warm nutritious meal? It's the cook. It's always the cook who gets the fuzzy end of the lollypop. It's the cook who stays behind to cook the meals, when everyone else is out taking in the sights. It's the cook who's always stuck below making sandwiches in a fly-infested cabin, while everyone else is up on deck soaking up the rays on a hot summer's day. It's the cook who's always up at the crack of dawn, slaving away, cooking breakfast, while everyone else gets to sleep in. It's a lonely, thankless job."*

True or not, that's the argument I made a long time ago when the crew decided that since it was the cook's responsibility to keep their spirits lifted and their bellies full, it was THEIR responsibility to do the dishes and take care of the clean up. Well, once we came to an understanding, and I didn't have to worry about doing the dishes anymore, I figured I could sit back, relax, with a Drambuie in one hand, a pipe filled with a fine English blend in the other, and enjoy the sunset. Dream on. I don't know which was harder; doing it myself or sitting in the cockpit watching the Laurel and Hardy show below, as those clowns made a very simple task extremely complicated. One crew member thought that all you had to do was throw everything in a fish net bag, add a whole lot of dish detergent and drag it behind the boat. Another was so fastidious you'd think he was wrapping a Christmas present instead of garbage and then he would insist on polishing the plastic knives and forks before putting them away. Then there was my personal favorite, Louis Pasteur; he thought you had to boil 30 gallons of water to sterilize everything we touched, including toothpicks and bottle caps.

I know! I don't do the work, so I shouldn't complain. Right? Well I'm not. I just thought you'd like to know that there is an easier approach to the clean-up problem than what those guys go through.

1) Forget about using the sink in the galley for doing the dishes. If yours is like mine, you can't even get a plate in it, so it's definitely too small to get the job done. Get a large bucket, one that can accommodate your Dutch oven, frying pan, plates, utensils and cups all at the same time (one of those plastic pails that pool chemicals come in is perfect). It's not necessary to put everything in all at once, but

under certain circumstances, it does come in handy. Like when the seas are really rough and you wisely choose to wait until it calms down a little; or maybe you'd rather do the dishes elsewhere, like out on the deck, on the beach or even in the shower room/bath house.

2) Use lots and lots of water. You're surrounded by it, so use it. Use lots of soapy, bio-degradable, sudsy water to wash with. Don't drain your holding tanks to do dishes, because at this stage it doesn't matter if it's fresh or salt water or whether it's hot or cold; the important thing is that the water is soapy and sudsy, because the detergent contains a disinfectant that will help kill all those nasty little bacteria and viruses that we're worried about. But make sure you use lots and lots of water to rinse away all that soapy sudsy water, because any soap residue left behind can also create problems.

3) Caked on, baked on, burnt on food, cemented to the bottom of the pan; it's not supposed to happen, but it does. When it does happen, at home or on the boat, you don't have to use a hammer and a chisel to get it out. Just add a little water, bring it to a boil, and take your wooden or plastic spatula and gently scrape it off. If it needs a little more friendly persuasion, add some dish detergent. Still stubborn? Try adding some bleach. If that doesn't work, throw the pan out and send the recipe to NASA.

4) Some people are comfortable at this point just to dry everything with a clean dish towel. But to play it safe, before I dry, I like to bathe my utensils in a couple cups of boiling hot water. Then I pour that water from glass to glass, ending up with a light rinse over the top of the plates. If you are washing in salt water, I strongly suggest that you tap your holding tank and give everything a final hot, fresh water rinse.

5) After we're all done scrubbing, washing, cleaning, sterilizing and drying the dishes, I like to give all my cutting and work surfaces a good rub down with a couple slices of fresh lemon or some lemon juice. Not only does it give the galley that lemony freshness that everybody seems to like, but the acid in the juice helps kill any bacteria that might be hanging around.

# Chapter 4

## GARBAGE & TRASH

I was always under the impression that boaters carried dinghies so they could either go ashore for supplies and to party when they anchored off or to get rid of the kids when they wanted to spend a quiet afternoon together. That's until I met Ken and Barby Goodie-Do-Right. Their boat was so squeaky clean, it'd make any hospital operating room look like a toxic waste dump. Heaven forbid, if a cigarette butt dirtied any of their ash trays for more than 12.7 seconds. In fact, the discarded ashes were removed from the ash trays and the surface was cleaned before you ever had a chance to finish your smoke. Everything was so spic and span. Their shorts, shirts, pants, handkerchiefs, socks, and shoelaces were all perfectly pressed and color-co-ordinated. I mean, these people were so obnoxiously neat, that even when they'd rise and shine each morning at 5:39 to do their yoga exercises their hair was perfectly coiffed. Oh well, that's a little off the subject. But you get the picture!

Anyhow, this couple thought they had come up with the hottest idea since sliced bread when it came to dealing with their garbage. After each and every meal, they simply shoved everything, including their designer chinette paper plates, stylish picnic flatware, and plastic wine glasses into a plastic trash bag and tossed it into the dinghy they were towing behind the boat. To their way of thinking, this practice not only eliminated any of the health and sanitary problems the garbage might create on board, but now all those nasty bugs and pesky flies would be hanging around the dinghy instead of the boat.

Now that idea is fine and dandy if you don't need or want to use the dinghy for anything else except garbage. But, I have to contend with a bunch of guys who like to venture out, go exploring, do some fishing, pick up refreshments and make a few water balloon attacks on hostile boats. We can't afford to have our dinghy filled up with garbage. We need it empty and ready for action! So how do we handle one or two weeks' worth of garbage? Simple. We just don't take it along to begin with.

That's not as stupid as it may sound. Most of us think of garbage as dinner leftovers, foods we don't use, goes stale or spoils. But that's only a small part of the waste problem we face aboard a boat. The major source of our garbage comes from the extra packaging our foods and supplies come in. Look at the instant hot cereals, cup-a-soups, and hot chocolate mixes for example. Since each portion is individually wrapped, the boxes they're sold in aren't needed. And who says rice has to be kept in the rice box or the pasta in the pasta box? There's no reason these and other dry food products can't be transferred to zip lock plastic storage bags. (If you're worried about losing the directions, you can either copy them down or tear them off the original box and keep them in the storage bag.) When empty, these single serving size envelopes and plastic storage bags compress into nice tiny little bundles of waste that are a breeze to handle. Whereas those stiff bulky cardboard boxes and commercial containers have to be crushed and trampled by a herd of elephants before they're suitable for the trash and even then, they're awkward to handle.

Another good idea is to get rid of some of the food waste before leaving the dock. Can you eat pork chops without the bone? Does a good steak really need that extra 2-inches of fat? Doesn't that recipe call for the chicken breast to be boned and skinned? What's wrong with seeding, removing the rind, and cutting the watermelon and cantaloupe into chunks beforehand? I know! All that stuff is considered natural and bio-degradable, so it's common practice to toss it overboard, but there's something about being anchored in a nice little cove at sunset and watching watermelon rinds float by, that bothers me. So get rid of all that junk first. Not only will it cut down on your garbage, but it cuts down on the amount of cold storage area you'll need and reduces the preparation time for the meals while you're out on the water.

This is going to be a very difficult subject for me to write about considering "WE" don't do what "I" preach. Every year, I try to convince everyone to leave their canned beverages (beer and pop) at home. I tell them to rely on juice concentrates, powdered drink mixes or just good old water to quench their thirsts. I've even tried appealing to the crew on a more mature level based on medical and scientific facts, I've explained that since we're out in the hot sun all day long, our biggest concerns are dehydration and heat exhaustion, and that the caffeine in pop and the alcohol in beer doesn't solve or prevent the problem, it only aggravates it. But no matter how well-documented my arguments are or how much I beg and plead with them, the crew still insists on taking them along.

Of course you realize the consequences of their decision!

When the cans are empty, we're stuck with them. We can't just toss them overboard. Not only is that an environmental NO! NO! but, where we come from, there's a 10 cent deposit on each can. Which means our inventory of empties is valued at over $15.60. And that translates into one free case, plus one free six-pack of beer (or 3 free cases of pop).

It also means, we have to store 6½ cases of empties until we get back to port and cash them in. In the mean time, 40 zillion flies, bees, yellow jackets and mosquitoes will discover this treasure-trove of sweet sugary liquids left behind fermenting in the empty cans and drive everybody aboard crazy.

The best way to keep this situation from happening is to thoroughly rinse all empties with water. Fresh or salt, it doesn't make any difference, just don't empty your holding tank to rinse any empties. Let them drain and dry for a little while. Then store them in a plastic garbage bag in some out of the way foot locker. 21

All the planning, all the shopping, all the pre-packaging and packing, all the time you spent organizing everything is paying off. The crew is ecstatic about their first meal aboard the boat. In fact it's all they can talk about. And now that they've witnessed for themselves the excellent cuisine in store for them on the cruise, they've enthusiastically agreed to the arrangement you had mentioned earlier. (That is . . . where you'll do the cooking, if they'll take care of the clean -up!)

Well, everything seems to be working out famously, just like the guy in **the Two Burner Gourmet** said it would. You're up on deck listening to a little Mantovani, sipping on Drambuie and enjoying a glorious sunset, while the crew is below cleaning up your mess. Then from the deepest bowels of the boat you hear. . . "What should we do with all this grease? Do you want to save this? What about the egg shells? Anybody want the rest of this pudding? Hey, don't throw that at me!"

You have now entered the Garbage Zone! The world of the greasy, the sleazy, the slimy, the grimy; the icky world of raw garbage.

It isn't the most esthetic or glamorous aspect of boating but it has to be dealt with. And it must be dealt with properly. For some unknown reason, naval architects have failed to provide boaters with adequate space to store their trash and garbage, In fact, consider yourself extremely fortunate if your boat does have a built-in trash bin. Most of us are lucky if we can find space to put a waste paper basket or have an out-of-the-way place to hang a plastic garbage bag. For that reason we must take this matter seriously. No pussy-footing around. Accumulating garbage calls for a frank and honest discussion. Because if it isn't, not only will it foul the nice, clean, fresh sea air and attract every fly, bug and pesky insect in the northern hemisphere, but its insatiable appetite for space will quickly devour the meager area designated for it and its gluttonous extremities will overflow, ending up sprawled all over the boat. Unsightly? Yes! . . . and smelly too.

The way I figure it, our on-board garbage falls into four different categories. First, there's the containers: cans, bottles, jars, plastic and paper bags. Second, there's absorbent solids such as paper products, bread, popcorn, onion skins, rice and Twinkies. Third is solid waste like scraps of meat, bones, egg shells, banana and potato peels. And finally you have liquids. They're left-over gravies, pan-juices, cooking oils, that sort of stuff. And although there are four different kinds of garbage we have to deal with, it doesn't mean we have to handle them separately, if we practice the old "crush and stuff" system of storing garbage.

To implement the old "crush and stuff" method, the first thing you have to remember is to make all the trash as small and as compact as

possible. If you want to dispose of a piece of paper, don't just wad it up in a ball and toss it, tear it into itty bitty pieces. Cut the bottom out of those cans and smash them flat like a pancake. Even those little boxes from fruit drinks and raisins should be broken down and flattened. Don't leave egg shells whole, crush them! Break up the bones into smaller, more manageable, pieces. You can reduce the space needed for almost everything if you just think about it. Heck, even leftover lettuce takes up far less room when it's chopped to smithereens with a cleaver.

Now, instead of dumping all this compacted, crushed, smashed and flattened junk into a garbage bag, I find it much more economical if I stuff all of it into one or two of the food containers we just emptied before they hit the old trash bin. The can those peaches or stewed tomatoes came in. That empty pickle jar or milk carton. Or even that large (gallon size) zip lock plastic storage bag we used to marinate the broccoli in. These containers make perfect receptacles for the meal's or the day's garbage. One of the additional beauties of using these containers is that after everything is crushed and stuffed and you think it's full, there's always room for the liquids. Note that it is imperative to add them last. The paper, bread and rice will absorb the liquids as they are added. The liquids will seep into the gaps and replace the air bubbles around the broken bones, crushed egg shells and flatten cans, and when you're all done, you'll end up with a nice neat little package of "La-Garbage". But if you try to stuff the paper, bread, bones and flattened cans into an empty carton half filled with left over gravy and grease, the mixture will act like a geyser bubbling, gushing and squirting up all over the place, and the only thing you'll end up with is a greasy, slimy mess.

From time to time you'll be faced with one of the most serious and dangerous aspects of handling garbage aboard any boat...The safe keeping of empty glass containers for disposal ashore. Although we try to avoid them like the plague, at times they're unavoidable. Cheez Whiz, marinated artichoke hearts, pimientos, pickles, mayo, Grey Poupon...some of the best things in life come in glass containers. So you're going to have to deal with them at some time or another, so you better know how to handle them.

Since glass containers are most susceptible to breakage when they are empty, I strongly suggest you practice the old "crush and stuff" technique with them first, before stuffing anything else. Then use them as part of the filling when you stuff some of the larger containers. If the jar happens to be larger than any of the other empty containers, after it's filled, place it in a large (gallon size) zip lock plastic storage bag, and continue to stuff the bag with garbage of the "soft kind" (lettuce, rice, bread crumbs, meat scraps, paper, etc.). This is kind of like placing an egg in a ball of cotton. It's now protected from any accidental blow. And if it should get whacked, the soft garbage stuffing inside the package will prevent any broken slivers of glass from doing any damage and will absorb any extra liquids.

Having a glass container or two on board isn't always a bad thing, you just have to know how to handle them. Not only do empty jars make an excellent depository for a couple of days' worth of discarded liquids during the cruise, but in a pinch, with their screw-on tops, they're a great substitute for a cocktail shaker.

The best garbage and trash receptacle for the old "crush and stuff" is the most overlooked or forgotten. Plastic Containers: empty milk cartons, Gatorade jugs, cooking oil bottles, large distilled water jugs. The reason they're probably overlooked is because they are the last containers to be emptied and the waste has already been "crushed and stuffed" into something else. Well, that isn't a good enough reason to leave these large containers filled with nothing but air. Even if you try to crush them, they still take up too much space. So cut off the top and stuff all the stuff you've already stuffed in those smaller containers in them. As long as you've got something larger to stuff everything in, keep doing it, and doing it, and doing it again. if you have too many large plastic containers, don't try crushing them, take a knife and cut them up into little pieces and stuff them. And what ever you do, DO NOT USE your good kitchen knives to do the cutting. I'm quite sure you can find a strong utility knife on board that is more than capable of doing the job. If not, use your teeth if you have to, but never, never use a good kitchen knife.

You may get your hands a little dirty using the old "crush and stuff" system, and I admit, it does take a little extra effort to make it work. But then again, you won't need a dinghy to stash a week's worth of garbage, will you?

# Chapter 5

## TOWARDS A BETTER UNDERSTANDING
### and the
### FINAL IMPLEMENTATION

The recipes in this cookbook are presented in a format I refer to as a **Group**. A **Group** is comprised of recipes for three meals a day (breakfast, lunch and dinner) for either a 2, 3, or a 5-day period. A 5-day **Group** represents the maxiumum amount of time I believe we can safely keep our fresh foods fresh, aboard our boat, without returning to port for ice and fresh supplies.

At the beginning of each Group, there is a detailed outline of the meals contained in that Group and when they are to be served. The reason for this rigid structure is four-fold:

1) No matter how good your refrigeration system is, unless you freeze it, fresh meats are going to spoil. Some faster than others. Therefore the meals are planned so we use the meats that are more susceptible to spoilage first, saving the heartier varieties for later (ground meat first, then chicken or pork, and beef last). Relying on fully cooked sausages, canned meats and pasta after that.

2) Nobody likes spending all their time in the galley. So what I've done is to arrange the meals in such a way as to minimize the amount of time we spend down there, yet at the same time maximizing your output by doing some of the preliminary tasks and pre-cooking stuff, for other meals, ahead of time.

3) Although it is entirely possible to take a cruise and never have to fire up the old stove to prepare a meal, I find it totally unacceptable to serve the crew a series of cold plate specials. Therefore, I've tried to strike a balance, keeping the daily fire-ups to a minimum. Not the bare minimum, just a minimum.

4) Food not only fuels the body but it lifts the spirit. Over the years I've noticed that during a cruise or a race, crews go through emotional high and low cycles that are quite predictable. The right meal at the right time can pull the crew out of the doldrums and snap them back to the fun life. And most of the time it doesn't have to be anything special or exotic either. These meal plans reflect those past experiences.

For each Group there is a complete shopping list located at the back of the book. The list contains everything you'll need to prepare all the meals for that particular Group. So now, when you're ready to go on your cruise, all you have to do is select a Group that looks good, grab the shopping list, and head for the store.

You may consider some of the meal plans a little too much. But from past experiences, I've found it's better to have too much than too little. Besides, you don't have to serve everything all at once. This isn't a sit-down-dinner. So take your time. It's not like we have to rush off to the opera or anything. And keep in mind, You Don't Have to Prepare Everything on the Menu, they're just suggestions.

I would be remiss in my duties as hospitable boater if I didn't include a section of drinks and hors d' oeuvres. Therefore, to close each Group, I've included a section called Time Out for Cocktails & Things. Although some of the recipes here might use some of the left-over ingredients from other recipes (such as the remaining half carton of sour cream, the rest of the hot dogs, or the unused smoked oysters), a good thing to remember is that **the ingredients for these drinks and appetizers are NOT on the shopping list.**

Now, how can you actually apply this system?

Simple! If you were going on a two-day cruise, you'd just select a meal plan from one of the two-day Groups. If you're going to be gone for three days, you'd pick from the three-day Groups. If you're going to be away for more than five days, you can simply extend the length of your meal plans by combining as many Groups as you need.

1 five-day Group + 1 two-day Group = 7 days

1 three-day Group + 2 five-day Groups = 13 days

4 five-day Groups + 2 three-day Groups = 26 days

Allow a day or two for pizzas, bar burgers and all the tourist stuff and you're all set.

(Note: When combining more than one Group for a cruise *watch your shopping list* for duplications in the **Condiments, Accent** and **Cooking Supply** sections. We don't need two jars of horseradish, 14 different bottles of salad dressing or six gallons of vegetable oil!)

## HOW TO READ
### the RECIPES

**A) the BANNER:** It answers everybody's question... "What's for Dinner?"

In the left hand margin you'll find the day and the meal we're dealing with in that particular group. The top line, in large print, indicates the main course. The line beneath that, in the smaller print, contains the side dishes. I think most of us are capable of making a salad, putting together a cheese and salami platter, opening a can of bean salad or cooking some instant rice, so I don't pay any attention to the instruction for those items. But all the ingredients you'll need to prepare them are on the shopping list. In situations where it is important, the recipe for any side dishes follows the instructions for the main course.

3rd day Dinner **PORK in ADOBO SAUCE**
salad • creole-style tomatoes & corn • watermelon sparkle

STORY ▶

*Anytime you mention you'll be serving Mexican food, somebody always wants a fire extinguisher kept nearby. Well, get ready, you're about to experience a rarity: a Mexican dish that isn't hot and spicy, but flavorful and mellow.*

**PRE-PACKAGED Ingredients** ▶

**MAIN Ingredients** ▶ ▶

| | | | |
|---|---|---|---|
| ¼ | cup vinegar | 1 | Tablespoon vegetable oil |
| 1 | 8-oz. can tomato sauce | 1 | medium onion, finely chopped |
| ¼ | teaspoon cumin | 2 | garlic cloves, minced |
| ½ | teaspoon oregano | | • • • • • |
| 1 | teaspoon salt | | |
| 2 | Tablespoons chili powder | 4 | pork loin chop, ¾ to 1-inch |
| 2 | Tablespoons flour | | thick |

Pre-package first 10 ingredients in a 18-oz. jar. (Shake jar after pre-packaging and before using.)
• • • • • •

**INSTRUCTIONS** ▶

Place pork chops in a large (gallon size) zip lock plastic storage bag. Add pre-packaged sauce. Seal and marinate overnight. (Turn package over every time you open ice chest.)

**BULLETS** ▶
• • • • • •
Transfer chops and sauce to a large skillet. Bring mixture to a boil. Reduce heat. Cover and simmer 45 minutes.

**MAKES** ▶   makes 4 servings

**CREOLE-STYLE TOMATOES & CORN**

| | | | |
|---|---|---|---|
| 1 | onion, chopped | ¼ | teaspoon salt |
| 1 | green pepper, chopped | ⅛ | teaspoon pepper |
| 1 | 14-oz. can tomatoes, drained | | Dash of hot sauce |
| 1 | 16-oz. can whole kernel corn, drained | | Dash of Worcestershire |

**SIDE DISH recipes** ▶

In a bowl, combine all ingredients. Mix well. Place mixture on a large sheet of foil. Form into a packet with all seams at top. Place in skillet during the last 15 minutes of cooking.

**WATERMELON SPARKLE**

| | | | |
|---|---|---|---|
| ½ | cup sugar | | |
| ⅓ | cup light rum | 4 | cups watermelon chunks |
| 3 | Tablespoons lime juice | | |

• • • • • •
In a small bowl, combine first 3 ingredients. Mix well. Place melon in a large (gallon size) zip lock plastic storage bag. Pour sauce over melon chunks. Seal and chill.

**TIPS & NOTES** ▶

**Tip:** Prepare dessert earlier in the day so it has time to chill before dinner.
**Note:** Keep a loaf of French bread handy, this sauce is fantastic for dunkin'.

**B) the STORY:** It's just my attempt to bring a smile to your face, a chuckle to your belly and a friend to your galley.

Since the story is not important to the preparation of the meal, (and it appears in a smaller, fancier print, which makes it extremely difficult to read at sea), I suggest that you read it at home during the off season, on a cold night, in front of a roaring fire, while sipping a warm brandy.

**C) the PRE-PACKAGED Ingredients:** The herbs, spices, dry ingredients and marinades that should be measured, mix, prepared and organized while you're still at home and not on the cruise. This way you can still run next door and borrow that extra ¼ teaspoon of turmeric or whatever if you have to.

You'll notice that the print for these ingredients and their instructions lean a little to the right and they are not as dark as the other print.

**D) the MAIN Ingredients:** All the stuff you'll need to create this culinary masterpiece. Note that they are all listed in the order they are needed.

**E) the INSTRUCTIONS:** They simply tell you what to do, when to do it and how long to do it.

**F) BULLETS:** They indicate stopping points. Use all the ingredients, do everything up to this point, and stop before proceeding any further. It's kinda like following steps 1, 2, and 3 without the numbers.

**G)MAKES:** Refers to the number of adult-size servings the recipe will produce. If you need a couple of extra servings just add a little more of main meat ingredient. Any time **"hearty"** appears, you'll have enough for a guest or two.

**H) SIDE DISH Recipes:** When there are any, these will always follow the instructions for the main dish.

**I) TIPS & NOTES:** This is my way of giving you a little extra information and a few suggestions of shortcuts that you might find handy.

# Chapter 6

## THE SECRETS TO SUCCESS

### Know the Territory

Before you start measuring, chopping and rattling all those pots and pans, read through the entire recipe and meal plan first. From start to finish. Then read through it again, visualizing what you'll have to do and how you're going to handle it. You don't have to study it like a text book. You don't have to memorize it. But it's a good idea to know what you're getting into before you get there. As they told Professor Harold Hill, "To be successful, you got to know the territory."

### Put a Lid on It!

Whenever you're heating or bringing anything to a boil, put a lid on it or cover it with a piece of aluminum foil. A covered or enclosed pot will heat 25% faster than an uncovered one. Which means you'll use less fuel.

Note: Once water comes to a rolling boil, reduce your heat to maintain a gentle roll. The water temperature will remain the same, but it won't evaporate (turn to steam) as fast.

### Fill it Up

I don't know if you noticed, but back on page 7, I included a pump thermos as one of the basic items I consider vital to cooking aboard a boat. For a long time many of my fellow sailors didn't understand my reasoning for this until they witnessed for themselves the value of its versatility. Not that it performs many different tasks. No! Just that many tasks can be performed with it. Its ability to keep boiling hot water boiling hot means any crew member can have a cup of instant coffee, cocoa, soup, broth, hot cereal or tea any time they want one. It means you no longer have to boil water just to make a batch of instant rice, mashed potatoes or stuffing mix. You can cook the pasta for Thursday night's Linguine with Red Clam Sauce on Monday and revive it with a bath of hot water just in time for dinner.

Boiling water takes too much time and burns far too much fuel to do it every time somebody needs a cup of hot water. But when we do boil water, like for major dish washing/clean-up projects, I boil extra for the pump thermos. Once we fill it up we've got boiling hot water, at the press of a button, for the next 24 hours.

## Everybody in the Water

### (Look Who's in Hot Water Now)

You've got to boil some water to make hard boiled eggs! You've got to boil some water to cook linguine. You've got to boil some water to cook seashell pasta. So why not save yourself some time, energy and fuel and do them all at once? In the same pot!

Place eggs in a 5-quart saucepan or pot and fill with water. Cover and bring to a rolling boil. Stir in some salt and a teaspoon of vegetable oil. Add linguine and seashell pasta, stir to prevent sticking. Reduce heat to a gentle boil. Cook for 8 minutes. With a slotted spoon remove eggs and seashell pasta, leaving the linguine in the pot to be drained and rinsed. (The secret to this little trick is that it is next to impossible to remove thin noodles, spaghetti, and linguine from boiling water with a slotted spoon.)

When pasta cools, store in large (gallon size) zip lock plastic storage bags.

To revive pasta for salads, just add salad dressing and other ingredients. For hot dishes, just add some hot water (from pump thermos), let it stand a while, then punch some holes in the bottom of the bag to drain.

Note: Fresh salt water is perfect for cooking eggs and pasta.

## Presto!

I think what I like best about using instant rice is that you don't have to be a genius to prepare it. Just boil some water, add the rice, stir it once or twice, then cover and remove it from the heat. A few minutes later and it's ready to serve. The trick is to do it without firing up the old stove! No big deal, if you're carrying a thermos of **HOT** water! Just place the rice in a bowl or pot, add the needed hot water, stir, cover and let stand. Presto! Instant rice. (The key to this is melting the butter or dissolving the seasonings in a small amount of hot water first.)

This technique also works well with instant mashed potatoes and stuffing mixes.

## Be Careful Out There

I wish I was more knowledgable about the pros and cons of all the different stoves. But, I'm not! So I'm not going to pretend I'm an authority on the subject. There's too much at stake. About the only thing I can tell you is...know your stove. Take the time to read the instructions. Twist and turn the old knobs. Make sure every part is working as smooth as silk and nothing is leaking. Then, to build up your confidence a little, fire it up a few times before you leave port.

**Safety Hints:** Don't wear any loose fitting long sleeve tops while cooking. Keep a lid handy just in case there's a flare up in one of the pans. I like to keep a damp wet dish towel around for any other burst of excitement. Use a funnel to refuel stove and never, never refuel while the stove is still hot. And Do Not, I repeat, DO NOT, mount a fire extinguisher right next to the stove. It may seem like the thing to do, but in close quarters, it's better to have it away from the action, but within easy reach and in the open.

## Show Time

Ever notice how many dishes a TV chef can prepare in just 30 minutes? Besides acknowledging the existence of the magical TV stove, (that can cook anything in just 10 minutes), have you ever wondered how he can do it? Well, the next time you see one of those shows, pay close attention to what he doesn't do! He doesn't do any measuring, any peeling, scraping, chopping or dicing. He doesn't even open his own cans on the air. Everything is ready to go before the lights go on and the cameras start to roll. (Pretty slick, ha!)

The trick is to do as much as you can ahead of time. Prepackage your spices, marinades and dry ingredients so you can just dump them in the pot. Clean, peel and slice a lot of the vegetables in advance and store them in individual zip lock plastic storage bags. Then when it's show time, just take out what you need, do any fine chopping (if necessary) and you're all set.

What's really neat about cutting all this stuff up in advance is anybody can do it at any time and they won't get in the cook's way. And when you're on a long leisurely cruise, the crew gets bored and they're just dying to find something to do. So let them help out. Let them slice the onions and mince the garlic. (P.S. Peeled and chopped garlic can be stored for a few days in a small jar with oil)

# Group 1
## a five day menu

| | BREAKFAST | LUNCH | DINNER |
|---|---|---|---|
| 1st day | **DONUTS**<br>juice • melon<br><br>beverage | **stacked**<br>**HAM & CHEESE**<br>**Sandwiches**<br>potato chips • 3-bean salad • pickles | **CHICKEN INDIENNE**<br>salad • rice • green beans<br><br>fruit pudding |
| 2nd day | **CEREAL**<br>juice • grapefruit<br><br>beverage | **SUPER NACHOS**<br>cheese & fruit platter | **CHINESE HONEY PORK**<br>rice • broccoli<br><br>sugar cookies |
| 3rd day | **CREAMED HAM & EGGS**<br>juice • peaches<br><br>beverage | **TUNA MELON BOATS**<br>cheese & crackers | **SKILLET ROUND STEAK**<br>salad • deviled eggs<br>saucy beans & noodles<br><br>fruit cocktail |
| 4th day | **BAGELS &**<br>**CRABMEAT SPREAD**<br>juice • pineapple<br><br>beverage | **MULLIGATAWNY SOUP**<br>crackers<br>cheese & salami platter | **SPAGHETTI &**<br>**SMOKED SAUSAGE**<br>salad • wrapped sticks<br><br>stuffed pears |
| 5th day | **CORN FRITTERS**<br>juice<br>sausage • applesauce<br><br>beverage | **HEARTY MACARONI SALAD**<br>crackers & fruit platter | **TUNA GUMBO**<br>salad • rice<br><br>pudding |

1st day
Breakfast
# DONUTS
Juice • melon • beverage

*Donuts and fruit may not be your idea of a gourmet breakfast. And I admit it, it isn't. But it does serve a purpose.*

*This menu represents the first meal, of the first day, of our long awaited vacation, aboard the boat. And since we want to get an early start and leave port at the crack of dawn...(ha, ha...I might just as well forget that line of thought). The fact of the matter is, things never go as planned. There are always a few last minute details to take care of before casting off. So, instead of preparing an elaborate breakfast buffet that nobody has or wants to take the time to eat anyway, I prefer to furnish the crew with an ample supply of fresh donuts and fruit.*

*Now, no matter what goes wrong, the crew can eat whenever and wherever they want, and I don't have to worry about throwing out good food.*

**Tip:** Try not to buy prepackaged store donuts. This is your vacation. Splurge. Go out and get a variety of fresh bakery donuts, filled with all that good creamy stuff you're not suppose to eat and you'll have a very happy crew.

33

# Stacked HAM & CHEESE Sandwiches
potato chips • canned 3-bean salad • pickles

*According to one of our crew members, the only way you can go wrong serving this great sandwich is by not cutting it in half properly. A good chef knows that "Sandwich Stupidstition" dictates that all sandwiches be cut in half DIAGONALLY. Not horizontally. Not vertically. But cut in half diagonally. The reason, according to him, is very clear. They taste better that way.*

**8   slices white bread**
**Butter**
**Mayonnaise**
**Lettuce**
**1   pound shaved cooked ham**
**Mustard**
**½   pound shaved Swiss cheese**

To make each sandwich, butter bread and assemble in order: slice of bread, mayonnaise, lettuce, ham, mustard, Swiss cheese, ham, mustard, Swiss cheese, mayonnaise, and buttered bread.

Dagwood Style:
Add any or all of the following: sliced onion rings, sliced green pepper, sliced cucumbers, sliced radishes, a dash of horseradish or Dijon mustard.

makes 4 sandwiches

**Tip:** Try to prepare the sandwiches ahead of time. Then wrap them in some paper toweling or a napkin and store in a zip lock bag. If somebody wants something different on his or her sandwich, identify it by labeling the bag with a felt tip pen.
**Note:** Prepare pudding for tonight's dessert so it has a chance to chill before dinner.

# CHICKEN INDIENNE
salad • white rice • canned green beans • fruit pudding

*Try to recall the most exciting sunset you've ever seen. Visualize its glorious array of golden yellows, oranges and reds. Remember the special sensation it created, sending tingles up and down your spine. Now imagine what it would be like if we could transfer these visual and emotional experiences to our taste-buds.*
*If it were possible to serve a sunset for dinner, I imagine it would taste something like Chicken Indienne.*

¼  cup flour
¼  teaspoon cayenne
1   teaspoon turmeric
1½ teaspoons paprika
2   teaspoons cumin
2   Tablespoons curry powder
• • • • • •

1   Tablespoon butter
2   Tablespoons vegetable oil
• • • • • •

1½ pounds boned and skinned
chicken breast, cut into bite
size pieces
• • • • • •

1   Tablespoon vegetable oil
1   onion, chopped
1   onion, sliced and separated
into rings
3   garlic cloves, minced
• • • • • •

1   cup water
1½ teaspoons instant chicken
bouillon granules
3   tomatoes, chopped
2   1½-oz. packages of raisins
Salt and pepper to taste

*Pre-package first 6 ingredients in a large (gallon size) zip lock
plastic storage bag.*
• • • • • •

Add chicken pieces to plastic bag containing the first 6 ingredients.
Shake and massage bag to thoroughly coat the pieces of chicken.
• • • • • •

In a large skillet, heat butter and oil over medium-high heat. Add
chicken and cook 5 minutes, stirring occasionally. With slotted spoon,
remove chicken from skillet and set aside.
• • • • • •

Add next 3 ingredients (oil, onions, and garlic) to skillet. Cover and
continue to cook over medium heat for 5 minutes.
• • • • • •

Add all remaining ingredients to skillet and bring mixture to a boil.
Return chicken to skillet and reduce heat. Cover and simmer 30
minutes.
Serve over rice.

makes 4 hearty servings.

**FRUITED PUDDING**

1   16-oz. can tapioca pudding
1   8-oz. can crushed pineapple,
drained

1   banana, chopped
• • • • • •
Maraschino cherries

In a bowl, combine first 3 ingredients. Chill. Top each serving with a cherry.

**Tip:** To heat canned green beans, simply drain beans and place on a
sheet of aluminum foil. Sprinkle with Italian-style salad dressing. Form
into a packet to fit inside skillet. Place on top of chicken during last 15
minutes of cooking.
**Note:** The weight of the meat is equal to 4 chicken breast halves. If you
have more than four guests at dinner, simply add one chicken breast half
for each. There's no need to add anything else.

## CEREAL
juice • grapefruit • beverage

*Cereal. Plain old dry cereal. It's appeared on the American breakfast table since 1872. Although it wouldn't win any culinary awards, it does have its advantages. Once a person is able to hold a spoon without assistance, he is perfectly capable of making his own breakfast. This means the chef no longer has to get up at the crack of dawn to give the crew a nutritious breakfast.*

**Tip:** Try buying cereal in variety-packs so everyone can have something different if they so desire. Plus, you can eat it right out of the carton, which means nobody has to do dishes.
You can "beef up" the cereal with sliced fruit, raisins or nuts.

## SUPER NACHOS
cheese & fruit platter

*So a few members of the crew are a little upset about having to make up their own cereal bowls, pour their own milk and slice their own grapefruit for breakfast this morning; while you, their cook, their chef, sleeps in. Well, never fear. Super Nachos will get you out of the dog house. In fact, not only will they get you out of the dog house, they will transform the hostile natives into your docile worshippers.*

| | | | |
|---|---|---|---|
| 1 | teaspoon seasoned salt | 2 | 16-oz. cans refried beans |
| 1 | teaspoon chili powder | 2 | cups (8-oz.) shredded Monterey Jack cheese |
| ½ | teaspoon cumin | | • • • • • • |
| ¼ | teaspoon paprika | 1 | 4-oz. can chopped green chilies |
| ¼ | teaspoon salt | | |
| | Dash of turmeric | 1 | cup (4-oz.) shredded Cheddar cheese |
| | Pinch of cayenne | | |
| | • • • • • • | 1 | tomato, finely chopped |
| 1 | Tablespoon vegetable oil | ¾ | cup taco sauce |
| 1 | onion, chopped | | • • • • • • |
| 1 | garlic clove, minced | | Tortilla chips |
| 1 | pound ground beef | | |
| | • • • • • • | | |

*Pre-package first 7 ingredients in a plastic zip lock envelope.*
• • • • • •

In a large skillet, heat oil over medium-high heat. Add onion, garlic, and meat. Cook until meat is browned. Discard grease.

• • • • • •

In a large bowl, combine refried beans, Monterey Jack cheese and pre-packaged ingredients. Mix well. Add mixture to skillet and reduce heat. Cover and simmer 3 minutes.

• • • • • •

Distribute chilies, Cheddar cheese, and chopped tomatoes evenly on top of meat mixture in skillet. Top with taco sauce. Cover and simmer 5 minutes or until cheese melts.

• • • • • •

Tuck tortilla chips around the inside edge of skillet and garnish with any or all of the following: sliced black olives, chopped pimiento, stuffed green olives, chopped green onion, sour cream or guacamole.

makes 4 hearty servings

## GUACAMOLE

| | |
|---|---|
| 1    garlic clove, minced | 2    avocados, halved, pitted, |
| ½   teaspoon seasoned salt |      peeled and cubed |
| ⅛   teaspoon hot pepper sauce | 1    Tablespoon bacon bits, |
| 2    Tablespoons lemon juice |      crushed |

In a large bowl, mash together garlic and salt with the back of a spoon. Blend in hot pepper sauce and lemon juice.

Add avacado cubes and mash ingredients together with a fork. Stir in bacon bits. Transfer to smaller bowl and chill thoroughly.

makes 2 cups

> **Tip:** If the weatherman is calling for choppy seas, this meal can be served at cabin temperature. Just cook the meat mixture in the morning before leaving port. Make sure the meat is well-drained. You can finish preparing this dish at lunchtime without any additional cooking.
> Prepare the guacamole ahead of time to allow the flavor to develop.
> **Note:** If you want, you can substitute a commercially-produced taco seasoning mix for the first 7 ingredients.

2nd day **CHINESE HONEY PORK**
Dinner    white rice • steamed broccoli • sugar cookies

*During the course of our summer cruise, we have several crew changes. It never fails to amuse me, whether it's during the winter planning sessions or when they finally step on board, that the crew's first and primary concern is when we're having Honey Pork. They don't care where we're going, when we're going, or anything else. They just want to make sure I'll be serving Honey Pork when they're on board. Think I'm kidding? Just wait and see what happens after you serve it.*

½ cup honey
½ cup soy sauce
¼ cup red wine vinegar
1 teaspoon garlic salt
2 teaspoons ginger
2 ¾-oz. packages brown gravy mix

• • • • • •

2 Tablespoons vegetable oil

2 pounds pork steak, cut into bite size pieces

• • • • •

1½ cups water

• • • • •

4 carrots, thinly sliced
1 onion, cut into wedges
1 green pepper, cut into 1-inch squares

*Pre-package first 6 ingredients in a 18-oz. jar. (Shake jar after packaging and before adding to skillet.)*

• • • • • •

In a large skillet, heat oil over medium-high heat. Add pork and cook 15 minutes, stirring frequently. Discard excess grease.

• • • • • •

Add water and pre-packaged ingredients to the skillet. Stir to blend mixture. Cover and continue to cook over medium heat for 20 minutes.

• • • • • •

Add all remaining ingredients to skillet. Cover and continue to cook over medium heat for 20 minutes.
Serve over white rice.

makes 4 hearty servings

**Tip:** To steam broccoli, simply remove leaves, cut off the tough ends of stalks and separate into spears. Place in skillet on top of the Honey Pork during the last 15 minutes of cooking.
**Note:** Any cut of pork is a suitable substitute for the pork steaks.

---

3rd day **CREAMED HAM & EGGS**
Breakfast juice • canned peaches • beverage

---

*The first time I served this tempting tidbit, the crew almost mutinied. And that was before they were called to the table.*
*You know how everybody likes to peek in the pot to see what's cooking? When they looked inside this time, they were reminded of an old Army / Navy favorite: creamed chipped beef on toast (more commonly referred to as #%$'# on a shingle).*
*Well, appearances are deceiving. And they learned, as you will, you can't judge the book by its cover, until you taste it.*

1 Tablespoon butter
2 4-oz. cans sliced mushrooms, drained
1 garlic clove, minced

• • • • • •

1 10½-oz. can cream of mushroom soup

¼ cup milk
¼ cup dry sherry
2 6¾-oz. cans chunk ham, broken up

• • • • • •

4 hard-boiled eggs, sliced
Italian Bread, crumbled

In a large skillet, melt butter over medium heat. Add mushrooms and garlic. Cook until mushrooms are heated through.

• • • • • •

Add next 4 ingredients to the skillet. Stir to blend well. Cover and cook 5 minutes.

• • • • • •

Gently stir in sliced eggs. Reduce heat and simmer, uncovered, for 2 minutes.

Serve over crumbled slices of bread.

makes 4 hearty servings

> **Note:** Since you have to cook some hard-boiled eggs for breakfast anyway, now would be a good time to do the noodles for tonight's dinner and the spaghetti and the macaroni that you'll need later on.
> If you have electricity and a toaster, try this mixture over toasted English muffins or bread.

## 3rd day TUNA MELON BOATS
Lunch   cheese & crackers

*The year I added this hot little number to our meal plan, I learned two very simple but important lessons. First: How not to store melons. And second: Know the likes and dislikes of your crew.*

*It happened during the first leg of our cruise. We lovingly refer to it as "the Death March"... a one hundred ninety-three mile jaunt from our home port to the happy cruising waters north of us. One hundred ninety-three miles that we "have to cover" in three days or less, come hell, high water, or the ever feared...Nor-Northeaster.*

*Well, this one particular year we spent quite a few hours beating into a very nasty Nor-Northeaster. Around 4 a.m., a very tired crew member left the helm and headed straight to his bunk for some well deserved sleep.*

*Enter lesson number one: As the boat rolled and pitched in the bad weather, so did the unsecured melons that were stored in the cubbie, directly over the head of one tired sailor.*

*Lesson number two: When a very, very, very tired sailor, who doesn't like cantaloupes to begin with, is exposed to lesson number one, he will have a tendency to propel said melons overboard.*

*Needless to say, later that day we enjoyed tuna fish sandwiches instead of those fancy dancy little tuna boats I had planned.*

| | |
|---|---|
| 2 | 6½-oz. cans tuna, drained and flaked |
| 1¼ | cups chopped mixed nuts |
| 1 | cup finely choppped celery |
| ⅔ | cup finely chopped onion |
| 2 | teaspoons lemon juice |
| 1 | Tablespoon prepared mustard |
| 5 | Tablespoons mayonnaise |

• • • • • •

2   cantaloupes, halved and seeded
    Sliced kiwi and grapes for garnish

In a large bowl, combine first 6 ingredients. Blend in mayonnaise, a little at a time, until desired degree of moisture is reached.

• • • • • •

Spoon tuna mixture into each half of melon. Garnish with kiwi and grapes.

makes 4 servings.

**SKILLET ROUND STEAK**
salad • deviled eggs • saucy beans & noodles • canned fruit cocktail

*Its name gets straight to the point. Skillet Round Steak. No fancy nouns, adverbs, adjectives or foreign phrases. In plain English, it tells you what you're going to be eating. Round steak that was cooked in a skillet. Yet, hidden beneath this crude, but honest, spartan dish, lies a mouthwatering treasure smothered in mysterious and intriguing flavors.*

¼  cup flour
¼  teaspoon pepper
1  teaspoon salt
• • • • • •

1  pound boneless round steak, ½-inch thick
2  Tablespoon butter
• • • • • •

1  teaspoon Worcestershire sauce

1½ Tablespoons Dijon mustard
• • • • • •
1  teaspoon Worcestershire sauce
1½ teaspoons instant beef bouillon granules
3  Tablespoons butter
¼  cup Brandy
½  cup water
1  onion, thinly sliced

*Pre-package first 3 ingredients in a small (quart size) zip lock plastic storage bag.*
• • • • • •

Trim all excess fat from steak. Cut meat into 4 serving size pieces and pound each to ¼-inch thickness. Dredge steaks in pre-packaged flour mixture.
• • • • • •

In a large skillet, melt butter over medium-high heat. Add steaks to skillet and brown on both sides. Remove steaks from skillet.
• • • • • •

In a cup, combine Worcestershire sauce and mustard. Mix well. Spread sauce on both sides of steaks and set aside.
• • • • • •

Add remaining ingredients to skillet and bring to a boil. Stir mixture to dissolve bouillon granules. Return steaks to skillet and reduce heat. Cover and simmer 30 minutes.

makes 4 servings

### HAM DEVILED EGGS

4  hard-boiled eggs
• • • • • •
2  Tablespoons mayonnaise
1  2½-oz. can deviled ham

2  Tablespoons finely chopped green pepper
• • • • • •
¼  cup (1-oz.) shredded Cheddar cheese

Slice eggs in half lengthwise. Remove yolks. In a bowl, combine yolks and next 3 ingredients. Mix well. Stuff egg whites with mixture and top with cheese.

**SAUCY BEANS & NOODLES**

¼ cup sugar
1 Tablespoon cornstarch
¼ cup vinegar
• • • • • •

1 15-oz. can 3-bean salad, drained
   and liquid reserved
• • • • • •

4 ounces egg noodles, cooked
¼ cup chopped walnuts

In a large saucepan, combine first 3 ingredients plus reserved liquid and mix well. Stirring occasionally, cook mixture over medium heat until thick and bubbly. Stir in beans and cook 2 minutes more. Serve over cooked noodles topped with chopped walnuts.

> **Tip:** You don't need a meat mallet to flatten the round steak. Simply place it inside a plastic bag and pound with the flat side of a winch handle or the bottom of a wine bottle.
> **Note:** If you don't normally carry brandy, pick up a few small (airline style) bottles for this recipe, because you can't do without it this time.
> Prepare the crabmeat spread for tomorrow morning's breakfast.

---

4th day **BAGELS & CRABMEAT SPREAD**
Breakfast  juice • canned pineapple slices • beverages

---

*One of my all time favorites for breakfast is bagels and cream cheese. It's quick, It's simple. And it's filling. But it sounds pretty boring. Since this is our vacation, I like to dress up my old favorite, give it a little class and a little extra zip, just for the crew. And this crabmeat spread does the trick.*

1 8-oz. package cream
   cheese, cubed and
   softened
½ cup mayonnaise
• • • • • •
½ cup (2-oz.)shredded Cheddar
   cheese

1 teaspoon pepper
2 4½-oz. cans crab meat,
   drained
• • • • • •
4 bagels, cut in half

In a large bowl, blend together cream cheese and mayonnaise until creamy.
• • • • • •
Add next 4 ingredients and blend well.
Spread mixture on each bagel half.

makes 4 servings.

> **Tip:** Make the spread the night before to allow the flavors to blend.
> **Note:** Any extra spread can be used to make cocktail sandwiches later on.

---

4th day **MULLIGATAWNY SOUP**
Lunch  crackers • cheese & salami platter

---

*Hold on there. No need to skip past this recipe. Just because there happens to be 15 or so ingredients in it, doesn't mean that it would be more difficult to prepare than canned soup. In fact, it only takes about 15 minutes longer to cook this hearty soup, then it does to heat up a couple of cans of Campbell's.*

½ teaspoon dried parsley flakes
1 teaspoon curry powder
2 whole cloves
  Dash of nutmeg
• • • • • •
¼ cup butter (½ stick)
1 onion, sliced
1 carrot, chopped
1 green pepper, chopped
1 celery stalk, chopped
1 apple, peeled, cored, and sliced

2 6¾-oz. cans chunk chicken, broken up
• • • • •
¼ cup flour
• • • • • •
2½ cups water
1 16-oz. can whole tomatoes, undrained and chopped
3 teaspoons instant chicken bouillon granules
  Salt and pepper to taste

*Pre-package first 4 ingredients in a plastic zip lock envelope.*
• • • • • •
In Dutch oven, melt butter over medium-high heat. Add next 6 ingredients and saute 10 minutes.
• • • • • •
Stir in flour. Saute until flour turns light brown (about 5 minutes).
• • • • • •
Add pre-packaged spices and all remaining ingredients. Bring mixture to a boil. Reduce heat. Cover and simmer 15 minutes.

makes 4 hearty servings

**Tip:** Since you don't have to cook anything for breakfast, you might want to prepare this soup in the morning before you leave port and store it in a wide-mouth thermos until lunch.
P.S. Yes, you can substitute canned soup, stew or a chowder if you wish. Just remember to add it to your shopping list.

---

4th day
Dinner
# SPAGHETTI & SMOKED SAUSAGE
salad • wrapped sticks • stuffed pears

---

*Good Lord, I hope my mother doesn't see this. She would kill me if she knew I was using or was even thinking about using a canned or jarred spaghetti sauce. "Good cooks use fresh tomatoes and let their sauce simmer." That's fine and dandy, but when you're bouncing around in 4 to 6 foot waves, you really don't want to be simmering anything for 3 hours, even if it does taste heavenly and your stove is gimbled.*

*Therefore, we have to use a little imagination to enhance the so-called "unacceptable". Dress it up. Make it look good and taste great. This recipe may not please great Italian cooks or Mama, but you'll have no complaints from the crew.*

1 pound fully cooked smoked sausage, sliced into ½-inch pieces
1 onion, chopped
2 4-oz. cans sliced mushrooms, drained
• • • • • •

1 16-oz. jar prepared spaghetti sauce
• • • • • •
8 ounces spaghetti, cooked
1 cup (4-oz.)shredded Cheddar cheese
  Chopped green and black olives

42

In a large skillet, over medium heat, cook first 3 ingredients until sausage is browned. Discard excess grease.

• • • • • •

Add spaghetti sauce to skillet and heat through.

Divide cooked spaghetti into serving portions. Cover with sauce mixture. Top with grated cheese and garnish with olives.

makes 4 servings

### Wrapped BREAD STICKS

| | |
|---|---|
| 12  bread sticks | 1  8-oz. jar processed cheese |
| | 12  thin slices of salami |

Cover ¾ of each bread stick with cheese. Wrap each stick with a slice of salami.

### Stuffed PEARS

| | |
|---|---|
| 2  ounces Blue cheese, crumbled | |
| 2  teaspoons plain yogurt | 1  16-oz. can pear halves, drained |

In a cup, combine cheese and yogurt. Mix well. Stuff pear halves with mixture.

**Tip:** By cooking the spaghetti ahead of time and storing it in a plastic bag, all you have to do now to get this dish ready is pour in some hot water, let it stand awhile, then poke some holes in the bottom of the bag to let it drain and presto! The spaghetti is ready for the sauce.

---

5th day
Breakfast
# CORN FRITTERS
juice • sausage • applesauce • beverage

---

*Never heard of a corn fritter, hey?*

*Well, I'm not surprised. Until several years ago, neither did any of the other members of the crew, or for that matter anybody at the club. In fact, when I first mentioned to the crew that we would be having fritters for breakfast, they thought I was joking. They envisioned fritters as those creepy, crawly, furry little creatures covered with chocolate, that were a popular novelty way back when.*

*Let me assure you, so you can reassure your crew: Fritters are not members of the insect family. Fritters are members of the pancake family. Lumpy first cousins to be exact.*

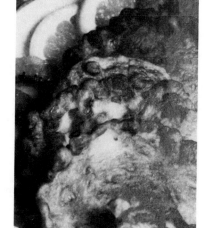

1  cup flour
1  teaspoon salt
1  Tablespoon sugar

• • • • • •

2  eggs, beaten
½  cup milk
  Dash of hot pepper sauce

• • • • • •

1  16-oz. can whole kernel corn, drained
  Vegetable oil

*Pre-package first 3 ingredients in a small (quart size) zip lock plastic storage bag.*

• • • • • •

In a large bowl, combine eggs, milk, and hot sauce. Mix slightly. Gradually add pre-packaged dry ingredients. Mix until smooth.

• • • • • •

Stir in corn.

In a large skillet, heat ¼-inch deep oil until hot. For each fritter, pour or spoon ¼ cup of mixture into the hot oil. Cook for 3 minutes per side or until golden brown.

makes 12 (4-inch) fritters

> **Tip:** You might want to try adding a little finely chopped green onions, green pepper or chopped pimiento to the batter. But just a little.
> If you're out of fresh milk you can use canned evaporated milk mixed with an equal amount of water.
> **Note:** Unlike pancakes, fritters have one smooth side and one bumpy side, so don't be surprised the first time you serve them. You didn't do anything wrong.

---

5th day
Lunch

# HEARTY MACARONI SALAD
crackers & fruit platter

---

*There are not too many sure things in life. But I can guarantee you one sure thing: If you serve this macaroni salad on a plate instead of in a bowl, you'll end up cleaning it from the deck, the table, the floor, the cockpit, dinghy and even the anchor locker. For some unknown reason, crew members have a tendency to think of macaroni salad as a mobile type of lunch; take it with you so to speak. Nothing wrong with that. Just make sure it's in a bowl.*

| | | | |
|---|---|---|---|
| 6 | ounces elbow macaroni, cooked | 1 | cup chopped celery |
| 2 | 6¾-oz. cans chunk ham, broken up | ½ | cup chopped onion |
| 1½ | cups (5-oz.) diced sharp cheddar cheese | ½ | cup chopped sweet pickle |
| | | ½ | cup sour cream |
| | | 2 | Tablespoons prepared mustard |

In a large bowl, combine all ingredients. Gently toss to mix. Transfer salad mixture to a large (gallon size) zip lock plastic storage bag. Seal and chill.
Serve in lettuce lined bowls.

makes 4 hearty servings

> **Tip:** In the morning, while you're cooking the corn fritters, have another crew member prepare the macaroni salad for lunch.
> **Note:** This tip only works if you have cooked the macaroni a day or two ahead of time.

*Paul Prudhomme, eat your heart out.*

*With no disrespect to the famous chef of K-Paul's Louisiana Kitchen intended, here's a quick and simple little gumbo that'll knock their socks off. I realize this "amateur" gumbo doesn't even rate in the same league as one prepared by the great Paul Prudhomme. But, when you're rocking and rolling on the high seas, it sure comes in a close second.*

| | |
|---|---|
| ¼  teaspoon thyme | ¼  cup chopped parsley |
| ½  teaspoon salt | 2  teaspoons instant chicken |
| 1  Tablespoon flour | bouillon granules |
| 1  bay leaf | 1  16-oz. can whole tomatoes |
| Dash of cayenne | undrained and chopped |
| • • • • • • | • • • • • • |
| 2  Tablespoons butter | 1  10-oz. can cut okra, drained |
| 1  onion, chopped | 2  6½-oz. can tuna, drained |
| 1  green pepper, chopped | 1  teaspoon lemon juice |
| • • • • • • | 1½ teaspoons Worcestershire |
| 1¼ cups water | sauce |
| • • • • • • | |

*Pre-package first 5 ingredients in a plastic zip lock envelope.*
• • • • • •

In Dutch oven, melt butter over medium-high heat.  Add onion, green pepper and garlic.  Saute 5 minutes.
• • • • • •

Combine water and pre-packaged spices. Mix thoroughly. Stirring constantly, add mixture to Dutch oven.
• • • • • •

Add next 3 ingredients to Dutch oven and bring to a boil.  Stir mixture to dissolve bouillon granules.  Reduce heat.  Cover and simmer 30 minutes.
• • • • • •

Add all remaining ingredients to Dutch oven. Cover and simmer 10 minutes.

Serve in bowls over rice.

makes 4 hearty servings.

**Tip:** Try topping your canned pudding with some chopped nuts and raisins.

45

# Time Out For Cocktails & Things

Have you ever noticed how friendly and sociable boaters are? It seems that every time you turn around, they've got a drink in their hand. And they're never shy about asking others to come aboard and join in. Well, contrary to popular beliefs, they're not a bunch of lushes, social drunkards, or misfits. Nope! They're just a dedicated group of individuals, preserving an ancient seafaring tradition of camaraderie and bonding. A way of celebrating a job well done.

It seems that a long, long time ago, after surviving a treacherous storm or after an excellent display of teamwork and seamanship, to reward them for their performance, the skipper would order up an extra ration of drink for his crew. So the way I see it, cocktail time, is just another way of keeping in touch with our heritage.

Since everybody knows that rum has always been considered the traditional drink of sailors, I think it only appropriate that I dedicate this first installment of Time Out For Cocktails to pleasures of Rum.

## CHEESE & BEEF BALL

| | |
|---|---|
| 1 | 8-oz. package cream cheese, cubed and softened |
| ¼ | cup grated Parmesan cheese |
| ¼ | cup chopped pimiento-stuffed green olives |
| 2 | teaspoons horseradish |
| 2½ | ounces dried beef, finely chopped |

• • • • • •

| | |
|---|---|
| ¾ | cup chopped pecans |

In a large bowl, combine first 5 ingredients. Mix well. Form into a ball and roll in remaining pecans. Seal in plastic wrap and chill. Serve crackers.

## SHRIMP & CUCUMBER SPREAD

| | |
|---|---|
| 1 | 3-oz. package cream cheese, cubed and softened |
| 2 | Tablespoons mayonnaise |
| 1 | Tablespoon catsup |
| 1 | teaspoon dry mustard |
| | Dash of garlic powder |

• • • • • •

| | |
|---|---|
| 1 | 4½-oz. can shrimp, drained and chopped |
| ¼ | cup finely chopped cucumber |
| 1 | Tablespoon finely chopped onion |

In a large bowl combine first 5 ingredients and mix well. Stir in remaining ingredients. Transfer to a smaller bowl and serve with cocktail breads and crackers.

## NORDIC DIP

| | |
|---|---|
| 1 | 3¾-oz. can smoked sardines in mustard sauce |

• • • • • •

| | |
|---|---|
| 1 | 3-oz. package cream cheese, cubed and softened |
| 1 | 2-oz. jar chopped pimiento, drained |
| 1 | teaspoon horseradish |
| 1 | teaspoon Dijon mustard |
| ½ | teaspoon Worcestershire sauce |
| ⅛ | teaspoon garlic powder |

• • • • • •

| | |
|---|---|
| 1 | 8-oz. carton plain yogurt |

In a large bowl, mash sardines with a fork. Add next 6 ingredients and blend well. Stir in yogurt. Transfer to a smaller bowl and chill. Serve with vegetables and crackers.

## BEEF ROLL-UPS

Cream cheese
Dried beef
Green onions, finely chopped
Pitted black olives, finely chopped

Spread cream cheese on a slice of dried beef. Sprinkle it with some onions and olives. Roll it up jelly roll fashion. Serve whole or sliced.

**Tip:** You might want to try using the SHRIMP and CUCUMBER spread to stuff some cherry tomatoes or some mushroom caps.

## HOT BUTTERED RUM

1     16-oz. package brown sugar
½     cup (1 stick) butter, softened
½     teaspoon ground cinnamon
½     teaspoon ground nutmeg
½     teaspoon ground cloves
      Dash of salt
      • • • • • •
      Rum
      Hot water
      Cinnamon sticks
      Lemon slices

In a large bowl, combine first 6 ingredients. Blend well. Store mixture in a 16 oz. jar. Keep cool.
      • • • • • •
To serve: Place 1 heaping Tablespoon butter mixture in a mug. Add 1½ ounces rum and a cinnamon stick. Fill with hot water and garnish with a slice of lemon.

## PINEAPPLE RUM SPRITZER

1½    ounces (1 jigger) white rum
3     ounces (2 jiggers) unsweetened
      pineapple juice
1     Tablespoon fresh lime juice.
6     ounces club soda

Combine all ingredients in glass over ice. Stir well.

## RANGOON RACQUET CLUB PUNCH

¼     cup pineapple juice
¼     cup lemon juice
¼     cup orange juice
½     cup sugar
      • • • • • •
1½    ounces dark rum
1½    ounces Curacoa
1½    ounces red wine
      • • • • • •
      Half bottle brut Champagne, chilled
1     cup chilled club soda

Combine first 4 ingredients. Stir until sugar dissolves. Add next 3 ingredients and chill. Add champagne and soda just before serving. Serve over ice.

## SURBER'S REVENGE

1½    ounces light rum
1     teaspoon honey
      Juice of half a lime
      Crushed ice
      • • • • • •
6     ounces chilled Champagne

In a screw top jar, combine rum, honey and lime juice. Add crushed ice. Secure lid and shake well. Strain into a glass and add Champagne.

# Group 2
## a five day menu

| | BREAKFAST | LUNCH | DINNER |
|---|---|---|---|
| 1st day | **COFFEE CAKE**<br>juice • orange slices<br>beverage | **CHILI**<br>crackers<br>cheese & salami platter | **SAVORY ALMOND DIN**<br>salad • rice • green beans<br>pudding |
| 2nd day | **BEER PANCAKES**<br>juice • eggs • sausage<br>beverage | **SPINNAKER CLUB<br>Sandwiches**<br>corn chips • pickles | **CHICKEN CONTINENTAL**<br>salad • rice • sunshine carrots<br>sugar cookies |
| 3rd day | **HOT CEREAL**<br>juice • peaches<br>beverage | **FRENCH DIP**<br>potato chips • 3-bean salad • pickles | **MEXICAN BEEF STROGANOFF**<br>salad • egg noodles • broccoli<br>lost wafers |
| 4th day | **POLYNESIAN<br>BREAKFAST CAKES**<br>juice • applesauce<br>beverage | **ALOHA CHICKEN SALAD**<br>cheese & crackers | **LINGUINE with CLAM SAUCE**<br>salad • bread sticks<br>strawberries & orange marsala |
| 5th day | **SPANISH SCRAMBLED EGGS**<br>juice • melon<br>beverage | **MACARONI-CRABMEAT SALAD**<br>cheese & crackers<br>fruit platter with coconut-honey dip | **HAM & POTATO SKILLET**<br>salad • deviled eggs<br>pudding |

1st day
Breakfast
# COFFEE CAKE
### juice • fresh orange slices • beverage

*One summer we had some real landlubbers join us for the second leg of our cruise. I mean their nautical experience was limited to floating around the swimming pool on an air mattress. But what they lacked in experience, they made up for in enthusiasm. It's customary for our departing and replacement crew members to get together the night before the changeover and down a few Brewskies together. As this particular night progressed, it became obvious that the newcomers were wide open for a little Tom Foolery.*

*We explained to them how everybody pitched in with the chores, and that they were expected to do their fair share. No problem! They were more than willing to do whatever we asked.*

*Well, the time finally came to set the bait for our little prank. I explained to them that it was time for me to return to the boat because I had to get up early to prepare breakfast. They were extremely disappointed and demanded that I stay. I insisted that there was really too much work to be done in the morning for me to be hanging around any longer. I was promptly reminded by them that everyone on board shared in the work load, and they immediately volunteered to help if I stayed around.*

*When we finally returned to the boat, I told the newcomers that I would write down the instructions as to what I wanted them to do in the morning. I would also set the alarm for them, but under no circumstances were they to wake me. Just follow the instructions.*

*The alarm went off at 5 a.m. They read their instructions, executed them and were back at the boat by 6:30 a.m. ready for the 7 a.m. departure.*

*What were their instructions? To pick up a pineapple almond coffee cake and two thermoses of hot coffee at the bakery 2 miles south of town. But, for some reason I forgot to mention the courtesy bicycle at the Harbor Master's office. Oh well, at least it was a nice morning for a walk.*

*I love chili. I love making chili. I love eating chili. In fact, I have 18 of the world's best chili recipes that I use as references when I make my hit or miss, one of a kind, one time only chili. Some of these recipes have over 35 ingredients in them, which is fine if you're whipping together a huge batch of chili at home. But right now, we're on a boat and need something just a little less ostentatious and I think I have found the ideal "on board" chili recipe. It may not be original or up to the standard of a true chili connoisseur, but it works.*

*Purchase your favorite canned chili and add a little spark to it with a dash of Worcestershire, hot sauce, or some chopped hot pepper rings and add a litte beer for good measure.*

*Rolaids, anyone?*

| | | | |
|---|---|---|---|
| 1 | 25-oz. commercially canned chili with beans | 1 | cup (4-oz.) shredded Cheddar cheese |
| 1 | 16-oz. commercially canned hot chili with beans | ½ | cup finely chopped onion |

• • • • • •

In Dutch oven, cook canned chili over medium heat until throughly heated.

• • • • •

Top each serving with cheese and onion.

**Note:** One of the proofreaders believes that since this is a cookbook, I should be talking about original chili recipes instead of canned. And she's right! So if you've got the time, you might want to try this award winning recipe by Jim Adamski. But, one word of warning. Prepare it at home, not on the boat. (Ingredients not on shopping list)

**Homemade CHILI**

| | | | |
|---|---|---|---|
| 3 | pounds ground beef | 3 | ounces chili powder |
| | • • • • • | ¼ | cup barbecue sauce |
| 3 | pounds round steak, trimmed and cut into cubes | ¼ | cup catsup |
| | | ¼ | cup hot pepper sauce |
| 2 | 28-oz. cans stewed tomatoes | 2 | teaspoons cumin |
| 1 | 46-oz. can V-8 juice | 2 | teaspoons instant beef bouillon granules |
| 2 | 1½-oz. packages dried onion soup mix | | |
| | | 2 | teaspoons salt |
| 1 | large Spanish onion, chopped | 1 | teaspoon oregano |
| 3 | celery stalks, chopped | 1 | teaspoon onion powder |
| 2 | green peppers, chopped | ½ | teaspoon black pepper |
| 2 | pickled mild banana peppers, seeded and chopped | | Dash of crushed red peppers |
| | | | Dash of basil |
| ½ | cup banana pepper juice | | Dash of thyme |
| ½ | cup white vinegar | 1 | dried red pepper |
| 2 | garlic cloves, crushed | | • • • • • |
| 1 | bay leaf | | 1 to 2 cups beer, or to taste |

In a large stock pot, brown beef over medium-high heat. Drain and discard any excess grease.

• • • • • •

Except for the beer, add all remaining ingredients. Bring mixture to a boil. Reduce heat. Cover and simmer 2 hours.

• • • • • •

Add beer and simmer 1 hours.

makes 6 quarts

# SAVORY ALMOND DIN

1st day
Dinner

salad • white rice • canned french-cut green beans
canned pudding

*Hungarian? Romanian? German? Mexican? Chinese? Japanese? Americanese? This recipe has been part of our cruising repertoire for so long that I can no longer remember where it came from. I've searched my files, my logs, my notes and my cookbooks with no luck. It does have an oriental flavor of sorts, but I'm not sure. About the only thing I am sure of is that the crew loves it. And when something is this good, all you need to know is that it is good. Who cares where it came from? Maybe it's from Africa or Brazil. No, no, no . . . I think it's northern Italy. May be . . .*

| | | | |
|---|---|---|---|
| 2 | Tablespoons vegetable oil | 1 | 8-oz. can sliced water chestnuts, drained |
| 2 | pounds pork steaks, trimmed and cut into bite size pieces | 2 | teaspoons salt |
| | • • • • • | ⅛ | teaspoon pepper |
| 1 | cup sliced celery | 2 | teaspoon instant beef bouillon granules |
| 1 | green pepper, thinly sliced | | • • • • • |
| | • • • • • | ¼ | cup water |
| ¾ | cup water | 2 | Tablespoons cornstarch |
| 1 | 4-oz. can sliced mushrooms, drained | 1 | 8-oz. can pineapple chunks, drained |
| | | 1 | 4-oz. jar pimiento |

In a large skillet, heat oil over medium-high heat. Add pork and brown. Reduce heat. Cover and simmer 15 minutes.

• • • • •

Add celery and green pepper to skillet. Cover and simmer 15 minutes. Pour off pan drippings.

• • • • •

Add next 6 ingredients and bring to a boil. Stir mixture to dissolve bouillon granules.

• • • • •

In a cup, blend cornstarch and water. Add mixture to pork and vegetables in skillet. Continue to cook and stir till thick and bubbly.

Top with chunks of pineapple and pimiento. Reduce heat. Cover and simmer 5 minutes.

Serve over white rice.

makes 4 servings.

**Tip:** To heat, simply spread the French Cut green beans over the top of the pork mixture during the last 5 minutes of cooking. But remember to remove the green beans first, before they get mixed into the pork.

For dessert, try topping canned pudding with some whipped topping and crowning it with a cherry.

## BEER PANCAKES
juice • eggs • sausage • beverage

*When I was a little tot, I wasn't too big on eating breakfast. In fact, I'd do just about anything to stay away from the table. But every time I stayed at Gram's, I'd end up stuffing myself. It wasn't because I was force-fed. In fact, it was quite the opposite. I was told I couldn't eat. That is, when my grandmother made beer pancakes, my grandfather and uncle told me that they were only for grown-ups (real men) and that little boys couldn't handle a "real" breakfast like beer pancakes. So I'd just have to sit there and watch them eat. Of course, after they left the table I discovered that Grams had an extra stack of pancakes waiting just for me.*

| | | | |
|---|---|---|---|
| 2 | cups packaged biscuit mix | 5 | eggs, beaten |
| 2 | Tablespoons sugar | ½ | cup beer |
| ½ | teaspoon cinnamon | 2 | Tablespoons vegetable oil |
| | Dash of nutmeg | | |

• • • • • •

*Pre-package first 4 ingredients in a small (quart size) zip lock plastic storage bag.*

• • • • • •

In a large bowl, combine remaining ingredients and mix. Add pre-packaged ingredients and stir until moist.

For each pancake, pour ¼ cup batter onto a lightly greased griddle. Cook 2 minutes per side or until golden brown.

makes 12 (4-inch) pancakes

> **Tips:** Don't over-mix pancake batter! Just blend until ingredients are moist.
> The pancakes are ready to be flipped when most of the surface bubbles have popped.
> **Note:** You can vary the flavor of these pancakes by using different imported beers. But NEVER use any Lite beer.

---

## The SPINNAKER CLUB Sandwich
corn chips • pickles

*One of the most beautiful sights out on the water is a sailboat headed downwind carrying a full complement of multi-colored head sails. It's hard to believe that just a little puff of wind is propelling that massive hull through the water. It's hard to believe that those beautiful pieces of cloth are harnessing the uncontrollable winds of Mother Nature. It's not the labor of one lone sail, but the harmony and unity of all the sails that make it work. That's one of the reasons I call this sandwich the "Spinnaker" Club. All the ingredients work well individually but when they get together they can harness the uncontrollable hunger of any sailor.*

| | | | |
|---|---|---|---|
| 12 | slices white bread | | Mayonnaise |
| | Butter | 4 | slices Swiss cheese |
| | Mustard | 4 | ounces-plus shaved turkey |
| 4 | ounces-plus shaved ham | | Tomato slices |
| | Onion rings | | Lettuce |
| 4 | slices Cheddar cheese | | |

To make each sandwich, butter bread and assemble in order: slice of bread, mustard, ham, onion rings, slice of Cheddar cheese, slice of bread, mayonnaise, slice of Swiss cheese, turkey, slice of tomato, lettuce, and buttered bread.

makes 4 sandwiches

> **Note:** When you build a 3 tier sandwich, it's not a good idea to make them ahead of time, unless you have some really long toothpicks to make sure the sandwiches are secure. Keep in mind, toothpicks tend to punch holes in storage bags.

---

## 2nd day CHICKEN CONTINENTAL
Dinner  salad • white rice • sunshine carrots • sugar cookies

---

*Many years ago, in one of their movies, Fred Astaire and Ginger Rogers introduced the country to the "Continental," a dance that was classified as graceful elegance; the perfect blend of adventure and sophistication. I can't think of any other adjectives that could aptly describe this dish any better than those.*

*If you have any questions regarding the quality and style I'm referring to, or if your just an old romatic fool like me, try renting one of Fred and Ginger's old movies some cold wintery night.*

| | |
|---|---|
| ¼ **cup flour** | ⅓ **cup soy sauce** |
| ¼ **teaspoon pepper** | 1 **16-oz. can tomatoes, cut up** |
| ¼ **teaspoon thyme** | 1 **onion, sliced** |
| ½ **teaspoon paprika** | 1 **garlic clove, minced** |
| 1 **teaspoon salt** | • • • • • |
| • • • • • | ½ **cup sliced pitted black olives** |
| 3 **pounds prime chicken parts, cut up** | 1 **4-oz. can sliced mushrooms, and liquid** |
| 2 **Tablespoons vegetable oil** | |
| • • • • • | |

*Pre-package first 5 ingredients in a large (gallon size) zip lock plastic storage bag.*
• • • • •

Add chicken parts to plastic bag containing first 5 ingredients. Shake and massage bag to thoroughly coat chicken.

In a Dutch oven, heat oil over medium heat. Add chicken and brown.
• • • • •

Add next 4 ingredients and reduce heat. Cover and simmer 45 minutes.
• • • • •

Add remaining ingredients and bring to a boil. Reduce heat. Cover and simmer 5 minutes.

Serve over white rice.

makes 4 hearty servings

**SUNSHINE CARROTS**

| | | | |
|---|---|---|---|
| 6 | Tablespoons orange juice | | |
| 4 | Tablespoons maple syrup | 2 | 16-oz. cans small whole carrots, |
| 2 | Tablespoons orange marmalade | | drained |

• • • • • •

In a large skillet, combine first 3 ingredients. Stirring constantly, bring mixture to a boil. Add carrots and return to a boil. Reduce heat. Cover and simmer 5 minutes.

---

3rd day **instant HOT CEREAL**
Breakfast    juice • canned sliced peaches • beverage

*I'm a little embarrassed to suggest, or even mention, oatmeal or any other type of hot cereal for breakfast, because I can still remember how much I used to hate the stuff. I remember my mother trying unsuccessfully to trick me into eating that icky, pasty stuff by playing "air-o-plane" and "choo choo train." I remember that at summer camp only the nerds ate OATMEAL!!! Yuk! Now here I am telling you to "Eat your oatmeal!" Why the drastic change? First, thanks to modern technology, oatmeal no longer looks or tastes like paste. There are many new and intriguing flavors. Secondly, manufacturers now package it in individual serving sizes so everybody can have his or her own special flavor for breakfast (and not everybody has to eat it!). Thirdly, and most important, the only thing you have to do to make it is boil some water!*

**Tip:** To give it a little extra zip, try topping your hot cereal with some chopped dried fruit, peanut butter, sesame or sunflower seeds, walnuts or dates.

---

3rd day **FRENCH DIP**
Lunch    potato chips • canned 3-bean salad • pickles

*I used to just toss some slices of roast beef between two halves of a French roll, heat up some of the beef juice I'd saved, and in no time flat I had the classic French Dip.*
*Well, that was too simple, too ordinary, too pedestrian for me. I had a reputation to protect, so I had to create something just a tad different. Now, if you don't want to try something different, something spectacular, you can always play it safe and just toss some slices of roast beef between two halves of a French roll . . . but you won't. That's too simple, too ordinary, too pedestrian. You want to bask in the glory of all those compliments just like I do.*

| | |
|---|---|
| 2 | **Tablespoons butter** |
| 1 | **large onion, thinly sliced and separated into rings** |
| 2 | **to 3 Tablespoons chopped hot pepper rings** |

• • • • • •

| | |
|---|---|
| 1 | **pound shaved roast beef** |
| 4 | **French rolls** |

In a large skillet, melt butter over medium heat.  Add onions and pepper rings.  Saute until onions are soft (about 5 minutes).

• • • • • •

Increase heat to high and add roast beef.  Stirring constantly, cook until beef is heated through (about 1 minute).

Divide mixture evenly between split French rolls.

makes 4 sandwiches

### Dip

| | | |
|---|---|---|
| 4 | teaspoons instant beef bouillon granules | Dash of garlic powder |
| | | 2 cups hot water |

Combine all ingredients in a bowl. Stir until bouillon granules dissolve. Divide evenly among four cups.

---

3rd day **MEXICAN BEEF STROGANOFF**
Dinner  salad • egg noodles • steamed broccoli • lost wafers

---

*How may times have you been invited over to a friend's house for a dinner party and discovered that the main entree for the evening was stroganoff? Now, there's nothing wrong with beef stroganoff, mind you, but it seemed that for a while there, stroganoff was becoming the only socially correct entree to serve. I don't know if it's just that I was overexposed to it, or what, but I found myself becoming very bored with it and I was looking for a change. I found one... Mexican Beef Stroganoff! This one will definitely add zip and adventure to your cruise. I'll guarantee that you won't be bored with this one.*

| | | | | |
|---|---|---|---|---|
| 1 | teaspoon seasoned salt | | | |
| 2 | teaspoons paprika | 1 | teaspoon soy sauce |
| 2 | teaspoons chili powder | ⅓ | cup chili sauce |
| • • • • • • | | 1 | cup water |
| 2 | Tablespoons vegetable oil | • • • • • • | |
| ½ | cup chopped onion | ½ | cup sour cream |
| 1 | garlic clove, minced | 1½ | Tablespoons flour |
| 1 | pound boneless beef round steak, cut into bite size strips | 1 | 4-oz. can sliced mushrooms, drained |
| • • • • • • | | | | |

*Pre-package first 3 ingredients in a plastic zip lock envelope.*

• • • • • •

In a large skillet, heat oil over medium-high heat.  Add onion, garlic and meat.  Cook until meat is browned.  Pour off pan drippings.

• • • • • •

Add next 3 ingredients, plus pre-packaged spices, to skillet. Bring mixture to a boil.  Reduce heat.  Cover and simmer 50 minutes.

• • • • • •

In a cup, blend sour cream and flour. Add mixture and mushrooms to skillet. Continue to cook and stir until thick and bubbly. Cover and simmer 2 minutes.

Serve over egg noodles.

makes 4 servings

1    16-oz. can lemon pudding        **Whipped topping**
16  vanilla wafers                   **Maraschino cherries**
1    banana, sliced and dipped in
     lemon juice

In four clear plastic glasses, layer in order: pudding, wafers, bananas, pudding, and whipped cream. Top each with a cherry.

**Tips:** Now's the perfect time, not only to cook the noodles for the stroganoff, but some hard-boiled eggs, the linguine for tomorrow night and the macaroni for the crab meat salad later on.

To steam the broccoli, trim the leaves and cut off the tough ends of the stalks. Separate into spears and place in skillet on top of beef during the last 15 minutes of cooking. Remove broccoli before making the sauce.

Also, combine the fruit and sauce for tomorrow night's dessert.

**Note:** Some folks like to crumble the wafers for their dessert, so it's spoonable. But I've found that most kids, including bank vice presidents and stock brokers, enjoy digging the whole wafer out of the pudding. Who cares if they use their fingers.

---

4th day **POLYNESIAN BREAKFAST CAKES**
Breakfast juice • applesauce • beverage

---

*Talk about creativity! This breakfast entree takes the cake!*

*From the south sea islands we experience the gentle blend of pineapple, pork, and soy sauce accented by a smidgeon of dry mustard. All aboard get ready for heaven! Close your eyes and imagine yourself on a tropical island. As you bite into these delightful breakfast cakes you can almost hear the rustle of grass skirts and the sound of a ukelele playing in the background. But keep your eyes closed or you'll discover that these exotic little creatures are actually ham fritters on vacation from the mainland.*

⅔  *cup flour*
1  *teaspoon baking powder*
¼  *teaspoon dry mustard*
  • • • • • •

2  **eggs, beaten**
⅓  **cup milk**
1  **teaspoon soy sauce**
  • • • • • •

2  **6¾-oz. cans chunk ham, chopped**
1  **8-oz. can crushed pineapple, drained**
¼  **cup finely chopped green pepper**

*Pre-package first 3 ingredients in a small (quart aize) zip lock plastic storage bag.*
  • • • • • •

In a large bowl, combine eggs, milk, and soy sauce. Mix slightly. Gradually add pre-packaged dry ingredients. Mix until smooth.
  • • • • • •

Stir in remaining ingredients.

In a large skillet, heat ¼-inch of vegetable oil over medium-high heat. For each fritter, pour or spoon ¼ cup mixture into hot oil. Cook for 3 minutes per side or until golden brown.

makes 16 (4-inch) fritters

**Tip:** If you have a deep skillet or frying pan, now's the perfect time to use it. Its straight sides prevents the oil from sloshing over the edge.
**Note:** Unlike pancakes, these fritters will have only one smooth side. The other side will resemble the surface of the moon.

---

4th day **ALOHA CHICKEN SALAD**
Lunch   cheese & crackers

*If you were having a very uppity, high society, puttin' on the ritz, type of luncheon and you wanted to impress your guests with something special, this would do the trick. Not only does it taste great, but it looks terrific! The presentation of colors in the ingredients resting gracefully atop a lettuce lined plate, accented with a sprinkling of pecans and kissed by coconut flakes seem to give it that "gourmet look" of elegance, appropriate for such occassions.*

*Of course, here we are dealing with a bunch of wild, crazy sailors, so you might want to forget about the fine china and waterford crystal, and break out the beer and stuff the salad mixture into some pocket bread like I do.*

| | | | | |
|---|---|---|---|---|
| 2 | 6¾-oz. cans chunk chicken, broken up | 1 | 11-oz. can mandarin orange segments, drained |
| 2 | celery stalks, sliced | ½ | cup chopped pecans |
| 1 | Tablespoon finely chopped onion | ⅓ | cup flaked coconut |
| 2 | 8-oz. cans pineapple chunks, drained | ¾ | cup mayonnaise |
| | | 2 | teaspoons instant chickend bouillon granules |

In a large bowl, combine all ingredients. Toss to mix. Transfer to a large (gallon size) zip lock plastic storage bag. Seal and chill. Serve in lettuce lined bowls.

makes 4 hearty servings

---

4th day **LINGUINE with CLAM SAUCE**
Dinner   salad • bread sticks • strawberries & orange marsala

*Forget anything you've ever heard about clam sauce! Forget you've ever tasted clams in any form before this! You are about to prepare one of the most mouth-watering pasta sauces you've ever tasted. And what's so surprising is that it's so simple! It almost takes you longer to cook the pasta than it does the sauce.*

| | | | |
|---|---|---|---|
| 2 | Tablespoons vegetable oil | ¼ | teaspoon pepper |
| 2 | garlic cloves, minced | | Dash of cayenne pepper |
| | • • • • • | | • • • • • |
| 1 | 16-oz. can tomatoes | 1 | 10-oz. can whole baby clams, |
| ½ | 8-oz. can tomato paste | | drained with liquid reserved |
| 1 | Tablespoon chopped parsley | | • • • • • |
| ¾ | teaspoon salt | 6 | ounces cooked linguine |

In a large skillet, heat oil over medium heat. Add garlic and cook until lightly browned.

• • • • • •

Add next 6 ingredients, PLUS reserved clam juice, and bring mixture to a boil. Stir well and break up tomatoes. Reduce heat. Cover and simmer 15 minutes.

• • • • • •

Add clams and heat through.

Divide cooked linquine into serving portions. Cover with sauce mixture and garnish with lemon slices.

makes 4 servings

### STRAWBERRIES & ORANGE MARSALA

| | | | |
|---|---|---|---|
| ½ | cup sugar | 1 | pint strawberries, rinsed, hulled |
| ½ | cup water | | and halved |
| ½ | cup Marsala | 2 | oranges, peeled and sectioned |
| ½ | teaspoon anise seeds | | |
| | • • • • • • | | |

To pre-packaged syrup, combine first 4 ingredients in a medium saucepan. Stirring constantly, simmer over low heat for 15 minutes. Strain into a 12-oz. jar. Let cool. Secure top.

Place strawberries and oranges in a large (gallon size) zip lock plastic storage bag. Pour pre-packaged syrup over fruit. Seal and chill overnight.

**Tips:** If you've already cooked the linguine ahead of time and stored it in a plastic bag, simply add some hot water and let stand a minute or so, then poke some holes in the bottom of the bag and let drain and it's ready to go.

It's a good idea to prepare the sauce for the dessert at home and bring it aboard rather than to cook it during the trip. Add fruit the day before serving.

**Note:** There are two reasons I use a skillet instead of a saucepan to cook the clam sauce. 1) The large cooking surface (bottom) of the skillet allows the sauce to heat faster. 2) Most of the time I don't carry a saucepan; only a Dutch oven and a large skillet.

---

5th day
Breakfast

# SPANISH SCRAMBLED EGGS
juice • melon • beverage

---

*Sure you can have plain old scrambled eggs if you like. Nothing wrong with that. But that would be like going on a vacation cruise and never leaving port or like pulling in the sails and heading back to the dock just as the wind started to pick up.*

*We're on vacation and we're looking for adventure! So forget the everyday routine! You'll be back to that soon enough. For now, we're looking to put a little spice and excitement in our scrambled eggs.*

| ¼ | cup butter (½ stick) | 1 | 4-oz. can chopped green |
|---|---|---|---|
| 1 | bunch green onions, finely | | chilies, drained |
| | chopped | 1 | 4-oz. jar diced pimiento, |
| 1 | tomato, chopped | | drained |
| 2 | 4-oz. cans sliced mushrooms, | 3 | Tablespoons Bac-O's |
| | drained | ½ | teaspoon Worcestershire |
| | • • • • • • | | sauce |
| 10 | eggs, beaten | | Dash hot pepper sauce |

In a large skillet, melt butter over medium heat.  Add onions, tomato, and mushrooms.  Cook until tender (about 5 minutes).
• • • • • •
In a large bowl, combine remaining ingredients. Blend well. Add egg mixture to skillet. Stirring frequently, cook until eggs are firm but still moist.

makes 4 hearty servings

> **Tip:** For nice fluffy eggs, cook slowly over low heat. If your stove or range can not provide a low heat, you can control or slow the cooking by removing the skillet from the burner whenever you stir the eggs.

---

5th day
Lunch
# MACARONI-CRABMEAT SALAD
cheese & crackers • fruit platter with coconut-honey dip

---

*I used to be totally turned off by macaroni salads.  Not because I didn't like them, but because I was overexposed to them.  It was always the same old tuna and macaroni swimming in a sea of mayo, time after time. Whenever I went to a picnic, family reunion, a softball outing, everywhere I went, there it was, the same old T&M salad! There were 10, 20, a good 30 of them and they were all alike. Probably from the same recipe. And do you know why everybody brought them? They were easy to prepare and the kids love them. Well, if you're tired of the same T&M salads, just like I am, try this recipe with a little crab meat and discover that macaroni salads aren't just for kids anymore.*

| 8 | ounces shell macaroni, | 1½ | Tablespoons sweet pickle |
|---|---|---|---|
| | cooked | | relish |
| 2 | 6½-oz. cans crab meat, | 2 | teaspoons lemon juice |
| | drained and flaked | ½ | teaspoon salt |
| 2 | celery stalks, chopped | ½ | teaspoon pepper |
| 1 | onion, chopped | | • • • • • • |
| 3 | hard-boiled eggs, chopped | ¾ | cup mayonnaise |
| 3 | Tablespoons Bac-O's | ½ | cup chopped parsley |

In a large bowl, combine first 10 ingredients, in order, tossing to mix after each is added.

• • • • ••

Add mayonnaise, a little at a time, until desired consistency is reached. Add more if needed. Blend in parsley. Transfer to a large (gallon size) zip lock plastic storage bag. Seal and chill.

Serve in lettuce-lined bowls.

makes 4 hearty servings

### COCONUT-HONEY DIP

1   16-oz. carton creamy-style cottage cheese
¼   cup plain yogurt

¼   cup honey

• • • • ••

¼   cup flaked coconut
1   teaspoon grated orange rind

In a small bowl, combine first 3 ingredients. Mix well, Stir in flaked coconut and orange rind.

Tip : If you've already cooked the macaroni, have another crew member prepare the salad in the morning while you're doing the eggs.

---

5th day **HAM & POTATO SKILLET**
Dinner   salad • deviled eggs • canned pudding

---

*I know, just about everybody turns their nose up at the mere mention of instant or dehydrated potatoes, but you have to understand one thing: next to cleaning the greasy exhaust fan over a huge 15 burner stove, the worst job anyone can pull on K.P. is peeling P-O-T-A-T-O-E-S.*

*For those of you who have never had the opportunity to experience the thrill of shaving the skins from 150 pounds of those starchy little devils, you can only imagine our enthusiasm when we discovered a meal that tastes great and uses packaged potatoes instead of freshly peeled ones.*

⅛   *teaspoon pepper*
¼   *teaspoon garlic salt*
½   *teaspoon basil*
• • • • • •

2   **Tablespoons butter**
1   **12-oz. can ham patties, cut in half**
• • • • • •

⅔   **cup condensed milk**
2¾  **cups water**
2   **carrots, thinly sliced**
1   **5½-oz. box instant scalloped potato mix**
• • • • • •

1   **zucchini, thinly sliced**
1   **tomato, chopped**

*Pre-package first 3 ingredients in a plastic zip lock envelope.*
• • • • • •

In a large skillet, melt butter over medium heat. Add ham patties and cook until lightly browned. Remove from skillet.

• • • • •

Add next 4 ingredients to skillet. Stirring frequently, bring mixture to a boil. Reduce heat. Cover and simmer 20 minutes.

• • • • •

Stir in zucchini and tomatoes. Return ham patties to skillet. cover and simmer 10 minutes.

makes 4 hearty servings

## DEVILED EGGS with SMOKED OYSTERS

| | | | |
|---|---|---|---|
| 4 | hard boiled eggs, shelled | ¼ | teaspoon sweet pickle juice |
| • • • • • • | | 8 | smoked oysters (from 3⅓-oz. can), |
| 2 | Tablespoons mayonnaise | | chopped |
| ½ | teaspoon mustard | | Dash of salt and pepper |

Slice eggs in half lengthwise. Remove yolks. In a small bowl, combine yolks and remaining ingredients. Using a fork, blend well. Fill egg whites with mixture.

**Tip:** Try topping the canned pudding with some flaked coconut, chopped kiwi and raisins.

# Time Out For Cocktails & Things

Planning can take all the fun out of everything. Some of our most memorable experiences are those that happen at the spur of the moment. A spontaneous reaction to our environment and mood. Take the time we went up to the club just to check out the boat. A hellatious storm had just gone through and we thought we'd go out for a little sail and catch the sunset. Well, after a few verses of Route 66, a couple of hot toddies and a few rounds of Rum & Coca-Cola, we came to the conclusion that it would be a shame to waste a good strong offshore breeze. So we decided it was time to head for our favorite watering hole, 23 miles across the bay, for last call. Three hours later, we were sitting in the Riverside sipping Long Island Ice Teas and downing our favorite sawdustburgers. With that in mind, I'd like to dedicate this Time Out for Cocktails to the owner/skipper of **DECADENCE** and her crazy crew.

## BEER CHEESE SPREAD

| | |
|---|---|
| 1 | cup (4-oz.) shredded sharp cheddar cheese |
| 1 | cup (4-oz.) shredded Swiss cheese |
| ½ | teaspoon Worcestershire sauce |
| ½ | teaspoon dry mustard |
| • • • • • • | |
| ¼ | cup beer |

In a small bowl, combine first 4 ingredients. Mix well. Gradually add beer while beating with a fork. Stir until texture of spread is consistent. Serve with crackers.

## SPINACH DIP

| | |
|---|---|
| 1 | 15-oz. can spinach, well drained and chopped |
| 1 | 1.8-oz. package Konorr's dried vegetable soup mix |
| 1 | cup sour cream |
| 1 | cup mayonnaise |
| 1 | onion, chopped |

In a large bowl, combine all ingredients and mix well. Transfer to a smaller bowl and chill. Serve with crackers and vegetables.

## SMOKED OYSTER CHEESE BALL

| | |
|---|---|
| 1 | 4½-oz. package Camembert cheese, cubed and softened |
| 1 | 3-oz. package cream cheese, cubed and softened |
| 2 | Tablespoons butter, softened |
| • • • • • • | |
| 1½ | teaspoons brandy |
| ½ | 3¾-oz. can smoked oysters, drained, rinsed and chopped |
| | Chopped pecans |

In a large bowl, combine first 3 ingredients. Mix until smooth. Add brandy and blend well. Stir in oysters. Form into a ball and roll in nuts. Seal in plastic wrap and chill. Serve with cocktail breads and crackers.

## LIVER POPS

Liverwurst
Almonds, finely chopped
Thin pretzel sticks

Shape pieces of liverwurst into 1-inch balls. Roll in chopped nuts and stick in one pretzel.

## ORANGE-CRANBERRY REFRESHER

3  cups orange juice
1  bottle sweet white wine
16  ounces cranberry-juice cocktail
• • • • • •
32  ounces club soda, chilled
Orange slices

Combine first 3 ingredients and chill. Add club soda. Serve over ice and garnish with a slice of orange.

## BOWL WEEVIL

3  ounces rum
3  ounces grenadine
3  ounces prepared sweet-and-sour mix
8  ounces orange juice
½  ounce Galliano
1½  ounces tequila
1½  ounces vodka
• • • • • •
Orange slices
Maraschino cherries

In a screw top jar, combine first 7 ingredients. Secure top and shake well. Serve over ice and garnish with a slice of orange and a cherry.

## TEQUILA SUNRISE

1½  ounces tequila
3  ounces orange juice
½  ounce grenadine
• • • • • •
Wedge of lime
Maraschino cherry

Stirring after adding each, combine the first 3 ingredients in a glass of ice. Garnish with lime and cherry.

## CARMEL FOG

¼  ounce half-and-half
1  ounce cream of coconut
1  ounce orange juice
2  ounces pineapple juice
3  ounces white wine
½  cup crushed ice

In a screw top jar, combine all ingredients. Secure top and shake well. Strain into glass.
Makes a nice breakfast drink.

**Tip:** The BEER CHEESE spread works really great stuffed in pitted black olives or stalk of celery.

# Group 3
## a five day menu

| | BREAKFAST | LUNCH | DINNER |
|---|---|---|---|
| 1st day | **CEREAL**<br>juice • grapefruit<br>beverage | **REUBEN Sandwiches**<br>potato chips • 3-bean salad • pickles | **PICADILLO**<br>salad • rice • broccoli<br>pudding |
| 2nd day | **BREAKFAST ROLLS**<br>juice • melon<br>beverage | **BEEFARONI TOSTADA**<br>cheese & fruit platter<br>with peanut butter dip | **PORK CHOPS<br>in MUSHROOM SAUCE**<br>salad • corn<br>black forest trifle |
| 3rd day | **MEXICAN POACHED EGGS**<br>juice • pineapple slices<br>beverage | **ROAST BEEF Sandwiches**<br>corn chips • potato salad • pickles | **DRUNKEN CHICKEN**<br>salad<br>rice • green beans with mushrooms |
| 4th day | **WAKE-UP SANDWICHES**<br>juice • fruit cocktail<br>beverage | **VEGETABLE-BURGER SOUP**<br>crackers<br>cheese & salami platter | **PASTA with<br>SEAFOOD-ARTICHOKE SAUCE**<br>salad • french bread<br>fruit fans |
| 5th day | **STUFFED FRENCH TOAST**<br>juice • sausage • blueberries<br>beverage | **CHILI DOGS**<br>potato chips • pickles | **SAUSAGE SKILLET DINNER**<br>deviled eggs • mushroom salad with<br>mustard vinaigrette<br>pudding |

---

1st day **CEREAL**
Breakfast juice • grapefruit • beverage

---

*Cereal. Solo, seco, nada mas cereal.*

*Ha estado en la mesa de todo mundo para el almuerzo desde 1872. Aunque no ganaria ningun premio, si tiene sus ventajas. Una vez que la persona pueda sostener la cuchara sin asistencia, es muy capaz de hacer su propio almuerzo. Esto quiere dicir que el cocinero ya no tiene que levantarze al amanecer para darles a la trop un buen almuerzo. (for English translation see page 36)*

---

1st day **The CLASSIC REUBEN Sandwich**
Lunch potato chips • canned 3-bean salad • pickles

---

*A brilliant blue sky illuminated by a radiant sun.*
*A brisk wind whistles through the rigging.*
*A mountain range of clouds continues to build on the horizon.*
*The bow of the boat slices its way through wave after wave, sending a wall of salty spray over the deck. You can smell the freshness of the sea air, your heart quickens to the rhythm of the boat's passage.*
*A spirited day such as this, needs a spirited meal. 'Tis not the time for a glass of milk and an egg salad sandwich. Go for the gusto! The ultimate. The total experience. Go for a cold beer. A kosher dill. And the Classic Reuben Sandwich.*

| | |
|---|---|
| ½ cup sour cream | 8 slices rye bread |
| 1 teaspoon horseradish | 1 8-oz. can sauerkraut, drained |
| ¼ teaspoon salt | 1 pound shaved corned beef |
| 2 Tablespoons Chili sauce | 8 slices Swiss cheese |
| • • • • • • | Butter |

In a small bowl, combine first 4 ingredients and mix well.
• • • • • •

To make sandwiches: spread horseradish mixture on bread and assemble in order; slice of bread, Swiss cheese, corned beef, sauerkraut, corned beef, Swiss cheese and slice of bread.

Warm griddle or skillet over medium heat.

Butter outside of sandwich. (Butter the top first, place sandwich on griddle butter side down, then butter other side.) Grill until golden brown.

makes 4 sandwiches

> **Tip:** Even if you decide not to grill these sandwiches, it's not a good idea to prepare them ahead of time. The juice from the sauerkraut will make them mushy.

---

1st day **PICADILLO**
Dinner  salad • white rice • steamed broccoli • canned pudding

---

*WARNING: Never prepare an entree that contains raisins on those days when you're barely able to survive massive attacks of "Killer Flies". There's absolutely no way you'll be able to convince even your staunchest supporters that those little black things are sweet succulent California raisins.*

*You might just as well break out the double stuffed Oreos and the Kahlua & milk before the crew does.*

| | |
|---|---|
| | 1 garlic clove, minced |
| ¾ teaspoon salt | • • • • • • |
| ¼ teaspoon pepper | 1 tomato, chopped |
| ¼ teaspoon cinnamon | 1 apple, peeled and chipped |
| ¼ teaspoon ground cloves | 1 jalapeno pepper, seeded and finely chopped |
| • • • • • • | |
| 2 Tablespoons vegetable oil | 2 1½-oz. packages of raisins |
| 1 pound ground beef | ½ cup sliced pimiento-stuffed green olives |
| 1 onion, finely chopped | |

*Pre-package first 4 ingredients in a plastic zip lock envelope.*
• • • • • •

In a large skillet, heat oil over medium heat. Add meat, onion, and garlic. Cook until meat is browned.
• • • • • •

Add remaining ingredients, plus pre-packaged spices, and mix well. Reduce heat. Cover and simmer 20 minutes.

Serve over rice.

makes 4 hearty servings

**Tips:** To steam broccoli, simply remove leaves, cut off the tough ends of stalks and separate into spears. Place in skillet on top of the Picadillo during the last 15 minutes of cooking.

For dessert, you might want to try topping the canned pudding with some whipped topping and chopped nuts.

**Note:** This would be a great time to pre-cook the pork sausage for the Mexican Poached Eggs and the ground beef for the Vegetable-Burger Soup. Not only is it a time saver, but the spoilage factor is lessened.

---

## 2nd day **BREAKFAST ROLLS**
Breakfast juice • melon • beverage

---

*Never under estimate the appeal of fresh baked goods. Once we were laid over in a tiny, tiny, little port because gale force winds were whipping up some very nasty waves and nobody in his right mind was venturing out of a safe harbor. Needless to say, we hadn't planned on delays, so this was a real bummer that brought the whole crew down. Well, I figured a huge breakfast was just the thing to cheer everybody up. (Rule #148: When depressed. . . stuff your face.) We had ham and sausages, pancakes and eggs, fresh fruit cups with spiced rum, juices and a special blend mocha coffee. I pulled out all the stops. I even made up a double batch of Bloody Marys (twice). The mood did pick up a little, but there still was room for improvement.*

*Less than an hour after finishing breakfast, we were checking out the town when we came across a divine little bakery with the most exquisite pastries.*

*The tempatation was too great. Every single crew member came out of that bakery with a bag in his hand and a smile on his face. And these were the guys who just a little while ago couldn't possibly take another bite of food or muster a happy face.*

*Since then, whenever we're in port, I check out all the local bakeries. It's a lot easier serving a gooey, sticky, yummy breakfast roll and some fancy pastries from them, than it is to fry up some bacon and eggs.*

---

## 2nd day **BEEFARONI TOSTADA**
Lunch cheese & fruit platter with peanut butter dip

---

*Before the cruise, I check the crew for food preferences. Since most of them are single, I wasn't surprised to learn that most of them consider Chef-Boy-ar-dee to be a patron saint of the kitchen.*

*Although there's a selection of the Chef's canned "gourmet" pasta treats on board, I like saving those "goodies" for emergency situations (like a nuclear attack). But this one particular crew member insisted on having the Chef's finest. He even went so far as to present me with this recipe and offered to prepare the meal himself. What can I say? He made me an offer I couldn't refuse!*

| | |
|---|---|
| ¼ **teaspoon garlic powder** | ¾ **cup sliced pitted black olives** |
| 1 **Tablespoon chili powder** | 1 **cup (4-oz.) Cheddar cheese, shredded** |
| • • • • • | • • • • • |
| 1 **Tablespoon butter** | **Shredded lettuce** |
| ¾ **cup chopped green pepper** | **Tortilla chips** |
| ½ **cup chopped onion** | **Sour cream** |
| • • • • • • | **Chopped green onions** |
| 2 **15-oz. cans Beefaroni** | **Tomato wedges** |

*Pre-package first 2 ingredients in a plastic zip lock envelope.*
• • • • • •

In a Dutch oven, melt butter over medium heat. Add green pepper and onion and saute until onions are soft (about 5 minutes).

• • • • • •

Add Beefaroni and pre-packaged spices. Cook and stir until mixture is thoroughly heated. Stir in olives. Top with cheese. Cover and simmer until cheese melts.

• • • • • •

Serve on a bed of lettuce and tortilla chips. Garnish with tomato wedges, sour cream, and green onions.

makes 4 hearty servings

### PEANUT BUTTER DIP

| | | | |
|---|---|---|---|
| ½ | cup peanut butter | | |
| ½ | cup sour cream | ¼ | cup water |
| ¼ | cup frozen orange juice concentrate, thawed and undiluted | | |

In a small bowl, combine first 3 ingredients. Mix well. Stir in water. Blend well.

**Tip:** To keep peanut better from sticking to your measuring cup or spoons, coat them with vegetable oil first.

---

2nd day **PORK CHOPS in MUSHROOM SAUCE**
Dinner salad • canned corn • black forest trifle

---

*It's really quite amazing when you stop and think about it, but this is probably one of, if not, the most popular way of preparing pork chops in this country. (At least it seems that way to me.) Yet, you seldom see it listed as an entree in a restaurant. If you wanted the recipe, you'd have to ask someone you know who's made it before, because you'd be hard-pressed to find one like it in a cookbook. I imagine all the editors figured that since it was so easy to prepare, everybody must know how to make it. Well, I'm not taking anything for granted. If you already have a tried-and-true and family approved recipe, go ahead and use it. If not, have a whirl and pig-out with this one.*

| | | | |
|---|---|---|---|
| 8 | ½-inch thick pork chops | ½ | cup water |
| | Salt | 2 | Tablespoons Kahlua |
| | Pepper | | • • • • • • |
| | Garlic powder | 4 | potatoes, peeled and quartered |
| 1 | Tablespoon vegetable oil | | |
| | • • • • • • | 4 | small onion, quartered |
| 2 | 10½-oz. cans cream of mushroom soup | 6 | carrots, halved lengthwise |
| | | 2 | 4-oz. cans sliced mushrooms and liquid |

Season pork chops with salt, pepper and garlic powder. In Dutch oven, heat oil over medium-high heat. Add chops, a few at a time, and brown on both sides. Remove from Dutch oven and discard grease.

• • • • • •

Add next 3 ingredients to Dutch oven and stir to blend.
Return chops to oven. Add remaining ingredients and bring mixture to a boil. Reduce heat. Cover and simmer 45 minutes.

makes 4 servings

**BLACK FOREST TRIFLE**

| | |
|---|---|
| 3 cups chocolate cake chunks | 1 16-oz. can cherry pie filling |
| ¼ cup brandy | Whipped topping |
| 1 16-oz. can chocolate pudding | |

In four 10-oz. clear plastic glasses, layer in order: cake chunks, a sprinkle of brandy, pudding, pie filling, cake chunks, a sprinkle of brandy, pudding, pie filling, and whipped cream.

**Tip:** To heat canned corn, simply drain and place corn on a sheet of aluminum foil. Form into a packet just small enough to fit inside Dutch oven. Place on top of pork chops during the last 15 minutes of cooking. **Note:** You will not be able to brown all the chops at the same time, but after they're browned, you can pile them in the Dutch oven to simmer all at once.

For dessert, if there isn't any chocolate cake available, I'll use some chocolate cupcakes instead. You know! The ones with the cream filling!

---

3rd day
Breakfast
# MEXICAN POACHED EGGS
juice • canned pineapple slices • beverages

---

*Besides strange, what would you call a breakfast made of green peppers, green chilies, onions, potatoes, garlic, ground pork sausage and eggs? No idea? Well, if you took out the green chilies, garlic, and you replaced the pork sausage with leftover roast beef, you'd have my father's all-time favorite breakfast hash...hash topped off with a poached egg. Only this time we've spiced it up a bit and given it a South-of-the-boarder twist.*

| | |
|---|---|
| 1 | Tablespoon vegetable oil |
| ½ | pound bulk pork sausage |
| 2 | garlic cloves, minced |
| ½ | cup finely chopped green pepper |
| ½ | cup finely chopped onion |

• • • • • •

| | |
|---|---|
| 2 | potatoes, peeled and diced |
| 1 | 4-oz. can chopped green chilies |

• • • • • •

| | |
|---|---|
| 4 | eggs |

• • • • • •

Avocado slices
Taco sauce

In a large skillet, heat oil over medium-high heat. Add pork sausage, garlic, green pepper and onion. Cook, breaking up sausage, until pork is lightly browned.

• • • • • •

Stir in potatoes and green chilies. Cover and cook over medium heat for 15 minutes or until potatoes are tender.

• • • • • •

With a large spoon, make 4 indentations into sausage mixture. Break an egg into each depression. Cover and cook until eggs are set (about 5 minutes).

• • • • • •

Garnish with avocado slices and a dash of taco sauce.

makes 4 servings

**Tip:** Try browning the meat earlier in the trip.
**Note:** This would be a good time to cook up some hard-boiled eggs, the spinach noodles for the Seafood-Artichoke Sauce and the shell macaroni for the Sausage Skillet Dinner.

---

3rd day
Lunch
# ROAST BEEF Sandwiches
corn chips • canned potato salad • pickles

---

*You can stack them anyway you want and fill them with anything you want and the end results can be quite impressive.*

*You can mix and match all kinds of outlandish ingredients to create wild flavors and textures in your sandwiches. But sometimes, when they're that dramatic and that awesome, it's almost impossible to take a bite of the sandwich without dislocating your jaw.*

*You don't have to build a sandwich that resembles Mt. Everest to capture the attention and applause of the crew. The secret to a truly sensational sandwich is a distinctive sauce.*

*Go ahead! Let them add all that Dagwood JUNK if they want it! I'll lay odds if they take a bite of this roast beef sandwich first, they'll forget about all those superficial extras.*

½ cup sour cream
1 teaspoon horseradish
1 teaspoon Dijon-style mustard
Salt

Pepper
• • • • • •

4 poppy seed or Kaiser rolls
1 pound shaved roast beef
4 slices Cheddar cheese

In a small bowl, combine first 5 ingredients and mix well.
• • • • • •
To make sandwiches: slice rolls in half horizontally and spread with horseradish mixture. Divide roast beef evenly among rolls and top with slice of Cheddar cheese.
• • • • • •
Add any of the following: chopped hot pepper rings, sliced green pepper, slice of red onion, Swiss or crumbled Blue cheese, or slices of marinated mushrooms.

makes 4 sandwiches

**Tip:** Prepare the sandwiches earlier in the day. Wrap them in paper toweling or napkins and store in zip lock plastic bags. If anyone wants something different on their sandwich put a slip of paper with his or her name on it in the bag.

Dress up the canned potato salad with some chopped onions and grated carrots.

---

3rd day
Dinner
# DRUNKEN CHICKEN
salad • white rice • green beans with mushrooms

---

*One of the reasons I really love to cook on our boat is because the liquor cabinet is in the galley, so any time I feel like a little drinkie-poo, I don't have to wait for the resident bilge rat to serve me. I just kinda help myself.*

*Don't go shaking your finger at me. Being able to take a sip or two or three, or whatever, is a small consolation for being stuck down in a hot galley while everybody else is up on deck, in the cool fresh air, partying down. Besides, all the great chefs down through history have been known to hoist a few while cooking. How do you think they could create a saucy dish like Drunken Chicken if they weren't stewed as well. Cheers!*

| | |
|---|---|
| ⅛ teaspoon marjoram | ½ cup rum or dry sherry |
| ⅛ teaspoon thyme | 1 8-oz. can tomato sauce |
| ¼ teaspoon oregano | 1 6¾-oz. can chunk ham, chopped |
| ½ teaspoon chili powder | |
| ½ teaspoon salt | 1 1½-oz. package of raisins |
| 1 bay leaf | 8 pimiento-stuffed green olives, sliced |
| Dash of pepper | |
| • • • • • • | • • • • • • |
| 1½ Tablespoons butter | 3 pounds prime chicken parts, cut up |
| ¼ cup chopped onion | |
| ¼ cup chopped green onion | • • • • • • |
| 1 garlic clove, minced | 4 teaspoons cornstarch |
| • • • • • • | 2 Tablespoons water |
| ¼ cup water | |

*Pre-package first 7 ingredients in a plastic zip lock envelope.*
• • • • • •

In Dutch oven, melt butter over medium-high heat. Add onions, green pepper, and garlic. Saute until onions are tender but not browned.
• • • • • •

Add next 6 ingredients, plus pre-packaged spices, to Dutch oven and bring mixture to a boil. Stir to blend ingredients.
• • • • • •

Add chicken and reduce heat. Cover and simmer 45 minutes. Simmer an additional 15 minutes uncovered.

With slotted spoon, remove chicken and set aside.
• • • • • •

In a cup blend cornstarch and water. Add to mixture in Dutch oven. Continue to cook and stir till thick and bubbly. Pour sauce over chicken.

Serve on a bed of white rice.

makes 4 servings

### GREEN BEANS with MUSHROOMS

| | |
|---|---|
| 1 16-oz. can cut green beans, drained | 2 teaspoons chopped parsley |
| | 3 Tablespoons finely chopped onion |
| 2 4-oz. cans sliced mushrooms, drained | ¼ teaspoon salt |
| | ¼ teaspoon pepper |
| 1 2-oz. jar sliced pimiento, drained | |

In a large bowl, combine all ingredients. Toss to mix. Place mixture on a large sheet of foil. Form into a packet with all seams on top. Place in the Dutch oven during the last 30 minutes of cooking.

# WAKE-UP SANDWICHES
juice • canned fruit cocktail • beverages

*No matter how glorious and inspiring the sun rise may be, our crew, if they're up, always needs a little something extra to help them clean out those old cobwebs and shake the sleep from their eyes. A nice pale Bloody Mary. A cup of strong black coffee. Three or four non-filtered Turkish cigarettes. Or the ever popular, "One, two, three, four, heave-ho, over the side he goes," plunge-into-the-cool-refreshing-water trick.*

*Now everybody may prefer something different to get the old motor started at the break of dawn, but when it comes to getting those old taste buds to snap to attention that early in the morning, the whole crew agrees, the Wake-Up Sandwich is a pretty good call.*

1   **3-oz. package cream cheese, cubed and softened**
3   **Tablespoons milk**
• • • • • •
1   **3-oz. package thinly sliced corned beef, chopped**

½   **cup (2-oz.) shredded Swiss cheese**
¼   **cup finely chopped onion**
2   **hard-boiled eggs, chopped**
• • • • • •
2   **English muffins, halved and toasted**
1   **hard-boiled egg, sliced**

In a large bowl, combine cream cheese and milk.  Stir until smooth.  Add more milk if necessary.
• • • • • •
Stir in next four ingredients. Mix well.
Spread mixture on English muffins and garnish with egg slices.

makes 4 hearty servings

> **Tip:** If you don't have a toaster aboard, try sticking a fork into the side of an English muffin and toasting over the open flame. Kinda like hot dogs around the old campfire.

# VEGETABLE-BURGER SOUP
crackers • cheese & salami platter

*Every spring, we'd get out to the boat yard, wash the old boat down, rub it out, and then lay down 2 or 3 coats of wax to make that hull shine like new. Sure, it was a lot of work. Sure, it took a lot of time and elbow grease. But when we were finished, she sure looked good.*

*Then we discovered a product that made her hull look and shine just like new, without all that washing, and all that rubbing, and all that waxing. Plus it didn't take that much time to do it. We could accomplish our task in one Sunday afternoon session while watching a ball game and drinking beer.*

*Lesson #7: Just because something takes more time and effort, doesn't mean it's any better than something that's quick and easy. And if you have any doubts, you can either try using Pentatrol on the hull of your boat or try Vegetable-Burger Soup. It's quick and easy. There's no chopping, not much to measure, and as soon as it's hot, it's ready to serve. No sense slaving all day over a hot stove, when you can get something that tastes this good, this easy.*

½   **pound ground beef**
• • • • • •
1   **16-oz. can stewed tomatoes**
1   **8-oz. can tomato sauce**
1   **16-oz. can mixed vegetables, drained**

2   **cups water**
½   **1.375-oz. package onion soup mix (¼ cup)**
1   **teaspoon sugar**

In Dutch oven, brown meat over medium-high.  Discard grease.

• • • • •

Stir in remaining ingredients.  Bring to a boil.  Reduce heat.  Cover and simmer 20 minutes.

**Tip:** Try to brown meat a couple of days ahead of time.
**Note:** Any leftover dry soup mix can be combined with some sour cream to make a nice chip dip.

---

4th day
Dinner

# PASTA with SEAFOOD-ARTICHOKE SAUCE
salad • french bread • fruit fans

---

*It's amazing how narrow some people's perspectives on life can be. For a long time I was under the impression that the only way to serve spaghetti was with a thick, rich, meaty, tomato sauce. Some of my fellow shipmates used to believe that REAL Italian spaghetti was shaped like little "O's" and came in a can with a chef on the label.*

*Until a few years ago, we never realized that there was a wide variety of spaghetti or pasta sauces out there just waiting to tantalize our taste buds. We decided it was time to expand our pasta horizons. That's when we discovered this outrageous and exciting little creation.*

3    *Tablespoons flour*
½    *teaspoon salt*
¼    *teaspoon grated lemon peel*
⅛    *teaspoon white pepper*
• • • • • •
3    **Tablespoons butter**
• • • • • •
1    **10-oz. can baby clams, and liquid**
2    **6-oz. cans tiny shrimp, and liquid**

1    **5-oz. can condensed milk**
⅓    **cup water**
⅓    **cup dry white wine**
1    **14-oz. can artichoke hearts, drained and cut in half or quarters**
• • • • • •
12   **ounces spinach noodles, cooked**

*Pre-package first 4 ingredients in a plastic zip lock envelope.*
• • • • •

In a large skillet, melt butter over medium heat.  Stir in pre-packaged ingredients and blend until smooth.

• • • • •

Gradually stir in clam and shrimp liquid, condensed milk, water and wine.  Stir until thickened and bubbly.
Add clams, shrimp, and artichoke hearts and heat through.
Divide cooked spinach noodles into serving portions.  Cover with sauce mixture.

makes 4 servings

**FRUIT FANS**

2    **Tablespoons cream sherry**
½    **cup apricot preserves**
• • • • •
1½   **Tablespoons whipped topping**
1    **Tablespoon cream sherry**
• • • • •
1    **Tablespoon cream sherry**

4    **short cakes**
• • • • • •
**Strawberries, sliced**
**Banana, sliced**
**Blueberries**
**Whipped topping**

In a little cup, combine sherry and apricot preserves.  Mix well.  In another cup, combine whipped topping and sherry.  Spread the apricot mixture over each short cake first, then cover with cream mixture.  Arrange sliced strawberries around the outer edge of each cake.  Overlap with a circle of sliced bananas.  Pile blueberries in the center and top with whipped topping.

**Tip:** Since you've already cooked the spinach noodles and stored them in a plastic bag, just add some hot water, let it stand a minute or so, then punch some holes in the bottom of the bag to drain and it's ready to go.

## STUFFED FRENCH TOAST

5th day
Breakfast

juice • sausage • blueberries • beverage

*Do you want to have some fun with your crew and pick up some extra bucks at the same time?*

*Before they get a chance to check out what's on the griddle or see what you're doing, ask them how many slices of French toast they think they can eat. Then simply tell them you don't think they can do it. Hassle them a little and make a little wager against the possibility.*

*Look at it this way. I've never seen one of my crew members eat less than four "normal" half-inch thick slices of French toast. So if they say four, wait till they try downing four one and one-half inch thick slices of French toast stuffed with a walnut cream cheese mixture. As you can imagine, you'll have made a pretty safe bet.*

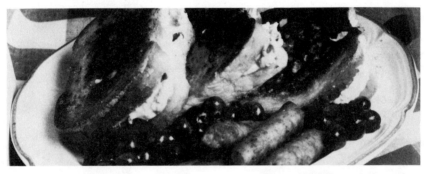

| | |
|---|---|
| 1   8-oz. package cream cheese, cubed and softened | 1   16-oz. loaf French bread, cut into 1½-inch slices |
| 1   teaspoon vanilla extract | • • • • • • |
| ½   cup chopped walnuts | 4   eggs, beaten |
| • • • • • • | 1   8-oz. carton heavy cream |
| | ½   teaspoon vanilla extract |
| | ½   teaspoon ground nutmeg |

In a large bowl, combine cream cheese and vanilla. With a fork, blend until mixture is fluffy. Stir in walnuts.

• • • • • •

Cut a pocket into the side of each slice of bread. Stuff pockets with cream cheese mixture.

• • • • • •

In a pie tin, combine remaining ingredients. Blend well with a fork.

For each piece of toast, dip both sides of stuffed bread in egg mixture. On a lightly grease griddle, over medium heat, cook for 3 minutes per side or until golden brown.

makes 10 to 12 slices.

**Delightful Sauce:** In a saucepan, combine a 12-oz. jar of apricot preserves and ½ cup orange juice. Stirring frequently, cook over low heat until warm. Pour over French toast.

**Tip:** Leave the cream cheese sit out over night to soften.
**Note:** Since the griddle will take up all the room on the stove, combine the ingredients for the sauce in an empty can and place it on the corner of the griddle. It'll heat and stay warm there and won't burn.

It's a good idea to cook the sausages first. Warm again just before serving.

---

5th day
Lunch

# CHILI DOGS
potato chips • pickles

---

*If some members of our crew had their way, we'd have chili dogs for breakfast, lunch and dinner every day of the cruise with a couple of Chinese Honey Porks thrown in for good measure!*

*Although they're one of the easiest foods to prepare, to create a truly authentic chili dog, one doesn't just pour sauce over a dog! No way! The secret to creating a true masterpiece is in cooking an all meat frankfurter in a big pot of chili for as long as possible. According to an old New York street vendor, "the very, very best dogs, are the ones on the bottom...the ones that have been there all day, soaking up all the good flavors."*

1   **16-oz. package hot dogs**
2   **15-oz. cans Chili with beans**
  • • • • • •
1   **package hot dog buns**
1   **cup (4-oz.) shredded Cheddar
    cheese**
½   **cup finely chopped onion**

In a large skillet, cook hot dogs in chili over medium heat. Simmer, covered, for 30 minutes. (The longer the dogs cook...the better they get).

Serve dogs in steamed buns with chili beans and sauce, topped with tons of cheese and lots of onions.

makes 4 servings

**Tips:** To steam buns, punch a bunch of holes in a sheet of aluminum foil, place it in the skillet over the chili and dogs, add buns and cover.

Nothing tops off a good chili dog like sauerkraut. So if there's any left over from the Reubens, bring it out!

---

5th day
Dinner

# SAUSAGE SKILLET DINNER
mushroom salad with mustard vinaigrette • deviled eggs
canned pudding

---

*On board our boat, every kid over the age of 30 loves this variation of their all-time childhood favorite, hot dogs with macaroni and cheese, smothered in catsup. Back in the good old days, any kid worth his salt could whip it together at a moment's notice whenever friends dropped over and mom and dad weren't around.*

*Well, now the kids are men and the men want to be kids again and there's nobody around to tell us what we can and can't do. So with a few extra spices, some smoked sausage instead of hot dogs, it's time to be kids again!*

| ⅛ | teaspoon oregano | 1 | green pepper, chopped |
| ¼ | teaspoon paprika | ½ | cup sliced celery |
| ¼ | teaspoon pepper | | • • • • • • |
| 1 | teaspoon chili powder | 2 | 8-oz. cans tomato sauce |
| | • • • • • • | 6 | ounces shell macaroni, |
| 2 | Tablespoons butter | | cooked |
| 1 | pound smoked sausage, cut | | • • • • • • |
| | into ¼-inch thick slices | ½ | cup (2-oz.) shredded Cheddar |
| 1 | onion, chopped | | cheese |

*Pre-package first 4 ingredients in a plastic zip lock envelope.*
• • • • • •

In a large skillet, melt butter over medium heat. Add sausage, onion, green pepper, and celery. Cook 5 minutes or until vegetables are tender.
• • • • • •

Add tomato sauce, cooked macaroni, and pre-packaged spices. Stirring frequently, bring mixture to a boil. Reduce heat. Cover and simmer 15 minutes.
• • • • • •

Sprinkle cheese over mixture and cook until cheese melts.

makes 4 hearty servings

## MUSHROOM SALAD with MUSTARD VINAIGRETTE

| ½ | teaspoon oregano | | |
| ½ | teaspoon tarragon | 3 | 4-oz. cans sliced mushrooms, |
| ¼ | teaspoon salt | | drained |
| ⅛ | teaspoon cayenne pepper | ½ | cup sliced pitted black olives |
| ¼ | cup Dijon mustard | | • • • • • • |
| ¼ | cup white wine vinegar | | Sliced tomatoes |
| ½ | cup vegetable oil | | Lettuce |
| | • • • • • • | | |

Pre-package first 7 ingredients in a 12-oz. jar. (Shake jar after packaging and before using.)
• • • • • •

Place mushrooms and olives in a small (quart-size) zip lock plastic storage bag. Pour pre-packaged marinade over vegetables. Seal and chill overnight. Serve over tomatoes on a lettuce-lined plate.
If fresh mushrooms are available, by all means use them.

## NIPPY DEVILED EGGS

| | | ¼ | teaspoon (or more) horseradish |
| 4 | hard-boiled eggs, shelled | | Dash of salt |
| | • • • • • • | | Dash of pepper |
| 2 | Tablespoons mayonnaise | | • • • • • • |
| ½ | teaspoon mustard | | Slice pimiento-stuffed green olives |

Slice eggs in half lengthwise. Remove yolks. In a small bowl, combine the next 5 ingredients. Mix well. Using a fork, fill egg whites with mixture and top with a piece of sliced olive.

**Tip:** Cook shell macaroni earlier in the trip.
For dessert, try some chopped banana and kiwi on top of the canned pudding.

# Time Out For Cocktails & Things

I don't know what it is about being out on the water, but it sure makes a person want to party hardy, no matter what time it is. I remember one time, a bunch of crazy sailors even radioed ahead to announce their arrival time. Then they proceeded to invite everybody (especially a girl named Zill) to a party, as soon as they got in.

Well, not everybody in port enjoyed being serenaded by a bunch of water-logged musicans at 1:30 in the morning. But for those who did and still remember us fondly, on behalf of the owner/skipper of **Bay Music** and her good-natured but misguided crew, I dedicate this unique Time Out For Cocktails to you.

## SALMON PARTY BALL

1   15½-oz. can red salmon, drained and flaked with all skin and bones removed
1   8-oz. package cream cheese, cubed and softened
1   Tablespoon lemon juice
1   Tablespoon grated onion
1   Tablespoon grated celery
1   teaspoon horseradish
¼   teaspoon salt
    Dash of hot pepper sauce
    • • • • • •

    Chopped pecans
    Chopped parsley

In a large bowl, combine first 8 ingredients. Mix well. Form into a ball, roll in nuts and sprinkle with parsley. Seal in plastic wrap and chill. Serve with cocktail breads and crackers.

## MUSTARD DOGS

Mustard
Apple jelly
Hot dogs, cooked and cut into ½-inch slices
Horseradish or hot sauce

In a saucepan, combine equal parts of mustard and jelly. Cook over medium heat. Add hot dogs and simmer, the longer the better. Serve hot or cold.

## PECAN CHEESE SPREAD

1   3-oz. package cream cheese, cubed and softened
⅓   cup crumbled blue cheese, softened
⅓   cup shredded sharp cheddar cheese, softened
2   Tablespoons minced onion
1½  Tablespoons sherry
½   cup finely chopped pecans

In a large bowl, combine all ingredients. Mix well. Transfer to a smaller bowl and serve with crackers.

## JALAPENO MEXICAN DIP

1   1.375-oz. package onion soup mix
2   cups sour cream
¼   teaspoon chili powder
3   Tablespoons hot Taco sauce
4   dashes hot pepper sauce
1   Jalapeno pepper, chopped
1½  Tablespoons chopped pimiento

In a large bowl, combine all ingredients and mix well. Transfer to a smaller bowl and chill. Serve with vegetables and chips.

**Tip:** Want to try something a little different this time? Spread some of the SALMON BALL over a piece of lettuce and roll it up.

## FRENCH 125

½  ounce lemon juice
1½  ounces brandy
1  teaspoon powdered sugar
• • • • • •
4  ounces chilled champagne
Strip of lemon peel

Combine first 3 ingredients and stir until sugar dissolves. Add ice and slowly pour in champagne. Twist lemon peel above then drop into drink. Nice breakfast drink.

## HONOLULU FIZZ

1  bottle white wine
1½  cups pineapple juice
¼  cup apricot liqueur
• • • • • •
7  ounces club soda, chilled
Pineapple chunks, chilled

Combine first 3 ingredients and chill. Add club soda. Serve in wine glass over pineapple chunks.

## DIFFERENT DRUMMER

¾  cup Jamaican rum
¾  cup Kahlua
3  cups orange juice
• • • • • •
Orange slices

In a screw top jar, combine first 3 ingredients. Secure top and shake well. Serve over ice and garnish with a slice or orange.

## FOGCUTTER

½  ounce gin
¾  ounce brandy
¾  ounce rum
3  ounces pineapple juice
1  ounce prepared sweet-&-sour mix
½  cup crushed ice
• • • • • •
Wedge of lemon
Wedge of lime

In a screw top jar, combine first 6 ingredients. Secure top and shake well. Strain into glass. Squeeze lemon and lime above, then drop into drink.

Psst! Hey you! Yeah you over there! Come here. I want you to try these recipes. But you've gotta promise never ever to tell anybody about them. Officially, this page does not exist. After all, I've spent many years perpetuating the image of a Drunken Sailor and if anybody finds out that I actually like and encourage people to drink these wimpy punches, I'll be ruined! My reputation will be shot!

## TROPICAL FRUIT DRINK

1  46-oz. can pineapple juice
1  15.5 oz. can cream of coconut
1  12-oz. can frozen orange juice
   concentrate
7½  cups water

In a pitcher or beverage thermos, combine all ingredients.
Serve over ice.

makes 16 (8 ounce servings)

## TROPICAL COOLER

1  ¾ cups water
3  Tablespoons sugar
1  Tablespoon instant ice tea
   granules
• • • • •
1  12-oz. can apricot nectar
1  6-oz. can frozen lemonade
   concentrate
2  12-oz. cans Sprite
   Lemon slices

In a pitcher or beverage thermos, combine first 3 ingredients. Stir until sugar dissolves.
Add all remaining ingredients and mix well. Serve over ice and garnish with a slice of lemon.

makes 8 (6 ounce servings)

## GINGER TEA

2  cups water
¼  cup sugar
2  Tablespoons instant ice tea
   granules
2  cups ginger ale
   Juice of 2 oranges
   Juice of 1 lemon
• • • • •
   Orange & lemon slices

In a pitcher or beverage thermos, combine first 5 ingredients. Stir until sugar and granules dissolve. Serve over ice and garnish with fruit slices.

makes 6 (6 ounce servings)

## APRICOT COOLER

½  cup instant lemonade powder
   mix
2  12-oz. cans apricot nectar
2  12-oz. bottles Sprite

In a pitcher or beverage thermos, combine all ingredients. Mix well. Serve over ice.

make 8 (6 ounce servings)

# Group 4
## a five day menu

| | BREAKFAST | LUNCH | DINNER |
|---|---|---|---|
| 1st day | **HOT CEREAL**<br>juice • peaches<br>beverage | **Grilled TRIPLE DECKER**<br>potato chips<br>eight-vegetable marinated salad | **JAMBALAYA**<br>salad<br>melon-mint julep |
| 2nd day | **BEEF FOO YONG PATTIES**<br>juice • applesauce<br>beverage | **EGG SALAD SANDWICHES**<br>potato chips • pickles | **BEEF BIRMINGHAM**<br>salad • egg noodles<br>green beans in tomato garlic sauce<br>pudding |
| 3rd day | **COFFEE CAKE**<br>juice • fruit cocktail<br>beverage | **the RAG-BAGGER SUB**<br>corn chips • potato salad • pickles | **PORK in ADOBO SAUCE**<br>salad<br>creole-style tomatoes & corn<br>watermelon sparkle |
| 4th day | **FRENCH TOAST**<br>juice<br>orange slices • sausage<br>beverage | **GAZPACHO with CLAMS**<br>st. louis cocktail sandwiches<br>fruit cocktail | **CHINESE SPAGHETTI**<br>honeydew salad<br>with apricot cream sauce |
| 5th day | **HASH BROWN SKILLET**<br>juice • pears<br>beverage | **YANKEE SEASHELL SALAD**<br>melba toast<br>crackers & cheese spreads | **HAM, YAM, AND APPLES**<br>salad<br>fruit cocktail |

---

1st day **Instant HOT CEREAL**
Breakfast juice • canned sliced peaches • beverage

---

*Todavia me da verguenza sujestionar, o mencionar, avena o otro tipo de cereal caliente para el almuerzo porque siempre recuerdo que mi madre me hacia travesuras para que me comiera yo ese atole, pegajoso, jugando el "aero-plano" y el "trenesito". Y ahora me encuentro aqui diciendoles a ustedes: "Comanse su avena!" Porque el cambio radical? Primeramente, gracias a la tecnologia moderna, la avena no parece ni sabe a pegamiento. Hay muchos nuevos e interesantes sabores. Segundo, las companias lo empaquetan en tamanos individuales para que todo mundo puede tener su almuerzo favorito, con su sabor favorito tambien (y no todos nos lo tenemos que comer!). Tercero, y mas importante, la unica cosa que tienes que hacer es hervir agua! (refer to page 54)*

**Note:** Now would be an excellent time to cut up some melon and prepare the dessert for tonight's Jambalaya.

---

1st day **Grilled TRIPLE DECKER**
Lunch potato chips • eight-vegetable marinated salad

---

*I don't know who invented the grilled cheese sandwich, but on behalf of kids, college students and bachelors everywhere, I thank you. Next to pouring milk on cereal or tossing dry soup mix into boiling water, grilled cheese sandwiches are one of the simplest meals to prepare. And if it weren't for peanut butter and jelly, it would probably be the most popular sandwich in the world. But if you had guests over for the weekend, would you serve them grilled cheese sandwiches? Heck no! How come? Not fancy enough for your friends? Well, just like the little scrubgirl, Cinderella, all you have to do is throw on the right trappings and poof! A fairy princess appears, or in this case a scrumptious gastronomic creation.*

79

| 1 | 3-oz. package cream cheese, cubed and softened | 12 | slices white bread |
|---|---|---|---|
| ¼ | cup chopped green pepper | 4 | slice provolone cheese |
| ¼ | cup chopped pitted black olives | 4 | slices tomato |
| | | 4 | slices red onion |
| 1 | 2-oz. jar chopped pimiento, drained | 4 | slices cheddar cheese |
| ¼ | teaspoon Worchestershire sauce | | • • • • • |
| | • • • • • • | | Butter, softened |

In a large bowl, beat cream cheese and couple drops of milk with a fork until light and fluffy. Stir in green pepper, olives, pimiento and Worcestershire sauce. Spread mixture on bread.

• • • • • •

To make sandwiches, assemble in order: slice of bread (spread side up), provolone cheese, tomato, slice of bread (spread side down), red onion, cheddar cheese, and top with a slice of bread (spread side down).
Warm griddle or skillet over medium heat.
Butter outside of sandwich. (Butter the top first, place sandwich on griddle butter side down, then butter the other side.) Grill until golden brown.

makes 4 sandwiches

### EIGHT-VEGETABLE Marinated Salad

| 1 | cup vinegar | 1 | 15½-oz. can kidney beans, drained |
|---|---|---|---|
| 1 | cup sugar | 1 | 8-oz. can lima beans, drained |
| ½ | cup vegetable oil | 1 | 8-oz. can whole kernel corn, drained |
| | • • • • • • | | |
| 1 | 16-oz. can cut green beans, drained | 2 | carrots, scrapped and sliced |
| | | 3 | onions, chopped |
| 1 | 16-oz. can cut wax beans, drained | 2 | green peppers, chopped |

In a large skillet, combine first 3 ingredients and bring to a boil. Reduce heat and simmer 1 minute. Let cool. Place all remaining ingredients in a large (gallon size) zip lock plastic storage bag. Pour marinade over vegetables. Seal and chill.

**Tip:** Don't try getting fancy when flipping these sandwiches. Use TWO hands! Hold top portion in place with one hand while using a spatula to turn the sandwich over with the other.
When combining the vegetables for the salad, hold the bag closed and shake after adding each one. This helps mix things up a little more evenly.
**Note:** Although marinated stuff is supposed to sit around a while so the flavors have time to develop to their fullest, this recipe tastes great as soon as the sweet vinegar oil is added. But don't worry, you'll get a chance to see how the flavor improves with age, because this makes a healthy batch. (I can guarantee, it will disappear a lot faster than you think.)

*Over the years, it has become a tradition for us to stop at Mackinac Island before heading home at the close of our vacation. This is the perfect resort area to change crews, rent cottages, villas or rooms and have families and girlfriends join us during the stopover. By some strange coincidence, our stopovers just happen to coincide with race week, (a period when roughly 2,000 sailors on about 300 sailboats, their families and friends, plus the normal tourist traffic descend on the Island to celebrate the finishes of the Chicago to Mackinaw then the Port Huron to Mackinaw races).*

*Since this is one of the few times we're all together as a family, I like to prepare a special dinner in honor of the occasion. One particular year, I was going to serve Jambalaya. I had asked one of the oncoming crew members to bring about 3 pounds of fresh shrimp from home. Unfortunately, when he came over to the island on the ferry, he left the shrimp in the refrigerator in the hotel room back on the mainland. So much for our special family dinner.*

*The next day when we finally did get the shrimp, everybody was gone. So that put me in the enviable position of preparing enough Jambalaya to feed 12 to 14 people while there were only four of us still on board.*

*Needless to say, we made a lot of new friends that night, because anyone and everyone who passed our ship was offered a little bowl of Jambalaya.*

| | |
|---|---|
| ¼   teaspoon pepper | 1   garlic clove, minced |
| 1   teaspoon salt | • • • • • |
| 1   teaspoon thyme | 1   16-oz. can stewed tomatoes |
| 1   Tablespoon paprika | ¾   cup water |
| • • • • • • | ¼   teaspoon hot pepper sauce |
| 3   pounds prime chicken parts, cut up | 1   teaspoon instant chicken bouillon granules |
| ¼   cup vegetable oil | 1   6¾-oz. can chunk ham, broken up |
| • • • • • • | ½   cup instant rice |
| ½   cup chopped onion | • • • • • • |
| ½   cup chopped green pepper | 1   pound frozen cooked shrimp, thawed |
| ⅓   cup chopped celery | |

*Pre-package first 4 ingredients in a plastic zip lock envelope.*

• • • • • •

Rub chicken parts with pre-packaged spices. In Dutch oven, heat oil over medium-high heat. Add chicken and brown. With a slotted spoon, remove chicken from Dutch oven and set aside.

• • • • • •

Add next 4 ingredients to Dutch oven and saute for 5 minutes.

• • • • • •

Add next 6 ingredients and bring to a boil. Stir mixture to dissolve bouillon granules. Return chicken to Dutch oven and reduce heat. Cover and simmer 45 minutes.

• • • • • •

Add shrimp. Cover and simmer 5 minutes.

makes 4 hearty servings

## MELON-MINT JULEP

| | | | |
|---|---|---|---|
| ½ | cup unsweetened orange juice | 1 | 20-oz. can unsweetened pineapple chunks, drained and liquid reserved |
| ¼ | cup lime juice | | |
| 2 | Tablespoons honey | | |
| 2 | Tablespoons chopped fresh mint | 3 | cups watermelon chunks |
| 2 | teaspoons grated orange rind | 2 | cups honeydew chunks |
| 2 | teaspoons grated lime rind | 2 | cups cantaloupe chunks |

• • • • • •

In a small bowl, combine first 6 ingredients. Mix well. Add reserved pineapple juice and stir. Place fruit chunks in a large (gallon size) zip lock plastic storage bag. Pour juice mixture over fruit. Seal and chill.

**Tip:** Prepare dessert in the morning to let the flavors blend.

If you don't have a grater to grate fresh orange and lime rind, remove the outer (colored) layer of the fruit with a vegetable peeler, then mince it with a knife.

If you cut up all the melon for the trip, just remember to store the different varieties in different bags.

**Note:** Personally I prefer shrimp in the shell for this recipe. Not only does it add a little extra flavor to the dish, but it also gives the crew a chance to slow down and appreciate the meal as they peel the shrimp.

---

2nd day
Breakfast
# BEEF FOO YONG PATTIES
juice • applesauce • beverage

*One of our crew members simply cannot survive without McDonalds. Every time we're in port, he'll go to any lengths to seek out an Egg and Sausage McMuffin for breakfast. Now, I do agree that bringing fast food back for breakfast does make my job a whole lot easier. But, when you have to bribe the junior assistant harbor master to use his motor scooter to ride 34 miles up the coast just to find the golden arches, I think you're carrying things just a little too far. There had to be a tasty combination I could whip up, that would keep him on the boat for breakfast with the rest of the crew. It wasn't that we missed his charming personality at the table in the morning, but he held up our departures for a good 2½ hours.*

*These patties may not be classified as the All American Breakfast, but I thought they offered a great taste sensation that would keep everybody happy for breakfast. And they did! And they do satisfy the breakfast needs of all the crew . . . except one.*

| | | | |
|---|---|---|---|
| 1 | pound ground beef | 1 | 4-oz. can sliced mushrooms, drained |
| | • • • • • • | | |
| 6 | eggs, beaten | 1 | teaspoon salt |
| 1 | 16-oz. can chow mein vegetables, drained | | • • • • • • |
| | | | Vegetable oil |

In a large skillet, brown ground beef over medium-high heat. With slotted spoon, remove beef and drain on paper towel. Discard grease.

• • • • • •

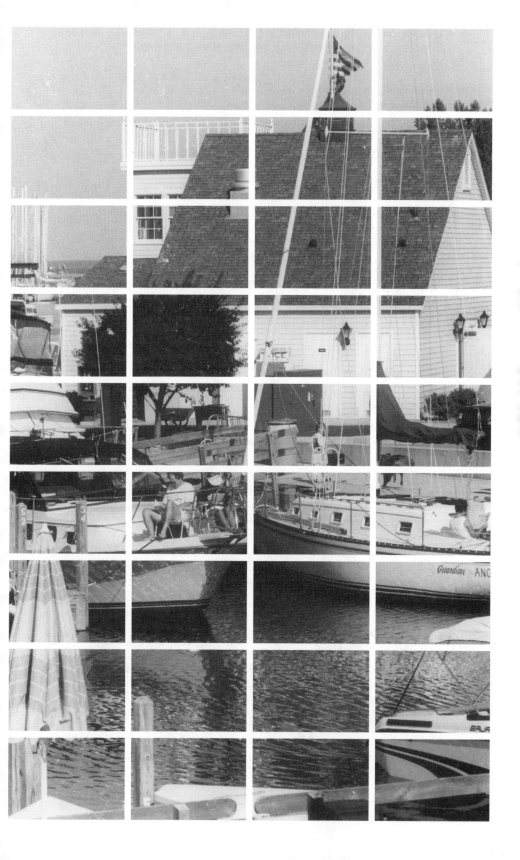

In a large bowl, combine all ingredients, including beef. Mix well.

In a large skillet, heat ¼-inch vegetable oil over medium-high heat.

For each pattie, pour ¼ cup mixture into hot oil. Maintain shape by pushing egg back into vegetable mixture to form patty. Cook until browned on both sides.

makes 10 to 12 (4-inch) patties

## BROWN SAUCE

| | | | |
|---|---|---|---|
| 1 | Tablespoon cornstarch | 1 | cup water |
| 2 | teaspoons sugar | 2 | Tablespoons soy sauce |
| • • • • • • | | 1 | teaspoon vinegar |

Combine cornstarch and sugar in a small saucepan.

• • • • • •

In a cup, combine remaining ingredients. Slowly add liquids to saucepan. Stir to dissolve. Cook over medium heat, stirring constantly till thick and bubbly. Reduce heat and simmer 1 minute.

> **Tip:** If you're not carrying a small saucepan, try using an empty can to cook the sauce in. Just substitute pliers for a handle and remember to use hot pads.
> **Note:** This would be a good time to cook up some hard-boiled eggs, the egg noodles for tonight's dinner, the pasta for Chinese Spaghetti, and the macaroni for the Yankee Seashell salad.

---

2nd day **EGG SALAD SANDWICHES**
Lunch  potato chips • pickles

---

*I've always loved egg salad sandwiches. But, I've also had a problem with them. Whenever I loaded the sandwich up with all the good fixin's, I'd take a bite and everything would squeeze out the sides and onto the floor. Can you imagine the problems that would create on a boat underway? Therefore, if the crew wanted them served during the cruise, I was forced to make them vending-machine style. That is to say, spreading the mixture thin and forgetting about any of the extras, including butter. Well, that was no-where! There had to be a better way.*

*Then one cold and windy day while we were stuck in port, I was having a hot toddy with another boater and telling her all about my egg salad sandwich predicament. She turned and looked at me straight in the eyes and told me to stuff it. At first I thought I had offended her. Then I realized she was talking about pita bread, not me!*

| | | | |
|---|---|---|---|
| 8 | hard-boiled eggs, coarsely chopped | ½ | teaspoon hot pepper sauce |
| 1 | celery stalk, chopped | ½ | cup mayonnaise |
| 1 | Tablespoon mustard | • • • • • • | |
| | | 4 | (6-inch) pocket bread rounds |

In a large bowl, combine first 5 ingredients and blend well. Add more mayonnaise if desired.

• • • • • •

Cut bread rounds in half. Before filling halves with egg mixture, line each pocket with any combination of the following: lettuce, sliced tomato, onion rings, green pepper rings, cucumber slices, slice of cheddar or Swiss cheese. After filling, top sandwich with slices of black olives.

makes 4 servings

**Tip:** Take it easy! Set out all the fixin's and let the crew have some fun. Let them create their own stuffed pita sandwiches for a change. Just remember it could get messy.

**Note:** Any leftover egg salad can be used during cocktail hour as a spread for crackers. If there is any left after that, feed it to the fish!

---

# BEEF BIRMINGHAM

salad • egg noodles • green beans in tomato garlic sauce canned pudding

---

*Not all my stories are about happy, smiling, well-fed sailors, who absolutely love and devour everything I cook for them. Take the time some of my fellow shipmates took one look at the food on their plates, then (after I went back down into the hot sticky galley), without even tasting it, they gave my creation the old heave-ho and deep sixed it over the side of the boat, all the while smiling and complimenting me on how great everything was. Later, when I discovered what had happened, I was really P.O'ed; not because they didn't like the food (I can handle people not liking something), but because they didn't even try it. They were judging a book by its cover. And according to the reaction of other crew members, they missed one hell of a great "book", because they scraped their plates clean and came back for seconds and thirds.*

| | | | |
|---|---|---|---|
| 2 | Tablespoons vegetable oil | 1 | cup water |
| 1 | garlic clove, minced | 1 | teaspoon instant beef |
| 3 | onions, sliced | | bouillon granules |
| 1 | cup sliced celery | ½ | teaspoon sugar |
| 1 | pound boneless beef, cut | 2 | Tablespoons peanut butter |
| | into bite size pieces | 2 | Tablespoons soy sauce |
| | • • • • • | | Dash of pepper |

In a large skillet, heat oil over medium heat. Add garlic, onions, celery, and beef. Cook until meat is browned.

• • • • • •

Add remaining ingredients, and bring mixture to a boil. Reduce heat. Cover and simmer 45 minutes.

Serve over cooked egg noodles.

makes 4 servings

### GREEN BEANS in TOMATO GARLIC SAUCE

| | | | |
|---|---|---|---|
| | | 2 | garlic cloves, minced |
| 1 | Tablespoon flour | | • • • • • • |
| 1¼ | teaspoons paprika | 2 | 8-oz. cans whole tomatoes, drained |
| | • • • • • • | | and liquid reserved |
| 2 | Tablespoons butter | 1 | 16-oz. can cut green beans, |
| 1 | onion, chopped | | drained |

Pre-package first 2 ingredients in a plastic zip lock envelope.

• • • • • •

In Dutch oven, melt butter over medium heat. Add onion and garlic. Cook for 3 minutes or until onion is softened. Stir in pre-packaged ingredients. Blend well. Cook 1 minute. Stir in reserved liquid from tomatoes. Stirring constantly, cook until sauce thickens (about 3 minutes). Add tomatoes and green beans. Reduce heat. Simmer uncovered 5 minutes.

**Tip:** If you didn't get a chance to cook the noodles in the morning, then do them now, along with some hard-boiled eggs, in the Dutch oven before cooking the green beans.

For dessert, try some whipped topping, crushed cookies and a cherry on top of the canned pudding.

Don't forget to marinate the pork for tomorrow night's dinner.

# COFFEE CAKE

juice • canned fruit cocktail • beverage

*Eines Sommers, schlossen sich einige echte Landratten, dem zweiten Teil unserer Sgelfahrt an. Ihre Marinekenntnis bestand darin, mit der Luftmatratze im Schwimmbad zu treiben. Begeisterung übertraf Erfahrung. Nun ist es bei uns ublich, das sich die abgelöste und die neue Bootsbesatzung, am Vorabend des Überwechselns, zu einigen ' Braulichkeiten' trifft. Im Verlauf dieses besonderen Abends, stellte es sich heraus, dass die Neuankömmlinge zum Vernarren reir waren.*

*Wir erklärten ihnen, wie ein jeder an Bord mithilft und das auch sie ihren Teil beisteuern müssten. Kein Problem! Sie waren bereit zu tun, was auch immer von ihnen verlangt wurde.*

*Schliesslich kam der Zeitpunkt, die Angel für den Streich auszuwerfen. Ich verkündigte, dass es für mich Ziet wäre, zum Boot Zurückzukehren, da ich früh aufstehn müsste, um das Frühstück zu bereiten. Sie waren Zutiefst enttäuscht und baten mich, länger zu bleiben. Ich bestand jedock darauf, dass es am Morgen zu viel zu tun gäbe, um noch länger herumzusitzen. Sofort erinnerten sie mich daran, dass man an Bord die Arbeiten teilt und ich mit ihrer vollen Unterstützung rechnen könnte. Deshalb solite ich doch noch bleiben.*

*Als wir schliesslich an Bord warren, verriet ich den Neulingen, dass ich ihnen schriftliche Anweisungen hinterlassen würde, was sie am Morgen zu tun hätten. Ich würde für sie den Wecker stellen. Unter keinen Umständen, sollten sie mich wecken. Nur den Anweisungen folgen.*

*Der Weckerging um 5 Uhr los. Sie lasen meine Mitteilung, befolgten sie und kehrten um 6:30 Uhr zum Boot zurück, bereit u abstosen, um 7 Uhr.*

*Welche Anweisungen hatten sie? In einer Bäckerel, 2 Meilen südlich der Stadt einen Annanas-Mandelkuchen und zwei Thermosflaschen, gefüllt mit heissem Kaffee, einzukaufen. Aus irgendeinem Grund, verfass ich jedock, zu erwähnen, dass sie das Fahrrad des Hafenmeisters benutzen könnten. Was soll's - es war doch ein schöner Morgen für einen Spaziergang. (see page 49 for English translation)*

---

# The RAG-BAGGER SUB

corn chips • canned potato salad • pickles

*At five o'clock, it's a mad dash from the office to the boat. No time to run home, change clothes and grab something to eat. No time to do anything, except get to the boat and get out on the water. If we want anything to eat, there's always nacho chips and picante sauce on board. Once in awhile, if we were lucky, someone would have time to stop for a bucket of chicken or pick up some grease burgers at the nearest drive-thru. That was before we discovered Nick's. The little deli down the street from the office, that made the most fantastic subs, hoagies, or heros you could ever want, and they would deliver them promptly at 4:55 p.m. From that time on, whether it was race night, party night, boys' night out, girls' night out, weekend out with the family, whatever the reason, it was subs forever. We were addicted to Nick's subs.*

*Well, that very summer, when we were off on our vacation cruise, it happened. A sub-attack. The unrelenting urge for one of Nick's super subs. No matter how many times we called, no matter how desperately we pleaded with him, Nick refused to deliver one of his masterpieces. To the office, fine. But to the North Channel — no way Jose. If we wanted a sub, we'd have to fend for ourselves. Create it with our own little hands. So we did. And we discovered that with a little imagination and lots of creativity (not to mention a cast iron stomach) anyone can create a glorious super sub.*

| | |
|---|---|
| 1   16-oz. loaf Italian bread | Shredded lettuce |
| Mayonnaise | • • • • • • |
| ½  pound-plus shaved turkey | Onion rings (thinly sliced) |
| Mustard | Green pepper, thinly sliced |
| ½  pound-plus shaved ham | Tomato, thinly sliced |
| Dijon mustard | Hot pepper rings, chopped |
| ¼  pound thinly sliced Swiss | Italian salad dressing |
| cheese | ¼  pound thinly sliced Cheddar |
| ½  pound-plus hard salami | cheese |

Split the loaf of bread lengthwise horizontally, but don't cut through. It should look like a giant hot dog bun. Scoop or pick out some of the center pulp from both upper and lower sections. Lay bread so both center sections are exposed as one (so it looks like a butterfly). Treat both halves as one foundation and start building your sandwich by spreading a generous amount of mayonnaise on bread. Then add in order: turkey, mustard, ham, Dijon mustard, Swiss cheese, salami, and a layer of lettuce.

• • • • • •

On bottom half only, continue building sandwich with onion rings, green peppers, tomato slices, and hot pepper rings. Sprinkle both halves with Italian dressing, top with Cheddar cheese and close. Cut in fourths.

makes 4 hearty servings

> **Tip:** Definitely prepare this sandwich in the morning as it takes up a lot of counter space. Wrap it in paper toweling and seal in plastic wrap.
> You can dress up the potato salad with some chopped celery and green pepper.
> **Note:** You don't have to unwrap it to cut it. The wrapping helps to hold this monster sandwich together while you're trying to take a bite.

---

3rd day **PORK in ADOBO SAUCE**
Dinner    salad • creole-style tomatoes & corn • watermelon sparkle

---

*Anytime you mention you'll be serving Mexican food, somebody always wants a fire extinguisher kept nearby. Well, get ready, you're about to experience a rarity: a Mexican dish that isn't hot and spicy, but flavorful and mellow.*

| | |
|---|---|
| ¼  cup vinegar | 1  Tablespoon vegetable oil |
| 1  8-oz. can tomato sauce | 1  medium onion, finely chopped |
| ¼  teaspoon cumin | 2  garlic cloves, minced |
| ½  teaspoon oregano | • • • • • • |
| 1  teaspoon salt | |
| 2  Tablespoons chili powder | 4  pork loin chop, ¾ to 1-inch |
| 2  Tablespoons flour | thick |

*Pre-package first 10 ingredients in a 18-oz. jar. (Shake jar after pre-packaging and before using.)*
• • • • • •

Place pork chops in a large (gallon size) zip lock plastic storage bag. Add pre-packaged sauce. Seal and marinate overnight. (Turn package over every time you open ice chest.)

• • • • • •

Transfer chops and sauce to a large skillet. Bring mixture to a boil. Reduce heat. Cover and simmer 45 minutes.

makes 4 servings

### CREOLE-STYLE TOMATOES & CORN

| | |
|---|---|
| 1 onion, chopped | ¼ teaspoon salt |
| 1 green pepper, chopped | ⅛ teaspoon pepper |
| 1 14-oz. can tomatoes, drained | Dash of hot sauce |
| 1 16-oz. can whole kernel corn, drained | Dash of Worcestershire |

In a bowl, combine all ingredients. Mix well. Place mixture on a large sheet of foil. Form into a packet with all seams at top. Place in skillet during the last 15 minutes of cooking.

### WATERMELON SPARKLE

| | |
|---|---|
| ½ cup sugar | |
| ⅓ cup light rum | 4 cups watermelon chunks |
| 3 Tablespoons lime juice | |

• • • • • •

In a small bowl, combine first 3 ingredients. Mix well. Place melon in a large (gallon size) zip lock plastic storage bag. Pour sauce over melon chunks. Seal and chill.

**Tip:** Prepare dessert earlier in the day so it has time to chill before dinner.
**Note:** Keep a loaf of French bread handy, this sauce is fantastic for dunkin'.

---

4th day **FRENCH TOAST**
Breakfast juice • fresh orange slices • sausage • beverage

---

*As a kid, one of my all-time favorite things to make was French toast! It was so messy to make and so yummy to eat! Thank God I had a loving mummy, who didn't mind cleaning up after I had a full tummy.*

*Now you may be asking yourself; "If this is such a mess to make, why is he suggesting that we make it?"*

*The answer: Because it still tastes yummy in the tummy. As for the mess, mummy may not be around, but remember we're supposed to have a helpful crew around to take care of the clean up.*

*(Seriously, if you don't let a six-year-old kid and his friend Fluffy make your French toast, there won't be any mess to clean up.)*

| | |
|---|---|
| 4 eggs, beaten | 4 Tablespoons honey |
| 1 cup milk | Dash of soy sauce |
| 1 teaspoon vanilla extract | Dash of salt |
| 2 teaspoons ground cinnamon | • • • • • • |
| | 12 slices white bread |

In a pie tin, combine first 7 ingredients. Blend well.

• • • • • •

For each piece of toast, dip both sides of bread in egg mixture. Then on a lightly greased griddle, over medium heat, cook for 3 minutes per side or until golden brown.

makes 4 servings

**Tip:** It's a good idea to cook the sausage first, then shove them to the edge of the griddle to keep warm while you prepare French toast. Serve each crew member as soon as toast is ready.

Forget about using fresh bread. The best French toast is made with bread that is just a little stale. Not moldy, but firm, dry, stale, two-day-old bread.

Add a touch of class by sprinkling toast with some powdered sugar or cinnamon. Just remember, they're not on the shopping list.

---

4th day **GAZPACHO with CLAMS**
Lunch   St. Louis cocktail sandwiches • canned fruit cocktail

---

*They say "Real Men don't eat gazpacho!" It's only served to the refined ladies of high society during their afternoon garden parties. (Tsk! tsk!)*

*That's a bunch of malarkie!*

*I've experienced the dry 105° heat off southern California. I've suffered through the high humidity and 97° weather in the upper Great Lakes, and I can tell you one thing. . . nothing satisfies and refreshes a 210 pound sailor on one of those days like a cool bowl of gazpacho. Not even a double cheeseburger deluxe, with an order of large fries and a chocolate malt!*

| | | | |
|---|---|---|---|
| 3 | tomatoes, chopped | 3 | 6-oz. cans tomato juice |
| 1 | cucumber, chopped | 2½ | Tablespoons red wine vinegar |
| ½ | green pepper, chopped | | |
| 3 | green onions, and tops, thinly sliced | 2 | Tablespoons lemon juice |
| | | 1 | Tablespoon vegetable oil |
| 2 | celery stalks, thinly sliced | 1½ | Tablespoon Worcestershire |
| 2 | garlic cloves, minced | | Dash of hot sauce |
| 1 | 6½-oz. can minced clams | | Dash of horseradish |

Combine all ingredients in a large (gallon size) zip lock plastic storage bag. Seal and chill overnight.

Serve in bowls garnished with lemon and cucumber slices.

makes 4 hearty servings

**ST. LOUIS Cocktail Sandwiches**

| | | | |
|---|---|---|---|
| 4 | hot dogs, finely chopped | ¼ | cup mayonnaise |
| | • • • • • • | 1 | Tablespoon chopped parsley |
| ¼ | cup finely chopped onion | | • • • • • • |
| ¼ | cup sweet pickle relish | 8 | slices of bread, crust removed |

In a large bowl, mash chopped hot dogs with a fork. Add next 4 ingredients. Mix well. Spread mixture over 4 slices of bread and top with remaining slices. Cut each sandwich into quarters.

**Tip:** You don't have to do all the chopping and slicing at the same time. Any time prior to this that you are cutting up some celery, green pepper, garlic, green onion, cucumber or tomatoes, chop a little extra for the Gazpacho and store it in the plastic bag. Then when the time comes, all you have to do to complete the recipe is open a few cans.

Wanna try something a little different? Take an empty can and cut the slices of bread into circles for round sandwiches and cut into wedges.

**Note:** The extra hot dogs can be used to make Mustard Dogs for cocktail hour. (see page 76)

# CHINESE SPAGHETTI

salad • honeydew salad with apricot cream sauce

*Chinese spaghetti? Spaghetti with bamboo shoots? Water chestnuts? Green onions, ginger root and soy sauce?*

*Why not? That's possibly the way it was first served to Marco Polo when he was venturing through the Orient. And he liked it so much that he brought it back to Italy so the rest of the civilized world could enjoy it, too.*

*Well, we're adventurous adventurers just like old Marco, so why not celebrate pasta properly, the Chinese way? (I'm just thankful it isn't made with Tofu.)*

| | |
|---|---|
| 1 Tablespoon sugar | 3 Tablespoons vegetable oil |
| 1 Tablespoon flour | • • • • • • |
| 3 Tablespoons shredded gingerroot | 2 red peppers, cut into thin strips |
| ¼ cup soy sauce | 4 green onions, thinly sliced |
| ¼ cup sherry | 1 4-oz. can sliced mushrooms, drained |
| 4 garlic cloves, minced | 1 8-oz. can sliced water chestnuts, drained |
| • • • • • • | 1 8-oz. can bamboo shoots, drained |
| 1½ pounds pork steak, trimmed and cut into bite-size pieces | • • • • • • |
| ½ cup water | 8 ounces spaghetti, cooked |
| • • • • • • | |

*Pre-package first 6 ingredients in an 8-oz. jar. (Shake jar after pre-packaging and before using.)*

• • • • • •

Place pork in a large (gallon size) zip lock plastic storage bag. Pour pre-packaged sauce over meat. Add ½ cup water. Seal and marinate overnight. (Turn package over every time you open ice chest.)

• • • • • •

In a large skillet, heat oil over high heat. Add pork and cook 5 minutes, stirring occasionally.

• • • • • •

Add vegetables and any leftover marinade. Cook until red pepper strips start to wilt and sauce has thickened.

Divide cooked spaghetti into serving portions. Cover with sauce mixture.

## HONEYDEW SALAD with APRICOT CREAM SAUCE

| | |
|---|---|
| 1 8-oz. carton sour cream | 2 Tablespoons apricot preserves |
| ¼ cup chopped pecans | • • • • • • |
| ¼ cup flaked coconut | 4 cups honeydew chunks |

In a small bowl, combine first 4 ingredients. Mix well. Divide fruit chunks among four individual serving bowls. Top with cream mixture.

**Tip:** If you've already cooked the spaghetti and stored it in a plastic bag, just add some hot water, let stand a minute or so, then punch some holes in the bottom of the bag to drain and it's ready to go.
**Note:** The longer the pork is in the marinade, the more robust the flavor. I love all the garlic and gingerroot flavor, so I marinate it overnight.

*It's Sunday morning. The thermometer registers well below freezing and a gentle, steady snow has fallen during the night. Although the world is covered with the beauty, splendor and purity of winter, a subtle depression fills the hearts of sailors yearning and dreaming for summer's return.*

*The call comes... brunch at the skipper's! Mimosa's. Spiked fruit cocktail. Cheese and vegetable trays. Quiche Lorraine. Videos of last years' sailing season, and talk of this year's summer cruise. All of a sudden the doldrums of winter simply disappear.*

*I'd like to recreate that special spirited brunch for the crew when we are on the cruise. The only problem is how to make a pastry crust for the quiche? There's no oven. Well, I found one solution. It may not be as fancy and as elegant as the classic Quiche Lorraine, but it works...*

| | | | |
|---|---|---|---|
| 1 | 6-oz. package hash brown potato mix | 1 | onion, chopped |
| | • • • • • • | 1 | green pepper, chopped |
| 1 | Tablespoon butter | | • • • • • • |
| 1 | pound fully cooked smoked sausage | 3 | Tablespoons butter |
| 1 | 6¾-oz. can chunk chicken, broken up | | • • • • • • |
| | | 6 | eggs, well beaten |
| 1 | 4-oz. can sliced mushrooms, drained | 1 | cup (4oz.) shredded sharp Cheddar cheese |

Pre-soak hash browns according to package directions.

• • • • • •

In a large skillet, melt butter over medium heat. Add the following 5 ingredients and cook until onion and green pepper are tender. Remove mixture from skillet and drain on paper towel. Discard grease.

• • • • • •

Add 3 Tablespoons butter to skillet. When butter has melted, add potatoes and spread them evenly over the bottom and up the sides (like a pie shell). Cook uncovered, over medium-high heat for 8 minutes or until crisp and lightly browned.

Spread sausage mixture evenly over hash browns. Pour in beaten eggs. Reduce heat. Cover and cook 5 minutes or until eggs are slightly firm. Top with cheese. Cover and cook until cheese melts and eggs are firm.

makes 4 hearty servings

**Tip:** If you wipe the sides of the skillet with oil before you begin, it will help prevent sticking.

The secret to success for this recipe is slow cooking. So don't get impatient and turn the heat up. You'll only burn the hash browns and spoil breakfast.

# YANKEE SEASHELL SALAD

melba toast • crackers & cheese spreads

*Aahhh! Those lazy, hazy, crazy days of summer. Days that are so beautiful, so sunny, so magnificent that you don't want to go anywhere, or do anything. Just kick back and let the sun and gentle breeze play games with your body and soul.*

*(Translation: The days are too damn hot to cook; there's no wind to ward off pesky flies; you've run out of gas, or you're hopelessly stranded and the crew is at each others' throats.)*

*For days like these, this marvelous, light, elegant salmon and pasta salad is just the thing to refresh the crew and lift their spirits. Of course, a couple of good belts from Captain Morgan couldn't hurt either.*

| | |
|---|---|
| 8 | ounces large shell macaroni, cooked |
| 1 | cup sliced celery |
| ½ | cup diced carrots |
| ½ | cup chopped parsley |
| ¼ | cup chopped green onion |
| ¼ | cup chopped green pepper |
| 1 | 8-oz. can sweet peas, drained |
| ½ | cup Italian salad dressing |
| 2 | Tablespoons lemon juice |

• • • • • •

| | |
|---|---|
| 1 | 15½-oz. can Pink Salmon, drained |
| | Lettuce |

In a large bowl, combine first 9 ingredients. Toss well to blend. Transfer mixture to a large (gallon size) zip lock plastic storage bag. Seal and chill.

• • • • • •

Before serving, break salmon into large pieces and add to salad mixture. Shake and massage bag to thoroughly coat and mix ingredients.

Serve on a bed of lettuce.

makes 4 servings

> **Tip:** In the morning, while you're busy preparing the Hash Brown Skillet for breakfast, have another crew member toss together the shell macaroni, vegetables and dressing for the salad. Finish the preparation by adding the salmon just before serving.

---

# HAM, YAM, AND APPLES

salad • canned fruit cocktail

*What a spoiled crew I sail with! You should have seen their noses turn up the first time I mentioned to these ingrates, that a sailor of old would gladly have given his soul to the devil to feast on our canned meat rather than the tart pickled or salty dried meat they had to choke down way back then.*

*After that stern lecture, the crew sat silently around the cabin table. Not silently as in meekly, but silent as in defiant. They were determined not to touch anything that I served. They were challenging my authority.*

*Then I put the old Ham-yam and apples in front of them. Its sweet aroma lowered their resistance and melted their opposition. And after just one little taste, the flavor stole their souls. So much for culinary snobbery.*

1   16-oz. can cooked boneless
    ham, cut into 8 slices
2   Tablespoons vegetable oil
    • • • • • •
1   17-oz. can sweet potatoes,
    drained
2   red apples, cored, quartered
    and cut into ½-inch slices
¼   cup orange juice
2   Tablespoons brown sugar

In a large skillet, brown ham slices in hot oil over medium-high heat.
    • • • • • •
Arrange sweet potatoes and apples around ham. Add orange juice. Sprinkle with brown sugar. Reduce heat. Cover and simmer 15 minutes.

makes 4 servings

# Time Out For Cocktails & Things

Before the advent of the stereo tape deck, C.D's, VCR's and the portable generator, boaters had to rely on their own ingenuity and creative talents to keep themselves entertained while cruising isolated waters. With that in mind, I wish to dedicate this very elegant and very proper Time Out for Cocktails to the owner/skipper of the **Sara-Ann** and his loving family. For it was these good people who taught me how to appreciate a good vodka gimlet and to find a deeper meaning in life by reading the jokes, aloud, from Readers Digest while being attacked by ravenous black flies and squadrons of blood-thirsty mosquitoes.

## CAVIAR BALL

1   3-oz. package cream cheese, cubed
    and softened
2   teaspoons sour cream
    Dash of Worcestershire sauce
    Dash of garlic salt
    • • • • • •
1   3½-oz. jar black caviar, well
    drained
2   hard boiled eggs, chopped
1   onion, finely chopped

In a small bowl, combine first 4 ingredients and blend well. Form into an oval mound on a plate. Cover with caviar and surround with chopped eggs and onion. Serve with cocktail ryes and crackers.

## CRAB MEAT SPREAD

1   8-oz. package cream cheese, cubed
    and softened
½   cup mayonnaise
    • • • • • •
½   cup (2-oz.) shredded cheddar
    cheese
1   6-oz. can crab meat, drained and
    flaked
¼   teaspoon pepper

In a large bowl, combine first 2 ingredients. With a fork, beat until creamy smooth. Add remaining ingredients. Mix well. Transfer to a smaller bowl and serve with crackers.

## INDIA CUP

3 Tablespoons brown sugar
3 Tablespoons water
• • • • • •
1½ cups pineapple juice
1 cup golden rum
⅓ cup lime juice

Combine first 2 ingredients and stir until sugar is dissolved. Add remaining ingredients. Serve over ice.

## ZIPPY VEGETABLE DIP

1 cup mayonnaise
1 cup cream-style cottage cheese
¼ cup grated onion
1 teaspoon Worcestershire sauce
½ teaspoon caraway seeds
½ teaspoon dry mustard
½ teaspoon pepper
¼ teaspoon salt
⅛ teaspoon garlic salt
¼ teaspoon celery seeds
Couple of dashes of hot sauce

In a small bowl, combine all ingredients. Mix well and chill. Serve with vegetables and chips.

## STUFFED NUTS

Processed cheese spread
Large pecan halves

Spread cheese over pecan halves and stick them together like a sandwich or an Oreo cookie.

## MINT JULEPS

4 cups water
2 cups sugar
4 cups loosely packed fresh mint, chopped
• • • • • •
4 cups bourbon
Sprigs of fresh mint

In a saucepan, combine water and sugar and bring to a boil Reduce heat and simmer 10 minutes. Add mint and simmer 30 minutes. Remove from heat and let stand overnight. Strain.
Combine mint syrup and bourbon. Serve over crushed ice and garnish with mint (about a 1 to 1 ratio). You may want to add more bourbon.

## MIMOSA HAWAIIAN

1 12-oz. can apricot nectar
1 12-oz. can pineapple juice
1 6-oz. can frozen orange juice concentrate, thawed and undiluted
¾ cup water
• • • • • •
1 chilled bottle dry white champagne

Combine first 4 ingredients and chill. Stir in champagne just before serving.

**Tip:** For an exciting taste sensation, try scooping out ¾ of the pulp from the center of a 1-inch thick slice of cucumber and fill it with the CRABMEAT spread.

# Group 5
## a three day menu

| | BREAKFAST | LUNCH | DINNER |
|---|---|---|---|
| 1st day | **BREAKFAST ROLLS**<br>juice • melon<br>beverage | **MUFFULETTA Sandwiches**<br>potato chips • pickles | **PORK STEAKS ROMANOFF**<br>salad<br>egg noodles • mixed vegetables<br>peach ambrosia |
| 2nd day | **PORTUGUESE POACHED EGGS**<br>juice • strawberries<br>beverage | **TUNA FISH SANDWICHES**<br>corn chips<br>marinated mushrooms & vegetables | **CHICKEN & CHERRIES**<br>salad • rice • broccoli<br>fruit with sweet sauced sauce |
| 3rd day | **NUTTY ORANGE PANCAKES**<br>juice • eggs • sausage<br>beverage | **CHUNKY SALMON SALAD**<br>**Sandwiches**<br>corn chips • cucumber cooler | **PASTA with**<br>**SAUSAGE & VEGETABLES**<br>salad • bread sticks<br>lovin trifle |

---

1st day **BREAKFAST ROLLS**
Breakfast juice • melon • beverage

---

Man sollte nie die Anziehungskraft von etwas Frischegbackenem uterschätzen.

So geschah es eimmal, dass wir in einem winzig kleinen Hafen unterkommen mussten, da stürmisches Wetter holen Wellengang verursachte und niemand, der ganz bei Verstand war, sich ausserhalb des sicheren Hafens begeben hätte. Diese Verzögerung unsere Segelpartie war nicht eingeplant und stellte sich, als eine echte Enttäuschung, für die gesamte Besatzung, heraus. Żer allgemeinen Aufmunterung, schlug ich ein ausgiebiges Frühstück vor. (Regel Nr. 148: Im Falle einer Depressing... schlemmern). Wir luden uns die Bäuche voll mit Schinken, Bratwurstchen, Pfannkuchen und Eiern. Ich übertraf mich selbst. Weimal sogar, bereitete ich eine Doppelportion "Bloody Marys". Die Stimmung hob sich etwas, konnte jedoch noch verbessert werden. Knapp eine Stunde nach dem Frühstück, sahen wir uns die Ortschaft an und kamen an einer schmucken Bäckerei vorbei, die das feinste Gebäck ausstellte. Die Versuchung war zu gross. Ein jeder von uns verliess die Bäckerei, mit einer Tute in der Hand und einem Lächelm im Gesicht. Dies waren die gleichen Burchen, die noch vor Kürzester Ziet keinen Bissen mehr zu sich nehmen, oder eine zufriedene Miene zeigen konnten.

Seitdem, wenn auch immer wir in einem Hafen ankommen, schauich mir, vor allem, die örtlichen Bäckerein an.

Es ist bei weitem unkomplizierter, susse, klebrige Pasteten und feines Gebäck auf den Tisch zu bringen, als Schinken and Eier zu brutzeln. (for English version, see page 66)

**Tip:** Prepare the filling for Peach Ambrosia, tonight's dessert.

---

1st day **MUFFULETTA Sandwiches**
Lunch potato chips • pickles

---

*If you thought Captain Queeg was a little P.O.'ed when he discovered his strawberries were missing, you should have seen me when I found out that a couple of my fellow crew members had been snacking on the antipasto mixture I was going to use in our noon-time sandwiches... "But it tasted so good!" I could have keelhauled them! The marinated olives and pickled vegetable mixture is what gives the Muffuletta that heavenly, sinful flavor that makes it so distinctive. Now it's all gone. Oh well, what's done is done. We still had the meat and cheese so I just made up a bunch of plain old everyday sandwiches.*

*But I did learn one lesson. It's extremely important that the crew understands that they will incur the wrath of God (and the cook) if they disobey the supreme law of the high seas... ONLY THE COOK IS ALLOWED IN THE FOOD LOCKER.*

| | | | | |
|---|---|---|---|---|
| ½ | cup chopped pimiento-stuffed green olives | 3 | Tablespoons lemon juice |
| ½ | cup chopped pitted black olives | ⅓ | cup vegetable oil |
| ½ | cup chopped celery | • • • • • • |
| ½ | cup chopped pickled vegetables | 1 | 16-oz. loaf Italian bread |
| ¼ | cup chopped parsley | ½ | pound thinly sliced salami |
| 1 | garlic clove, minced | ½ | pound shaved ham |

½ cup chopped pimiento-
stuffed green olives
½ cup chopped pitted black
olives
½ cup chopped celery
½ cup chopped pickled
vegetables
¼ cup chopped parsley
1 garlic clove, minced

3 Tablespoons lemon juice
⅓ cup vegetable oil
• • • • • •
1 16-oz. loaf Italian bread
½ pound thinly sliced salami
½ pound shaved ham
½ pound thinly sliced provolone
cheese.
Shredded lettuce

Combine first 8 ingredients in a small (quart size) zip lock plastic storage bag. Seal and chill overnight.

• • • • • •

Cut loaf of Italian bread in half horizontally. Scoop or pick out some of the pulp from both halves.

Drain olive mixture, reserving liquid.

Brush cut sides of bread with reserve liquid. Start building sandwich with a layer of salami covered with half the olive mixture, then the ham, more olive mixture, provolone cheese and a nice layer of shredded lettuce. Drizzle any remaining liquid over the top and cover with top half. Cut in fourths.

makes 4 hearty servings

> **Tips:** To drain olive mixture, punch some holes in the bottom of the bag with a fork and hold over a small bowl to save liquid.
> Make sandwiches ahead of time. Wrap in paper toweling, then seal in in plastic wrap. You do not have to unwrap it to cut it.

---

1st day **PORK STEAKS ROMANOFF**
Dinner salad • egg noodles • canned mixed vegetables • peach ambrosia

---

*A few years back, a friend and I use to do some short bay crossing during the week. We'd slip out of work early, get on his boat and sail to a friendly port, eat or drink our dinner, then head back in time for work the next morning. After a couple weeks of this, we came to the conclusion we were spending too much time and money on booze and food in the local taverns. We figured we could do a lot better if we, at least ate on the boat. The only problem was, his boat was a sleek twenty-five footer designed for racing, not cooking. Which meant we had to prepare something simple, like Pork Steaks Romanoff.*

2 Tablespoons vegetable oil
4 pork steaks, trimmed of fat
• • • • • •
1 8-oz. can tomato sauce
1 5-oz. box Stroganoff
noodle mix
• • • • • •
2 Tablespoons cornstarch
¼ cup water

In a large skillet, heat oil over medium-high heat. Add pork steaks and brown. Remove steaks and discard grease.

• • • • • •

In skillet, combine tomato sauce and dry ingredients for Stroganoff sauce (cook noodles separately). Return steaks to sauce and bring to a boil. Reduce heat. Cover and simmer 35 minutes. Remove steaks.

• • • • • •

In a cup, blend cornstarch and water. Add to skillet. Continue to cook and stir until thick and bubbly. Pour over steaks and noodles.

makes 4 servings

### PEACH AMBROSIA

| | | | |
|---|---|---|---|
| 1 | 8-oz. can pineapple tidbits, drained | 2 | Tablespoons flaked coconut |
| 10 | grapes, sliced | 2 | Tablespoons sour cream |
| 4 | orange sections (from a 16-oz. can of Mandarin oranges) chopped | | • • • • • • |
| 2 | Tablespoons chopped miniature marshmallows | 4 | peach halves (from a 16-oz. can of peach halves) |
| | | 2 | Tablespoons chopped walnuts |

In a small bowl, combine first 6 ingredients. Mix well. Chill. Spoon mixture into each peach half and sprinkle with walnuts.

**Tip:** Since you've got to cook up some noodles for dinner anyway, you might as well cook up some hard-boiled eggs and the noodles for the pasta dish in a few days, all at the same time. Just remember to start everything a little bit earlier than normal.

Prepare the filling for dessert in the morning.

**Note:** Instead of leaving them whole, I like to cut the steaks into bite size pieces, that way the crew doesn't fight over who got the biggest piece of meat.

You won't be using the entire can of either the orange segments or the peaches. What's leftover, drain and store in a zip lock bag to use in tomorrow night's dessert, Fruit with Sweet Sauced Sauce.

2nd day
Breakfast
# PORTUGUESE POACHED EGGS
juice • strawberries • beverage

*Picture this: the stormy Atlantic, 1703. You're aboard a proud Portuguese ship of the line, returning from battle with the British in the East Indies. The captain's in his mess savoring the last of the chorizo stew. The cook rushes in with an egg he found in the deserted chicken coop. Suddenly the ship lunges; the cook stumbles and falls, breaking the egg in the captain's stew. It splashes the captain's last clean white shirt with the red sauce from the stew. He's furious. He has the cook thrown to the sharks. Upon returning to his table, the captain discovers that the egg has cooked in the sauce. Poached to perfection in his absence.*

*This morning as you sit down to enjoy this marvelous breakfast, I ask that you bow you heads in silence, in remembrance of the clumsy oaf who gave his life to create this meal. The cook.*

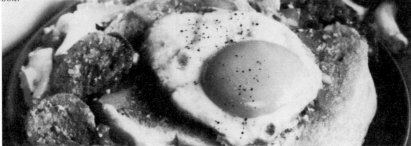

| | |
|---|---|
| 2 Tablespoons butter | 1 teaspoon instant beef bouillon granules |
| 2 onions, chopped | 1 teaspoon salt |
| 2 garlic cloves, minced | ½ teaspoon pepper |
| • • • • • • | • • • • • • |
| 1 cup water | 1 16-oz. can sweet peas, drained |
| 2 tomatoes chopped | 4 eggs |
| 1 pound Italian sausage, cut into ½-inch think slices | 4 1-inch thick sliced French bread |

In a large skillet, melt butter over medium heat. Add onions and garlic. Cook 5 minutes.

• • • • • •

Add next 6 ingredients and bring mixture to a boil. Reduce heat. Cover and simmer 15 minutes.

• • • • • •

Add sweet peas and cook until thoroughly heated.
Break one egg at a time into a cup, then slide it into the skillet. Cover and simmer 5 minutes or until eggs are set.
Serve poached eggs and meat sauce over a slice of French bread.

makes 4 servings.

**Tip:** If fresh strawberries aren't in season, buy a package of frozen, but store it in a plastic zip lock bag, so it doesn't drip all over the cooler.

---

2nd day **The Rodney Dangerfield TUNA FISH SANDWICH**
Lunch    corn chips • marinated mushrooms & vegetables

---

*Just mention subs, stacked ham & cheese, BLT's, club or Reubens! Tell the crew, the kids, the family; tell them they can have any one of these sandwiches for lunch, and their mouths begin to water!*

*Even if you respond to the old "What's for lunch?" with bologna sandwiches, you'll get an "allll RIGHT!" from at least one junior member of the lunch bunch. But answer with "tuna fish sandwiches" you'll get nothing. No response one way or the other. Everyone seems to be indifferent to tuna fish sandwiches.*

*Well, things are about to change! It's time the tuna fish sandwich got some respect.*

| | |
|---|---|
| 2 6½-oz. cans white tuna, drained and flaked | ½ teaspoon mustard |
| 2 Tablespoons chopped onion | ¼ cup mayonnaise |
| 2 Tablespoons chopped green pepper | Dash of Worcestershire |
| | • • • • • |
| 1 teaspoon chopped hot pepper rings | 4 hard rolls, split in half horizontally |
| | 4 slices Swiss cheese Lettuce |

In a large bowl, combine first 7 ingredients and blend well. Add more mayonnaise if desired.

• • • • • •

To make sandwich, spread one-fourth tuna mixture on each bottom half of the rolls. Cover with a slice of Swiss cheese, lettuce and top half of roll.

makes 4 sandwiches

**Marinated MUSHROOMS & VEGETABLES**

| | | | |
|---|---|---|---|
| 1 | teaspoon sugar | | |
| 1 | teaspoon basil | 1 | 16-oz. can whole carrots, drained |
| 1 | teaspoon oregano | 1 | 14-oz. can artichoke hearts, |
| 1 | teaspoon salt | | drained and halved |
| ¼ | teaspoon pepper | 1 | cup pitted black olives, halved |
| | • • • • • • | 1 | cup sliced celery |
| ⅔ | cup vinegar | 1 | 2-oz. jar sliced pimiento, drained |
| ⅔ | cup vegetable oil | | and chopped |
| ½ | cup chopped onion | 2 | 4-oz. can sliced mushrooms, |
| 2 | garlic cloves, minced | | drained |

• • • • • •

Pre-package first 5 ingredients in a plastic zip lock envelope.

• • • • • •

In a large skillet, combine the next four ingredients with pre-packaged spices. Bring mixture to a boil. Reduce heat. Simmer uncovered 10 minutes. Let cool. Place remaining ingredients in a large (gallon size) zip lock plastic storage bag. Pour marinade over vegetables. Seal and chill.

> **Tip:** After splitting the rolls in half, you might want to scoop out some of the pulp from the top half. It makes a nice little cap to hold in all the good fixin's.
> When and if they are available, substitute ½-pound fresh mushrooms (sliced) for the canned mushrooms in the side dish.
> Prepare tonight's dessert.

---

2nd day
Dinner
# CHICKEN & CHERRIES
salad • white rice • steamed broccoli • fruit with sweet sauced sauce

---

*If you want to raise a few eyebrows, just tell the crew you're serving "Chicken and Cherries" for dinner. After all, it does sound like a recipe a deranged four-year-old would dream up.*

*Cherries Jubilee. Chocolate covered cherries. Cherry pie. A cherry topping on an ice cream sundae. A Manhattan, straight up with a cherry. These classic cherry combinations. But Chicken and Cherries?*

*Although it isn't one of the most common cherry combinations, I can assure you that it is one of the most intriguing and delightful ones you'll ever try. At first, I served it as a novelty dish, but now the crew considers it one of our official celebration dinners, at home as well as on the water.*

| | | | |
|---|---|---|---|
| ¼ | *teaspoon ginger* | | |
| ½ | *teaspoon instant chicken* | 2 | **pounds boned and skinned** |
| | *bouillon granules* | | **chicken breast, cut into bite** |
| ¼ | *cup honey* | | **size pieces** |
| ¼ | *cup red wine vinegar* | | • • • • • • |
| ½ | *cup water* | 1 | **Tablespoon water** |
| 3 | *Tablespoons soy sauce* | 1 | **Tablespoon cornstarch** |
| | • • • • • • | 1 | **16-oz. can pitted tart red** |
| 2 | **Tablespoons butter** | | **cherries, drained** |
| 1 | **carrot, thinly sliced** | 3 | **green onions, sliced** |
| 1 | **garlic clove, minced** | | |

• • • • • •

*Pre-package first 6 ingredients in a 16-oz. jar. (Shake jar after pre-packaging and before adding to skillet.)*

• • • • • •

In a large skillet, melt butter over medium-high heat. Add carrots and garlic. Cook for 2 minutes then remove them with a slotted spoon.

• • • • • •

Add chicken and cook 5 minutes, stirring occasionally.
Stir in pre-packaged ingredients. Bring mixture to a boil.
Return carrots to skillet. Reduce heat. Cover and simmer 10 minutes.

• • • • •

In a cup, blend cornstarch and water. Add mixture to skillet.
Continue to cook and stir until thick and bubbly.
Stir in cherries and onions. Heat through.
Serve over white rice.

makes 4 hearty servings

### FRUIT with SWEET SAUCED SAUCE

½    cup sour cream
1½   Tablespoons brown sugar
1¼   teaspoons white rum                      Remaining canned Mandarin
1¼   teaspoons Irish whiskey                     oranges
1    Tablespoon chopped raisins               Remaining peach halves
                                             1    Banana, sliced

• • • • •

In a small bowl, combine first 5 ingredients. Mix well. Place fruit in a large (gallon size) zip lock plastic storage bag. Pour sauce over fruit. Seal and chill.

**Tip:** Prepare dessert earlier.
**Note:** Remember that you are using the leftover fruit from yesterday's Peach Ambrosia.

---

3rd day
Breakfast

# NUTTY ORANGE PANCAKES
juice • eggs • sausage • beverage

Picture this! After 53 years of hard work, pinching pennies, scrimping and saving, a sweet elderly couple finally escapes the hassels of the big city to retire to a nice cozy little lake-front community. They fulfill their life-long dream and open a tiny little mom and pop diner.

Although they don't know the first thing about the food service business, they figure that since this is such a small, laid back town they'd only be serving two or three customers at a time, so they'd be able to practice a little "on the job training." Learn as you go, so to speak. Besides how hard could it be, to serve up a couple cups of joe and scramble some eggs for a few new friends?

Simple enough. But unbeknownst to them, the same weekend they planned to open their doors the local yacht club was hosting an open invitation regatta. So instead of just a handful of boats in the harbor, there were 50 or 60. All with hungry crews. You should have seen their faces when we came in for breakfast singing "Double Shot of My Baby's Love." Actually they weren't surprised. They were stunned! They freaked out! This sweet adorable little gray-haired couple had no idea how to feed this---this...unshaven mass of humanity.

Fortunately, we weren't Blue Beard and his gang of cutthroats who had come to rape and pillage the town. Just a bunch of jovial sailors who love to cook and enjoy pitching in and lending a helping hand when needed. And they needed one. And everyone got served.

Now if you ever come across a little mom and pop operation that serves up a mean stack of Nutty Orange Pancakes, and that sweet little old lady who is serving you is always humming "Double Shot of My Baby's Love"...you don't even have to ask...because as Paul Harvey would say..."Now you know the rest of the story."

1¾ cups packaged biscuit mix          2    eggs, beaten
½ cup ground walnuts                  1    cup orange juice
• • • • •                             2    Tablespoons honey

Pre-package first 2 ingredients in a small (quart size) zip lock plastic storage bag.

• • • • •

In a large bowl, combine eggs, orange juice, and honey. Mix well.
Add pre-packaged ingredients and blend well.

• • • • •

For each pancake, pour or spoon ¼ cup batter onto a hot, lightly greased, griddle. Cook 2 to 3 minutes per side or until golden brown.

makes 12 (4-inch) pancakes

### Orange Butter

In a small bowl, combine ½ cup soft butter and 2 Tablespoons orange juice. Beat vigorously with a fork until well blended. Serve on pancakes.

> **Tips:** Don't over-mix pancake batter. Just blend until all ingredients are moist.
>   Pancakes are ready to be flipped when most of the surface bubbles pop.
>   Cook the sausages first and keep them warm around the edges of the griddle while you cook the pancakes.
> **Note:** There's a neat little trick to try if you're using a griddle that coveres both burners. After you finish cooking the pancakes, stack them on top of the sausages on one half of the griddle and turn that burner off. Coverfood with a sheet of aluminum foil to keep warm while you fry the eggs on the other half.

---

3rd day
Lunch

# CHUNKY SALMON SALAD Sandwiches
corn chips • cucumber cooler

---

*On our way north to our happy cruising grounds, we pass by or cross over some very prosperous fishing grounds. Not only can you catch a lot of big fish, but you can also win some big money and some very big prizes, if you enter some of the local tournaments. So a lot of people buy expensive boats and lots and lots of fancy equipment just to drag a couple of lines behind them with hopes of landing a few fish and winning a prize or two. Since we already have the quietest and most relaxing way to move across the water, we decided it was time that we dragged a line and won some of those beautiful prizes ourselves. (It sounded so good over a couple of beers)*

*We soon discovered that we had neither the temperament, the patience, nor the skill it took to be successful fishermen. Our lines crossed and tangled. We hooked the sails and got snagged in the rigging. Our reels developed birds' nests and our deep diving spinners skipped across the water. As the morning wore on, with no hits, no bites and no hope in sight, nerves wore thin. Names were called. Obscenities were uttered, and fights broke out. No fish. Not one, for all our efforts. Then I remembered an old trick my uncle taught me. A little while later the call went out...Fish On! Fish On! All bickering ceased. All animosities and hostilities came to a halt as the crew came together as one, united in our goal. The reel screamed. The pole bent to the max. Then we spotted the sparkle from below. The shiny silvery skin. "The landing net! Get the landing net!" Success at last.*

*What did we catch? Oh it wasn't much. Just a 16-ounce can of pink salmon. It was good for a laugh and great for lunch.*

1   **15½-oz. can pink salmon, drained**
1   **cup chopped celery**
2   **Tablespoons chopped sweet pickle**
1   **Tablespoon chopped green pepper**
1   **teaspoon chopped chives**
½   **cup mayonnaise**
2   **Tablespoons lemon juice**
   **Dash hot pepper sauce**
   • • • • • •
4   **(6-inch) pocket bread rounds**

In a large bowl, flake salmon and remove any skin and bones. Add all remaining ingredients, except bread, and blend well. Add more mayonnaise if desired.

• • • • • •

Cut bread rounds in half. Before filling halves with salmon mixture, line each pocket with lettuce, a slice of tomato, and onion rings.

makes 4 servings

## CUCUMBER COOLER

| | | |
|---|---|---|
| 2 | cucumbers, chopped | |
| ¼ | cup chopped onion | Lettuce |
| 1 | 12-oz. carton cottage cheese | Chopped green onion |
| 2 | Tablespoons mayonnaise | |

• • • • • •

In a small bowl, combine first 4 ingredients. Mix well. Serve on lettuce-lined plates and garnish with green onions.

**Tip:** Place chopped cucumber for side dish on some paper toweling. Pat dry to remove excess moisture. If you don't, the final mixutre may be a little more watery than you like.

---

3rd day
Dinner

# PASTA with SAUSAGE & VEGETABLES
salad • bread sticks • lovin' trifle

---

*It's difficult trying to figure out what it will take to satisfy a hungry sailor. If I cook up a five pound roast, they want more. If I grill a 24-ounce porterhouse steak, one for each member of the crew, they still want more. And they've never been satisfied with just one hamburger, a single chicken leg or only one meaty pork chop. That's why I can't understand why this recipe, using only one pound of sausage, can fill and satisfy the empty tummies of four hungry sailors. But it does.*

| | | | |
|---|---|---|---|
| ¼ | teaspoon garlic powder | | |
| 1 | teaspoon oregano | 3 | Tablespoons butter |
| | • • • • • • | | • • • • • • |
| ¼ | cup chopped green pepper | 1 | pound fully cooked smoked |
| ¼ | cup chopped onion | | sausage, cut into ½-inch |
| ½ | cup chopped zucchini | | thick slices |
| 1 | cup broccoli flowerets | 6 | cherry tomatoes, halved |
| 2 | 4-oz. cans sliced mushrooms, drained | | • • • • • • |
| | • • • • • • | 6 | ounces egg noodles, cooked |

*Pre-package first 2 ingredients in a plastic zip lock envelope.*

• • • • • •

In a large skillet, melt butter over medium heat. Add pre-packaged spices and all the vegetables, except tomatoes. Cook 5 minutes.

• • • • • •

Add sausage. Cover and cook 5 minutes.

• • • • • •

Add tomatoes and heat through.

Divide cooked noodles into serving portions. Cover with mixture and top with grated cheese.

makes 4 hearty servings

## LOVIN' TRIFLE

| | | | |
|---|---|---|---|
| 3 | cups angle food cake chunks | 1 | 16-oz. can blueberry pie filling |
| ¼ | cup rum | | Whipped topping |
| 1 | 16-oz. can vanilla pudding | | |

In four 10-oz. clear plastic glasses, layer in order: cake chunks, sprinkel of rum, pudding, pie filling, cake chunks, sprinkle of rum, pudding, pie filling and whipped topping.

**Tip:** If you've already cooked the egg noodles and stored them in a plastic bag, just add some hot water, let stand a minute or so, then punch some holes in the bottom of the bag to drain and you're all set.

For dessert, if you can't find any angle food, sponge or short cakes, try using some Twinkies instead.

# Time Out For Cocktails & Things

It doesn't matter whether you're dockside, at anchor, or still underway. There's a special time of the day when everyone just wants to sit back and relax. A time to share with friends and associates the joys of boating. A time to taste the forbidden fruits of the vine. (In other words, just get hammered.)

Some libation-stations have even set aside a certain period of the day so that we might observe this occasion. It's known as the Cocktail Hour. The precise hour of this ritual is of little importance. As one member of our crew correctly points out, "Somewhere in the world, it's post time, Right Now!". The important thing is that the crew participates in this daily celebration.

Why am I so adamant about them getting blasted out of their minds? It keeps them out of the galley and out from under my feet. Plus the fact, that after two or three drinks, they love anything I cook.

## PINEAPPLE CHEESE BALL

| | |
|---|---|
| 1 | 8-oz. package cream cheese, cubed and softened |
| 1 | Tablespoon finely chopped green pepper |
| 1 | Tablespoon finely chopped onion |
| 2 | Tablespoons drained crushed pineapple |
| 1 | teaspoon seasoned salt |
| ½ | cup chopped pecans |
| | • • • • • • |
| ½ | cup chopped pecans |

In a large bowl, combine first 6 ingredients. Mix well. Form into a ball and roll in remaining pecans. Seal in plastic wrap and chill. Serve with cocktail breads and crackers.

## SEAFOOD DIP

| | |
|---|---|
| 1 | 3-oz. package cream cheese, cubed and softened |
| 1 | 6 oz. can crab meat and liquid |
| 1 | 6½-oz. can shrimp and liquid |
| 2 | teaspoons grated onion |
| 1½ | teaspoons lemon juice |
| ¼ | teaspoon salt |
| 1 | Tablespoon mayonnaise |
| ¼ | teaspoon Worcestershire sauce |
| 2 | teaspoons chopped parsley |
| 3 | drops hot sauce |

In a large bowl, combine all ingredients. Mix well. Transfer to a smaller bowl and serve with crackers.

## MAI TAI

1½  ounces orange juice
1½  ounces pineapple juice
1½  ounces lime juice
1½  ounces cherry juices
1½  ounces rum
• • • • • •
Slice of lime
Maraschino cherry

Combine first 5 ingredients. Serve over ice and garnish with lime and cherry.

## IRISH COFFEE

1    cup coffee
1½  ounces Irish whiskey
2    teaspoons firmly packed
     brown
     sugar
• • • • • •
Whipped topping

Combine first 3 ingredients. Cover with whipped topping.

# Group 6
## a two day menu

|  | BREAKFAST | LUNCH | DINNER |
|---|---|---|---|
| 1st day | **DONUTS**<br>juice • melon<br><br>beverage | **MEX-TEX SALAD**<br>tortilla chips • cheese & fruit platter<br>tangy coconut fruit dip | **CHICKEN & PORK TABLECLOTH STAINER**<br>salad • rice<br><br>pudding |
| 2nd day | **FRANKS & EGGS**<br>juice • peaches<br><br>beverage | **HAM & CHEESE COMBO**<br>potato chips • 3-bean salad • pickles | **MEDITERRANEAN FISH CHOWDER**<br>salad • french bread<br><br>melon wedges with blueberry sauce |

1st day **DONUTS**
Breakfast juice • melon • beverage

*Buneulos y fruita quizas no sera su idea de un almuerzo elegante. Y yo sere el primero en admitir que no lo es! pero si sirve el proposito.*

*Este menu representa la primera comida, del primer dia, de una vacaccion que se esperaba por mucho tiempo, a bordo de un bote. Aun que teniamos que salir muy temprano y embarcarnos del puerto en la madrugada. . . (seria mejor olvidar este pensamiento). La realidad es que las cosas nunca pasan como uno las planifica. Siempre hay detalles que preparar al ultimo minito antes de despidirse. Asi es que en vez de preparar un almuerzo elegante que nadie quire o tiene tiempo para comerze, preferie tener bastantes bunuelos y fruta a mano para la tropa.*

*Ahora, no le hace que pueda suceder, la tropa pueda comer cuando y donde quieren, y no no tengo que preocuparme de hacer perdicion de buena comida. (see page 33 for translation)*

# MEX-TEX SALAD
tortilla chips • cheese & fruit platter • tangy coconut fruit dip

*How would I describe the Mex-Tex Salad?*
*Well, it's not totally a vegetable salad. It's not exactly a taco salad. It's not, yet it is, kinda like a sloppy Joe. That's a sloppy Joe that has crash landed on a salad! Sound awful? Well, it may not be what you'd want to serve to the Wednesday night bridge club, but if you've got a bunch of kids who are over 30, it's great fun to eat!*

2   **teaspoons chili powder**
1   **Tablespoon flour**
• • • • • •
1   **pound bulk pork sausage**
½   **cup chopped onion**
1   **garlic clove, minced**
• • • • • •
1   **8-oz. can tomato sauce**
1   **7½-oz. can tomatoes, cut up**
1   **4-oz. can green chili peppers, rinsed, seeded and chopped**
• • • • • •

1   **small head of lettuce, torn**
1   **15-oz. can garbanzo beans, drained**
¾   **cup sliced pitted black olives**
• • • • • •
1   **cup (4-oz.) shredded Cheddar cheese**
1   **cup cherry tomatoes, halved**
1   **green pepper, thinly sliced**

*Pre-package first 2 ingredients in a plastic zip lock envelope.*
• • • • • •
In a large skillet, cook meat, onion, and garlic over medium-high heat until meat is browned.  Discard excess grease.
• • • • • •
Add next 3 ingredients, plus pre-packaged spices, to skillet. Stirring occasionally, cook mixture over medium heat until thick and bubbly.
• • • • • •
In a large bowl, combine lettuce, beans and olives.  Toss to mix.
To serve:  Place lettuce mixture on individual serving plates or bowls.  Cover with meat mixture.  Top with shredded cheese, tomato halves, and green pepper slices.

makes 4 hearty servings

### TANGY COCONUT FRUIT DIP

1   **15-oz. can cream of coconut**

1   **6-oz. can frozen lemonade concentrate, thawed and undiluted**

In a small bowl, combine all ingredients. Mix well.

**Note:** You'll have no problem using frozen juice concentrates during the first couple of days of your cruise, if you just remember to store it in a zip lock plastic bag and keep it next to the ice. Of course it won't stay frozen that long.

# CHICKEN & PORK TABLECLOTH STAINER
salad • white rice • canned pudding

*Imagine yourself sitting at your grandmother's dining room table on Sunday. The platter is placed in the center of the table. You execute the old "boardinghouse reach" for a chicken leg or you thrust your fork into a thick chunk of pork, and while moving it onto your plate, the thick dark rich sauce coating the succulent morsel descends to desecrate your grandmother's precious white linen tablecloth.*

*Viola! You've just discovered the name of this fantastically delicious Mexican dish... and in doing so, probably got your pork ears boxed by Grams.*

¼ teaspoon ground cloves
¼ teaspoon cinnamon
2 teaspoons chili powder
2 teaspoons salt
• • • • • •
2 Tablespoons vegetable oil
1 pound pork loin, cut into bite size pieces
1 pound boneless chicken, cut into bite size pieces
• • • • • •
1 garlic clove, minced
1 onion, chopped
1 cup walnuts, chopped
• • • • • •

¼ cup chopped parsley
1 cup water
1 16-oz. can tomatoes
1 teaspoon instant chicken bouillon granules
• • • • • •
1 sweet potato, peeled and cubed
1 zucchini, sliced
1 apple, cored and sliced
• • • • • •
1 8-oz. can pineapple chunks, drained
2 bananas, peeled and sliced

*Pre-package first 4 ingredients in a plastic zip lock envelope.*
• • • • • •

In Dutch oven, heat oil over medium-high heat. Add pork and brown. With slotted spoon, remove pork and set aside. Brown chicken and remove. Discard all but 2 Tablespoons pan drippings.
• • • • • •

Add garlic, onions and walnuts to Dutch oven and cook for 5 minutes.
• • • • • •

Add next 4 ingredients and bring mixture to a boil. Stir to dissolve bouillon granules. Return pork and chicken to Dutch oven. Reduce heat. Cover and simmer 45 minutes.
• • • • • •

Add sweet potato and zucchini. Cover and simmer 15 minutes.
Add apple slices. Cover and simmer 15 minutes.

• • • • • •

Top with pineapple and bananas.
Serve over white rice.

makes 4 hearty servings

> **Tip:** You can brown the chicken and pork at the same time. The pork
> won't get as brown and crispy as some people would like, but after it
> simmers in the sauce for 45 minutes very few can tell the difference.
>    Keep some chunks of bread around to do some serious dunking. This
> sauce is too good to worry about table etiquette.
>    Top canned pudding with some chopped bananas and walnuts.

---

2nd day **FRANKS & EGGS**
Breakfast juice • canned sliced peaches • beverage

---

*Believe it or not, at one time I wasn't really big on breakfast. A piece of toast with some
peanut butter and a glass of juice was an early morning banquet for me. On the other hand,
some members of the crew couldn't function unless they devoured the entire contents of the
ice chest, including the ice, for breakfast.*

*Having had little experience preparing the different kinds of breakfast foods they
requested or sometimes demanded, I simply turned them loose in the galley to create
whatever their little hearts desired. Some of the stuff they came up with was pretty bizarre.
Some very weird. Some were just plain gross. And then again there were some dishes, like
Frank & Eggs, that were delightfully delicious.*

*Sometimes it does pay to let 9 and 11 year olds cook!*

| | | | |
|---|---|---|---|
| 1 | Tablespoon butter | 2 | Tablespoons milk |
| 1 | onion, chopped | 1 | Tablespoon mustard |
| 2 | green peppers, cut into bite size pieces | 1 | 2-oz. jar diced pimiento, drained |
| 8 | hot dogs, cut diagonally into 1-inch pieces | ½ | teaspoon salt |
| | | | Dash of pepper |
| | • • • • • | | • • • • • |
| 8 | eggs, beaten | 2 | Tablespoons butter |

In a large skillet, melt butter over medium-high heat. Add onions,
green peppers, and hot dogs. Cook until hot dogs are golden brown
on all sides. Remove mixture from skillet.

• • • • • •

In a large bowl, combine next 6 ingredients. Mix until well
blended.

Melt remaining 2 Tablespoons butter in the skillet. Add egg
mixture. Stirring frequently, cook over medium heat until eggs are
firm but still moist.

Push cooked eggs to the sides of skillet and spoon hot dog
mixture into the center. Reduce heat. Cover and heat through.

makes 4 servings

> **Tip:** I know that catsup is the acceptable accent for scrambled eggs, but
> this time, give some chili or taco sauce a chance.

# HAM & CHEESE COMBO
potato chips • canned 3-bean salad • pickles

**Com bo** *(kom bo), n. [pl. COMBOS (-bos)], a small jazz ensemble that really cooks, kicks butt and takes no prisoners; has lots of spirit and more energy, more flavor, and out performs groups with twice as many members. One that dishes up a fiery blend of the old classics with a contemporary beat.*

*This may not be the exact way Webster would define the word combo, but it's a pretty accurate description of our Ham & Cheese Combo.*

**1 cup (4-oz.) shredded Swiss cheese**
**2 6¾-oz. cans chunk ham, broken-up**
**½ cup finely chopped celery**
**1 Tablespoon Dijon mustard**
**4 Tablespoons mayonnaise**
**Salt and pepper to taste**

• • • • •

**8 slices rye bread**
**Butter**
**4 thin slices of apple**
**Lettuce**

In a large bowl, combine first 5 ingredients. Salt and pepper to taste.

• • • • •

To assemble sandwiches, butter bread, spread ham mixture on 4 slices of bread, top each with a slice of apple and some lettuce, and cover with a slice of bread.

makes 4 sandwiches

**Tip:** Feeling ambitious? Try these sandwiches grilled. Feeling really adventurous? Try preparing them like the French toasted salmon sandwiches on page 112.

---

# MEDITERRANEAN FISH CHOWDER
salad • french bread • melon wedges with blueberry sauce

*Many years ago, a beautiful high school graduate and her boyfriend signed on for part of our summer cruise. They were anticipating a very romantic experience on the high seas, and it might very well have been, had it not been for the presence of her father, her older protective brother and little old me. You see, under certain circumstances such as these, a 36-foot sailboat just isn't as big as it sounds. Needless to say, the young lovers didn't get to spend much time alone. Then one afternoon, after we were securely anchored in a nice little lagoon, the fair young maiden told me that if I could get her father and brother to go ashore with me and do some exploring, she wouldn't mind preparing dinner.*

*The only problem with that agreement was that she didn't know how to cook. She couldn't even boil water and she knew it. So she didn't even try preparing the Chicken Cordon Bleu with a Shrimp and Avacado Salad I had planned on serving that evening. Instead, we dined on a fine assortment of canned sardines, cheese puffs and Twinkies.*

*Lesson #67: Keep meal preparation as simple as possible, so anybody can cook. It's good to plan something like Mediterranean Fish Chowder, where the most difficult procedure is turning on the stove.*

| | | | |
|---|---|---|---|
| 1 | 8-oz. can tomato sauce | 2 | pounds frozen cod or perch fillets |
| 1 | 10¾-oz. can condensed Manhattan-style clam chowder | | • • • • • • |
| | | ⅓ | cup vegetable oil |
| 1 | 16-oz. can cut okra, drained | 1 | teaspoon salt |
| 1 | 16-oz. can tomatoes | ⅛ | teaspoon pepper |
| 2 | Tablespoons finely chopped parsley | 3 | Tablespoons flour |
| | • • • • • • | | |

Combine first 5 ingredients in Dutch oven (do not heat at this time). Stir to blend.

• • • • • •

Arrange frozen fish fillets on top of mixture in Dutch oven.

• • • • • •

In a cup, blend the remaining ingredients until smooth. Pour over fish fillets.

Place Dutch oven over burner and bring to a boil. Reduce heat. Cover and simmer 30 minutes.

makes 4 hearty servings

### MELON WEDGES with BLUEBERRY SAUCE

| | | | |
|---|---|---|---|
| ½ | cup strawberry halves | 2 | Tablespoons sugar |
| ½ | cup blueberries | | • • • • • • |
| ¼ | cup orange juice | ½ | cantaloupe, cut into 4 wedges and peeled |

Combine first 4 ingredients in a small (quart size) zip lock plastic storage bag. Seal and chill. To serve: place melon wedges on four individual serving plates and cover with fruit sauce.

**Tip:** If fresh blueberries aren't in season, you can use canned. Just drain them and rinse with fresh water to remove the heavy syrup.
**Note:** Using frozen fish fillet is no problem. In fact having frozen foods in the cooler is like having extra ice. Just remember to seal it well in a plastic bag, because this ice can smell when it melts.
You can substitute any fresh lean fish for the cod or perch.

# Time Out For Cocktails & Things

1989 was the year of the dragon. Bonzai Dragon that is! 1st place, first half. 1st place, second half. Boat of the year.

Not a bad club record. Yet, despite our victories, we received more notoriety for our hospitality, food and drink, than our skills and tactics on the race course. Although I'm not using his famous tequila and Gatorade recipe here, I would like to dedicate this Time Out For Cocktails to the owner/skipper of **Bonzai Dragon** and her spirited crew. Chop, Chop!!

## SEA BREEZE COCKTAIL

3    cups cranberry-juice cocktail
2    cups grapefruit juice
¾    cup vodka
• • • • • •
Lime slices

Combine first 3 ingredients. Serve over ice and garnish with a slice of lime.

## IGUANA

1    ounce vodka
1    ounce tequila
¾    ounce Kahlua
3    ounces lemon juice
1    teaspoon sugar
½    cup crushed ice

In a screw top jar, combine all ingredients. Secure top and shake well. Strain into a glass.

## MARINATED SHRIMP

½    cup vegetable oil
3    Tablespoons red wine vinegar
3    Tablespoons lemon juice
½    cup chopped parsley
1    clove garlic, minced
1    bay leaf
1    teaspoon dry mustard
1    teaspoon basil
1    teaspoon salt
¼    teaspoon pepper
• • • • • •
2    pounds cooked shrimp, shelled,
     deveined and tails removed
1    red onion, thinly sliced
2    lemons, thinly sliced
½    cup thinly sliced pitted black olives

In a screw top jar, combine the first 10 ingredients. Secure top and shake well. Layer shrimp, onion, lemon, and olives in a large zip lock storage bag. Add marinade. Seal and chill overnight.

# Group 7
## a three day menu

| | BREAKFAST | LUNCH | DINNER |
|---|---|---|---|
| 1st day | **CEREAL**<br>juice • pears<br>beverage | **FRENCH TOASTED SALMON Sandwiches**<br>corn chips • 3-bean salad • pickles | **HAWAIIAN PORK CHOPS**<br>salad • rice<br>honeydew fruit cups |
| 2nd day | **SHRIMP FOO YONG PATTIES**<br>juice • strawberries<br>beverage | **CALYPSO SALAD**<br>melba toast<br>crackers • cheese spreads | **CARPETBAGGER STEAKS**<br>salad<br>sweet potatoes • broccoli<br>pineapple compote |
| 3rd day | **BREAKFAST PIE**<br>juice • peaches<br>beverages | **TUNA CAKES**<br>corn chips • potato salad • pickles | **CHICKEN in LEMON & WINE SAUCE**<br>salad<br>rice • carrots in brandy sauce<br>cherry salad with honey-lime dressing |

---

1st day
Breakfast
# CEREAL
juice • canned pears • beverage

---

*Ganz einfache Frühstücksspeise aus Getreide. Die gibt es auf dem amerikanischen Frühstückstisch bereit seit 1972. Zwar gewinnt sie wohl kein kulinarische Auszeichungen, und dennoch hat sie ihren Vorteil. Kann ein Mensch erst einmal einen löffel in der Hand halten, so ist er auch imstande, sein Fruhstuck selbst zu bereiten. Dies bedeutet wiederum, dass der koch nicht mehr in aller Herrgotsfrühe auffstehen muss, um der Bestazung ein nahrhaftes Frühstück, zu bereiten. (refer to page 36)*

---

1st day
Lunch
# FRENCH TOASTED SALMON Sandwiches
corn chips • canned 3-bean salad • pickles

---

*Once we've cast off and are underway, we like to keep going. No dilly-dallying around. After all, there are places to go, things to see, people to meet and new bars to discover. No sense wasting precious time. Right?*

*For that reason, I generally try to steer clear of lunches that require any cooking while underway, but, as with everything else, there are exceptions. And this is one of them.*

*Although I've grilled these sandwiches while sailing on a broadreach, in fairly calm seas, it's much much more comfortable preparing them when you're not bobbing around.*

*So find a nice, quiet, out-of-the-way anchorage. Drop the sails or turn off the engines. Toss out the hook. And take time to enjoy. Because this is one time it's well worth it.*

| 1 | 7¾-oz. can red salmon, drained with liquid reserved |
|---|---|
| 2 | hard-boiled eggs, chopped |
| 2 | green onions with tops, chopped |
| 3 | Tablespoons finely chopped celery |
| 3 | Tablespoons mayonnaise |
| 2 | Tablespoons Seafood cocktail sauce |

| ¼ | teaspoon pepper |
|---|---|
|  | Dash of hot pepper sauce |

• • • • • •

| 8 | slices of white bread |
|---|---|

• • • • • •

| 2 | eggs, beaten |
|---|---|
| ⅓ | cup milk |
| ¼ | teaspoon salt |
|  | Reserved salmon liquid |

• • • • • •

1½ cup crushed potato chips

In a large bowl, combine first 8 ingredients. Blend well.

• • • • • •

Spread salmon mixture on 4 slices of bread and top with remaining slices.

• • • • • •

Combine next 4 ingredients in a pie tin. Mix well.

• • • • • •

Place crushed potato chips in another pie tin.

To toast sandwiches; dip both sides in egg mixture and then in crushed potato chips. Then on a slightly greased griddle, over medium heat, brown sandwiches on both sides.

makes 4 sandwiches

**Tip:** Don't try getting fancy when flipping these beauties. Use both hands! Hold the top portion in place with one hand while using a spatula to turn the sandwich over with the other.

---

# 1st day HAWAIIAN PORK CHOPS
Dinner salad • white rice • honeydew fruit cups

*Rule #64: Never start cooking a meal, no matter how fabulous it is, when approaching a harbor or port with real people, real restaurants, and real bars with real music. It doesn't make any difference if it's 1:37 in the morning. After being out on the high seas, away from civilization and around the same bunch of unshaven guys for more than a few days, as soon as the boat is tied off, the crew is going to abandon ship to head for the nearest pizza stand or bar to gorge themselves on junk food.*

*Take it from one who knows. I've been there before. When it happens you've got to stay loose and go with the flow. Remember, it's their loss; not yours. They'll learn. Just like my crew did. As soon as we were secure, they left me behind with a simmering pan of Hawaiian Pork chops, to dash off to some sleazy little waterfront bar to down a few greasy sawdustburgers. After tasting this, they now pledge "Never more."*

| | | | |
|---|---|---|---|
| 2 | Tablespoons vegetable oil | 1 | onion, sliced |
| 4 | pork loin chops, ¾ to 1-inch thick | 1 | green pepper, sliced |

• • • • • •

| | | | |
|---|---|---|---|
| ¼ | cup water | 2 | 8½-oz. cans pineapple chunks, drained |
| ½ | cup pineapple preserves | | |
| 1 | 6-oz. can pineapple juice | 1 | 16-oz. can sweet potatoes, (or yams) drained and cut into chunks |
| ½ | teaspoon instant chicken bouillon granules | | |

In a large skillet, heat oil over medium-high heat. Add pork chops and brown on both sides.

• • • • • •

Add next 6 ingredients and bring mixture to a boil. Stir to blend. Reduce heat. Cover and simmer 30 minutes.

• • • • • •

Add pineapple and sweet potato chunks to skillet. Cover and simmer 15 minutes.

Serve over white rice.

makes 4 servings

### HONEYDEW FRUIT CUPS

| | | | |
|---|---|---|---|
| 1 | 8-oz. carton plain yogurt | 1 | 15¼-oz. can pineapple chunks, drained |
| ¼ | cup dry pina colada cocktail mix | | |
| | | 4 | cups honeydew chunks |

• • • • • •

In a small bowl, combine first 2 ingredients. Mix well. Divide pineapple and honeydew chunks among four individual serving bowls. Top with sauce.

**Tips:** If you can find a butcher who has some smoked pork chops, by all means, give them a try in this recipe!
Dress up the presentation of the dessert fruit by serving it in lettuce-lined bowls and topping it off with a cherry.
**Note:** Since you're already making up a batch of rice for dinner, go ahead and make a little extra to use in the Breakfast Pie, day after tomorrow.

2nd day **SHRIMP FOO YONG PATTIES & GREEN PEA SAUCE**
Breakfast juice • strawberries • beverage

*Remember the crew member I mentioned a while back? The one who would go to great lengths to get to a McDonald's restaurant for breakfast? Well, the following year I discovered that the one thing he loves more than a Mickey-D's is shrimp. So when I came across this intriguing recipe I thought I had him. No way was he going off in search of an Egg McMuffin now. For once, everybody would eat and enjoy breakfast on board together (or at least that's what I had hoped).*

*When I finally served the patties for breakfast, everybody did enjoy them. Everybody, that is, except one. No, it wasn't the McMuffin freak. He absolutely loved them. It was another crew member, who just happened to have an allergic reaction to seafood. I forgot rule #34 section, B: Know what your crew can and can't eat.*

6   eggs, beaten
3   4½-oz. cans shrimp, drained
1   16-oz. can chow mein
    vegetables, drained

1   4-oz. can sliced mushrooms, drained
¼   cup chopped green onion
• • • • • •
Vegetable oil

In a large bowl, combine all ingredients. Mix well.

In a large skillet, heat ¼-inch vegetable oil over medium-high heat.

For each pattie, pour ¼ cup mixture into hot oil. Maintain shape by pushing egg back into vegetable mixture to form patty. Cook until browned on both sides.

makes 10 to 12 (4-inch) patties

### Green Pea Sauce

¾   cup water
1   teaspoon instant chicken
    bouillon granules
1   teaspoon sugar

1   Tablespoon soy sauce
1   Tablespoon cornstarch
• • • • • •
1   8-oz. can sweet peas, drained

In a small saucepan, combine the first 5 ingredients. Stir until smooth. Stirring constantly, cook over low heat until thick and bubbly.

• • • • • •

Add peas and heat through. With fork, mash half the peas. Stir to blend.

> **Tip:** Yes, you can cook these on a lightly greased griddle. BUT, they don't have the same crispy character and texture they do when cooked in the ¼-inch of vegetable oil.
> If fresh strawberries aren't available, buy them frozen. Just remember to store them in a zip lock plastic bag, so they don't drip all over everything when they thaw.

---

2nd day
Lunch
# CALYPSO SALAD
melba toast • crackers • cheese spreads

---

*Just as the beautiful sea nymph, Calypso, held Ulysses captive...*
*Just as the excitement of Calypso music captivates the free spirit...*
*This Calypso Salad will surely capture and titillate your taste buds.*

½   teaspoon ginger
1   Tablespoon curry powder
• • • • • •
¼   cup finely chopped onion
1   cup mayonnaise
1   Tablespoon catsup
1   Tablespoon soy sauce
1   Tablespoon lemon juice
    salad
• • • • • •
1   6½-oz. can crab meat
1   6¾-oz. can chunk chicken

1   6¾-oz. can chunk turkey
• • • • • •
1   8-oz. can sliced water
    chestnuts, drained
1   8-oz. can pineapple chunks, drained
1   4-oz. jar pimiento, drained
    and chopped
1½ cups chopped green pepper
2   cups seedless green grapes

*Pre-package first 2 ingredients in a plastic zip lock envelope.*

• • • • • •

**Dressing:**

In a small bowl, combine the next 5 ingredients. Stir in pre-packaged spices and blend well. Set aside.

**Salad:**

In a large bowl, break up and flake crab meat, chicken, and turkey.

• • • • • •

Add remaining ingredients. Toss to mix. Add dressing.

Transfer salad mixture to a large (gallon size) zip lock plastic storage bag. Shake and massage bag to thoroughly coat and mix salad.

Seal and chill.

Serve on a bed of lettuce and garnish with thin slices of melon.

makes 4 hearty servings

---

# CARPETBAGGER STEAK

2nd day
Dinner
salad • canned sweet potatoes • steamed broccoli
pineapple compote

---

*I don't carry a fancy grill or hibachi for barbecuing... just a couple of metal grills from a portable propane grill. (see pages 1 & 3) I don't wear a goofy lookin' chef's hat or a cute little apron with a clever saying. When I want to impress someone with my prowess for outdoor cooking, I simply throw on a couple of Carpetbagger Steaks. They look and taste so impressive, so magnificent, who would guess that they're as easy to cook as hamburgers. But what a difference!*

1 **Tablespoon butter**
1 **8-oz. can whole oysters,
   drained and chopped**
1 **4-oz. can sliced mushrooms,
   drained and chopped**
1½ **Tablespoons chopped
   parsley**

• • • • • •

1 **Tablespoon Bac O's**
¼ **cup bread crumbs**
2 **ounces blue cheese,
   crumbled**

• • • • • •

2 **1-pound boneless sirloin
   strip steaks**
3 **Tablespoons butter**

In a large skillet, melt butter over medium heat. Add oysters, mushrooms, and parsley. Cook for 3 minutes. Transfer mixture to a bowl.

• • • • • •

Add next 3 ingredients to oyster mixture. Blend well.

• • • • • •

Cut a pocket in the side of each steak. Stuff pockets with oyster mixture and secure with wooden toothpicks.

In a large skillet, melt butter over medium-high heat. Add steaks and cook 4 to 5 minutes per side.

Cut steaks in half to make 4 servings.

**PINEAPPLE COMPOTE**

1    16-oz. can pineapple chunks,
    drained
1    17-oz. jar pitted dark sweet
    cherries, drained

½    cup cherry brandy
    Garnish with flaked coconut

Combine all ingredients except flaked coconut, in a small (quart size) zip lock plastic storage bag. Seal and chill.

**Tips:** These steaks are fantastic on the outdoor grill, but they're just as sensational pan-broiled. The secret to pan-broiled is to sear the steak in a hot pan. The pan is hot enough only after the melted butter stops foaming or bubbling.

Try sprinkling the steaks with a little creole seasoning for a little extra southern flavor.

**Note:** You can either serve the sweet potatoes heated in their own liquid and drained or mashed with ¼-cup brown sugar, a tablespoon or so of butter and some rum. Top with flaked coconut and chopped pecans.

Steam broccoli on top of sweet potatoes.

---

3rd day **BREAKFAST PIE**
Breakfast juice • canned peaches • beverage

---

*One morning, after a particularly wild night in port, one very hung-over sailor decided it was too hard to climb up the hill and too far to walk into town, and asking too much to even consider purchasing fresh food stocks for breakfast. It would be much, much easier to use whatever stores and leftovers that we still had on board. Just throw everything into the pan, smother it with plenty of cheese, serve pale Bloody Marys\*, and they'll love it.*
*And they did!*

*\* A pale Bloody Mary: better known as the San Diego B.M. One whose consistency allows you to read the "Sunday Union" while looking through the glass.*

1    Tablespoon vegetable oil
1    onion, chopped
½    green pepper, chopped
1    garlic clove, minced
• • • • • •
1    cup cooked rice
1    2-oz. jar sliced pimiento,
    drained and chopped
1    4-oz. can sliced mushrooms,
    drained

2    6¾-oz. cans chunk ham,
    broken-up
• • • • • •
6    eggs, beaten
1½  Tablespoons water
1    teaspoon mustard
    Dash of horseradish
• • • • • •
1    cup (4-oz.) shredded cheddar
    cheese

In a large skillet, heat oil over medium heat. Add onion, green pepper, and garlic. Cook 5 minutes, or until green pepper is tender.

• • • • • •

Add next 4 ingredients to skillet and heat through.

• • • • • •

In a large bowl, combine eggs, water, mustard, and horseradish. Mix well. Add egg mixture to skillet. Reduce heat. Cover and cook 10 minutes.

• • • • • •

Sprinkle cheese over the top of the eggs. Cover and cook until cheese melts and egg mixture is firm.

makes 4 hearty servings.

**Tip:** If you wipe the sides of the pan with some oil before you start cooking, it will help prevent sticking.

**Note:** Use the extra rice you made for the Hawaiian Pork Chops. Prepare marinated broccoli for tonight.

---

3rd day
Lunch

# TUNA CAKES
corn chips • canned potato salad • pickles

---

*What do you do with cold hamburgers? Serve them to the seagulls, of course!*

*One year, I made up a whole bunch of super deluxe burgers for the crew and our guest. But some people were too busy frolicking in the water, flinging frisbees, or following felines to eat when everything was ready. And when they were ready to eat, what was hot, was not. So instead of being polite and gagging graciously on the cold burgers, they flung the patties into the harbor to the delight of zillions of seagulls.*

*What decadence! What waste! Never again! There had to be a better way!*

*There was! There is! There always will be! From now on, it's Tuna Cakes! Tuna Cakes forever!*

*Although tuna cakes are shaped like burgers, served in sesame seed buns like burgers, and can be topped off with lettuce, cheese, tomato and special sauce just like burgers, tuna cakes will never replace the Big Mac, Whopper or super double-cheeseburger deluxe in the hearts of true gut bomb connoisseurs. But, unlike the Great All-American Hamburger, Tuna Cakes are delicious served either hot or COLD.*

| | | | |
|---|---|---|---|
| 2 | **eggs, beaten** | 5 | **slices white bread, crumbled** |
| 2 | **6½-oz. cans tuna, drained and flaked** | 2 | **teaspoons lemon juice** |
| 1 | **zucchini, shredded** | ½ | **teaspoon salt** |
| ¼ | **cup finely chopped onion** | ½ | **teaspoon pepper** |

In a large bowl, combine all ingredients. Mix well. Shape mixture into 4 hamburger-style patties.

In a large skillet, heat ¼-inch vegetable oil over medium heat until hot. Cook patties for 4 minutes per side or until golden brown. Serve on a bed of lettuce with a slice of tomato.

makes 4 servings

**Tips:** Since you can serve these babies cold or at cabin temperature, you might want to cook them up in the morning while you're making the Breakfast Pie.

Try adding a little horseradish to some mayonnaise for a spread.

**Note:** If you decide to make these into burgers or sandwiches, try adding either a slice of American or Swiss cheese.

---

# CHICKEN in LEMON & WINE SAUCE
3rd day
Dinner
salad • white rice • carrots in brandy sauce
cherry salad with honey-lime dressing

---

*Some of the finest things in life are the simplest. This meal is a perfect example. It's so easy to prepare, yet if you went into some fancy French restaurant you'd probably find it on the menu. This is a perfect entree sure to please any guest at home or on a boat.*

*For that matter, this meal is so impressive, I'd get rid of the rest of the crew, the kids or any other extra baggage, put on some soft music, add a little candlelight, fill a pair of fluted champagne glasses with the bubbly, lay a red red rose on a table draped with lace, find an erotic verse from John Donne and I'd have a very romantic dinner for two.*

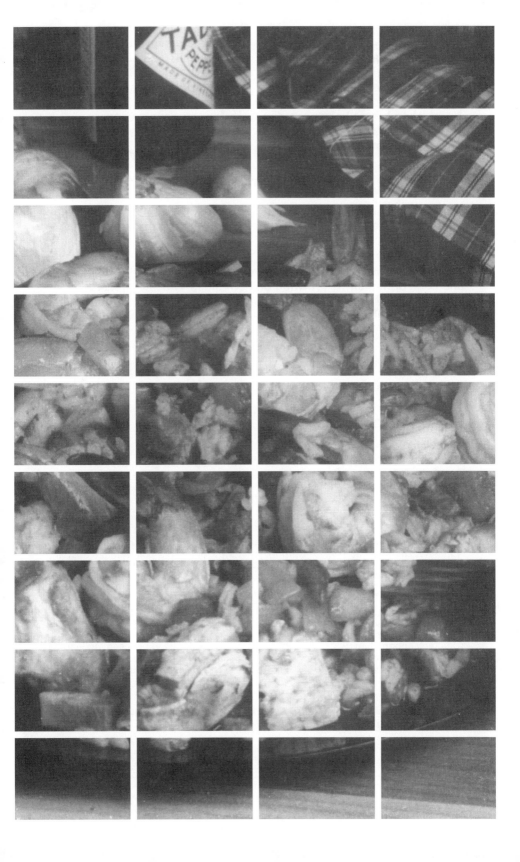

| ¼ | teaspoon sage | 1 | garlic clove, crushed |
| ¼ | teaspoon thyme | • • • • • • |
| ½ | teaspoon ginger | 1 | teaspoon vegetable oil |
| ½ | teaspoon dry mustard | 1 | teaspoon butter |
| | • • • • • • | • • • • • • |
| 4 | chicken breast halves, skinned and boned | ½ | cup dry white wine |
| 2 | Tablespoons lemon juice | 2 | 4-oz. cans sliced mushrooms, drained |

*Pre-package first 4 ingredients in a plastic zip lock envelope.*
• • • • • •

Sprinkle chicken with lemon juice and let stand a couple of minutes. Then rub with crushed garlic and sprinkle with pre-packaged spices.
• • • • • •

In a Dutch oven, heat butter and oil over medium heat. Add chicken and cook until slightly browned on both sides. Discard grease.
• • • • • •

Add wine and mushrooms and bring to a boil. Reduce heat. Cover and simmer 20 minutes.

Serve chicken breast on a bed of white rice and top with mushrooms.

makes 4 servings

### CARROTS in BRANDY SAUCE

| 2 | Tablespoons butter | 2 | Tablespoons brandy |
| 2 | Tablespoons flour | ½ | cup diced green pepper |
| | • • • • • • | ¼ | cup diced onion |
| 1 | cup water | 1 | 16-oz. can whole baby carrots, drained |
| 1 | teaspoon instant chicken bouillon granules | | |
| | • • • • • • | | |

In a large skillet, over medium heat, melt butter. Add flour. Stir until smooth. Cook 1 minute. Gradually add water. Stirring constantly, bring to a boil. Reduce heat and cook until thick and bubbly. Stir in brandy and gently add remaining ingredients.

### CHERRY SALAD with HONEY-LIME DRESSING

| ½ | teaspoon grated lime rind | 1 | 16-oz. can sweet cherries, drained and rinsed |
| 2 | Tablespoons lime juice | | |
| 2 | Tablespoons honey | 1 | 8-oz. can sliced peaches, drained and rinsed |
| ¼ | teaspoon salt | | |
| ¼ | cup mayonnaise | ½ | honeydew melon, cut into chunks |
| | • • • • • • | 1 | banana, sliced |

In a small bowl, combine first 5 ingredients. Mix well. Arrange fruit on four individual serving plates. Drizzle dressing over the top of each.

**Tip:** This time, don't combine fruit for the dessert ahead of time. Let the flavor of each stand out by itself and not blend with the others.

# Time Out For Cocktails & Things

The river was clogged by an armada of pleasure boats, waiting for the annual 4th of July fireworks to begin. As friends and families settled in for food and drink, a small flotilla of pirates infiltrates the perimeter. Those who refuse to pay tribute to the intruders suffer the consequences, a massive barrage of water balloons. Those who share their bounty and offer up to a drink or two to the buccaneers are spared. After downing their booty, they return to the mother ship. As they pass by their drenched victims, they are reminded that "pay backs are hell." But that's the price we pay for free drinks and good times.

Join with me and hoist a wine spritzer in a toast as I dedicate this Time Out For Cocktails to the ingenuity of **FANTASIA's** diabolical captain and the treachery of her fearless crew.

## DEVILED CHEESE DUNK

1    5-oz. jar pimiento cheese spread
1    2½-oz. can deviled ham
½    cup mayonnaise
2    Tablespoons minced parsley
1    Tablespoon minced onion
4    drops hot sauce.

In a small bowl, combine all ingredients and blend well. Serve with vegetables and chips.

## SHRIMP & CHEESE LOG

1    8-oz. package cream cheese, softened
¾    cup seafood cocktail sauce
1    6½-oz. can shrimp, drained
2    Tablespoons finely chopped green pepper

Place cream cheese on a plate. Cover with sauce and shrimp. Sprinkle with green pepper and serve with cracker.

## CHERRY BLIZZARD

1½   ounces cherry-brandy
     Chilled club soda
     Strip of lemon peel

Pour brandy over ice in a tall glass. Fill with soda. Twist peel above and drop into drink.

## CHERRY BOMB FIREWORKS

1    ounce rum
1    ounce vodka
1    ounce tequila
     dry pina colada mix
6    ounces water
     couple of drops cherry juice
     • • • • • •
     Maraschino cherry

Combine first 5 ingredients. Stir until dry mix is dissolved. Serve over ice and garnish with cherry.

# Group 8
## a two day menu

|  | BREAKFAST | LUNCH | DINNER |
|---|---|---|---|
| 1st day | **COFFEE CAKE**<br>juice • fruit cocktail<br>beverage | **SEAFOOD STEW**<br>french bread • cheese platter | **PORK in ORANGE SAUCE**<br>salad • rice • broccoli<br>bananas supreme |
| 2nd day | **ITALIAN VEGETABLE OMELETS**<br>juice • strawberries<br>beverage | **KING DELI Sandwich**<br>potato chips • potato salad • pickles | **COUNTRY CAPTAIN**<br>salad • rice • marinated asparagus<br>pudding |

1st day **COFFEE CAKE**
Breakfast juice • canned fruit cocktail • beverage

Un verano habia unos marineros que no les gustaba el agua. Pero se juntaron con nosotros en la secunda parte del viaje en el mar. Su experiencia marinera estaba limitada flotando nada mas en la alberca en un colchon de aire. Es costumbre que los miembros que se despida y los que remplazan se juntan la noche anterior del cambio ye se toman unas cheves juntos. Al progresar la noche era obvio que los marineros estaban listos para una noche de bromas.

Les explicamos que cada uno debe contribuir con el trabajo a mano. Ellos contestaron. "!No hay problema!" Estaban dispuestos hacer lo que se pidiera.

Se llego el tiempo para nuestra travesura. Le explique que me retiraba al bote porque tenia que levantarme temprano y preparar el almuerzo.

Se pusieron muy triste y insistieron me quedara. Yo insistice que tenia demaciado queacer en la manana y ya no podice demorar mas.

Me recordaron que todos teniamos que hacer la tarea en el bote, y se propusieron a dar su ayuda voluntariamente si you me quedaba.

Al fin regresamos al bote, les dije a lost marineros nuevos que les dejaria las instrucciones con su tareas listas para la manana. Les dije el dispertador listo, ye bajo ninguna circumstancia deberian de despertarme, nada mas seguir mis instrucciones.

El despertador seno a las 5:00 de la manana. Leeron sus instrucciones y regresaron al bote a las 6:30 de la manana listos para viajar a las 7:00 de las manana.

?Que eran sus instrucciones? Traer un biscocho de pina y dos termos de cafe caliente de una panaderia dos milas al sur del pueblo. Pero, por alguna razon se me olvido mencionar la bicicleta que podian usar de la **Oficina Marinera**.-Tal vez fue una buena manana para un paseo a pie. (turn to page 49 for English version)

---

1st day
Lunch
# SEAFOOD STEW
french bread • cheese platter

---

*While racing, it's extremely important to keep the body fueled with nutritious foods. So I try to serve the crew foods loaded with all that kind of good stuff. But we have one crew member, that even on the coldest, windiest, day would decline hot foods because he was "watching his weight."*

*Well, I came across this recipe that is just jam-packed with protein, low in fats and loaded with all kinds of good nutrients. And best of all, not even the most ardent weight watcher can pass this one up, because it contains only 150 calories per 8 ounce serving.*

| | |
|---|---|
| 1 teaspoon salt | 2 11-oz. cans tomatoes and liquid |
| ½ teaspoon oregano | 1 8-oz. can tomato sauce |
| ½ teaspoon basil | 3 Tablespoons chopped parsley |
| ¼ teaspoon paprika | |
| Dash of cayenne pepper | • • • • • |
| Dash of pepper | 1 4½-oz. can shrimp, and liquid |
| • • • • • • | 1 6½-oz. can minced clams and liquid |
| 1 Tablespoon vegetable oil | 1 16-oz. package frozen perch fillets, thawed and cut into bite size pieces |
| ½ cup chopped green pepper | |
| ¼ cup chopped onion | |
| 1 garlic clove, minced | |
| • • • • • • | |

Pre-package first 6 ingredients in a plastic zip lock envelope.

• • • • • •

In Dutch oven, heat oil over medium heat. Add green pepper, onion, and garlic. Cook for 5 minutes.

• • • • •

Add next 3 ingredients, plus pre-packaged ingredients, and bring mixture to a boil. Reduce heat. Cover and simmer 15 minutes.

• • • • •

Add all remaining ingredients. Cover and simmer 10 minutes.

makes 4 hearty servings

**Tip:** Prepare ahead of time and store in a wide mouth thermos.
**Note:** If you thicken it up with some cornstarch, flour, or a roux this stew makes a very intriguing pasta sauce that will feed 12. Keep that in mind when ever a dozen or so drunken sailors stop by for dinner.

1st day
Dinner
# PORK in ORANGE SAUCE
salad • white rice • steamed broccoli • bananas supreme

*If I were home and we were in a hurry, I might consider preparing our meal in the microwave oven. But I'm not home. I'm on a boat and we've just arrived in port. The crew is anxious to get off the boat and into town to have some fun. And there's no microwave to be found.*

*This is a perfect time to serve a stir-fry dinner. It's quick and easy to prepare. By the time the boat is secured and everybody has had a shower, dinner is ready and waiting. And since there's so little clean-up when you stir-fry, go ahead and use paper plates so nobody will be left behind doing the dishes when you take off to do the town.*

| | |
|---|---|
| 1 teaspoon sugar | 2 pounds pork steak, cut into bite size pieces |
| 2 teaspoons cornstarch | • • • • • • |
| ⅛ teaspoon ginger | ½ cup orange juice |
| • • • • • • | 2 Tablespoons soy sauce |
| 2 Tablespoons vegetable oil | 1 Tablespoon finely shredded orange peel |
| 2 carrots, thinly sliced | • • • • • • |
| 2 celery stalks, chopped | ½ cup chopped cashews |
| • • • • • • | |

*Pre-package first 3 ingredients in a plastic zip lock envelope.*
• • • • • •

In a large skillet, heat oil over medium-high heat. Add carrots and celery and stir-fry 3 minutes. With slotted spoon, remove from skillet.
• • • • • •

Add pork and stir-fry 5 minutes.
• • • • • •

In a cup, blend pre-packaged ingredients with orange juice, orange peel and soy sauce. Add mixture to skillet. Reduce heat. Continue to cook and stir until thick and bubbly.

Return vegetables to skillet and add cashews. Cover and simmer 5 minutes.

Serve over white rice.

makes 4 servings

### BANANAS SUPREME

| | |
|---|---|
| 4 bananas, sliced in half lengthwise | Whipped topping |
| 2 Tablespoons butter | ¼ cup coarsley chopped pecans |
| • • • • • • | ¼ cup spiced rum |
| ¼ cup flaked coconut | |

In a large skillet, melt butter over medium heat. Add bananas and cook 1 to 2 minutes per side. Remove to four indivudual serving plates. Top each with coconut and some whipped topping. Sprinkle with chopped pecans and spiced rum.

**Tip:** Separate broccoli into spears and steam in a skillet using ½ cup water and 1 Tablespoon soy sauce for the liquid.

# ITALIAN VEGETABLE OMELETS
juice • strawberries • beverage

*Try as I may, I've never had much success folding an omelet and I have no idea how those hinged omelet pans are supposed to work, so instead of embarrassing myself any longer, I simply gave up making omelets. UNTIL! Until I saw this technique demonstrated on TV by Jeff Smith (the Frugal Gourmet). It's so simple that even I can do it, and I use an electric fry pan.*

We will be making two omelets to be cut in half to serve four people.

### the Filling

½ **pound sweet Italian sausage, casings removed**
1 **onion, chopped**
1 **cup coarsely chopped broccoli flowerets**
½ **cup chopped green pepper**
• • • • • •

½ **cup chopped tomato**
1 **4-oz. can sliced mushrooms, drained**
• • • • • •
1 **cup (4-oz.) shredded Swiss cheese, reserved**

In a large skillet, cook first 4 ingredients over medium-high heat, until meat is browned.
• • • • • •
Add tomatoes and mushrooms. Cook, stirring frequently, 5 minutes. With slotted spoon, remove mixture and let drain on paper towel. Discard grease and wipe bottom and sides of the skillet with a paper towel.

### the Omelet

10 **eggs, beaten**
4 **Tablespoons water**
½ **teaspoon hot pepper sauce**
**Couple of dashes soy sauce**
• • • • • •

1 **Tablespoon vegetable oil**
1 **Tablespoon butter**
• • • • • •
1 **Tablespoon vegetable oil**
1 **Tablespoon butter**

Heat the same skillet used to make filling over medium-high heat. Add 1 Tablespoon oil and 1 Tablespoon butter. Rotate skillet to coat sides and bottom. When butter stops bubbling, immediately pour in half the egg mixture. With a spatula, gently draw an X through the eggs. As eggs begin to set up, push and lift set egg mixture from the edge to the center. This allows the uncooked portions to fill in and flow under to finish cooking.

When mixture is nearly set, shake skillet to make sure omelet isn't sticking to the bottom. If it is, run a spatula underneath to free it.

Spoon filling over the half of the omelet that is directly opposite the skillet handle. Sprinkle with half the cheese.

With the palm of your hand facing up, grab the handle of the skillet and remove it from the heat. Now, start to slide the omelet, filling side first, onto a plate. As soon as the filling half is on the plate, fold the remaining half over the top.

Wipe skillet clean with paper towel and repeat procedure for second omelet.

makes 4 servings

**Tips:** You can use any combination of ingredients to create your own filling. Just make sure they're not refrigerator-cold when you add them to the omelet.

For the best results, let the eggs come to room (cabin) temperature before using.

If fresh strawberries aren't available, use frozen and store in a plastic zip lock bag.

**Note:** Wiping the bottom and sides of the skillet with oil before cooking, helps prevent sticking.

Prepare marinated asparagus for tonight's dinner.

---

2nd day
Lunch
# KING DELI Sandwich
potato chips • canned potato salad • pickles

---

*Our story opens: Little Current, Ontario, 1975. Railroad swing-bridge stuck. Won't open for days. East-West passage blocked. Miles and miles from civilization, thousands and thousands of pleasure boats are stranded. Entire crew faces starvation as supplies run low. Hopelessly, helplessly they wait and wait.*

*With only six slices of bread remaining on their boat, two valiant young men set out on an old Indian trail they had discovered while exploring the shore line, in search of supplies, leaving their three brave but innocent shipmates behind to guard against pirates.*

*Successful in their quest, the young men return to their vessel with a couple cases of cold liquid vitamin "B" nutrients, only to discover that while they were away, their trusted shipmates had built and downed 3 scrumptious sandwiches from those remaining slices of bread, leaving the two of them only the crumbs as a reward for their efforts.*

*Despondent, our two heroes climb the cliff overlooking their boat. In their final act of despair and revenge they consume massive quantities of vitamin "B" nutrients and pelt their boat below with the empty cans.*

*Moral to the story: Make sure you've got enough sandwiches to feed the entire crew or it's "All cans on deck!"*

| 1 | 8-inch round loaf rye bread | ¼ | pound Swiss cheese, thinly sliced |
|---|---|---|---|
| • • • • • • | | | Mayonnaise |
| | Dijon mustard | | Horseradish |
| ½ | pound shaved pastrami | ½ | pound shaved roast beef |
| 1 | onion, thinly sliced | | Thin slices of tomato |
| | Mayonnaise | | Shredded lettuce |
| ½ | pound shaved turkey | | |

With serrated knife, slice bread horizontally into four layers.

• • • • • •

To build sandwich, spread bottom slice of bread with Dijon mustard and assemble in order: pastrami, onion, layer of bread, mayonnaise, turkey, Swiss cheese, layer of bread, mayonnaise, horseradish, roast beef, tomato, lettuce, and cover with top layer of bread.

To serve, slice into wedges.

Makes 1 huge or 8 tiny servings, or any number in between.

**Tip:** Dress up the canned potato salad with some chopped celery and green pepper.
**Note:** If available, you might want to consider making this beauty with a Dusseldorf mustard, some smoked turkey and a Jarlsberg Swiss cheese.

---

## COUNTRY CAPTAIN

2nd day
Dinner
salad • white rice • sweet spiced marinated asparagus
canned pudding

---

*This dish reminds me of an old retired sea captain, sitting on the porch of his tiny cottage that overlooks the harbor and waters he once sailed. His rocker is creaking back and forth, and he is taking an occassional draw from his pipe and sipping on a warm mug of rum. A devilish smile crosses his face as he remembers days gone by, of high sea adventure, of intrigue and romance, when sailing to far-off lands.*

*It was a captain such as this, who skippered one of those magnificent sailing schooners of long ago, that introduced us to this wonderful recipe that originated in India.*

*Even though it contains some wild, fiery and exciting spices, its character is reminiscent of the old sea captain's. Mellow and mature. A flavor that we enjoy and respect.*

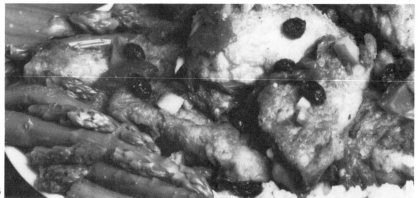

⅛ teaspoon pepper
½ teaspoon salt
½ teaspoon thyme
1 Tablespoon curry powder
⅓ cup flour
• • • • • •
3 pounds prime chicken parts
2 Tablespoons vegetable oil
• • • • • •
½ cup chopped onion
⅓ cup chopped green pepper

1 garlic clove, minced
• • • • • •
1 16-oz. can tomatoes and liquid, cut up
2 1½-oz. packages raisins
1 teaspoon instant chicken bouillon granules
2 Tablespoons chopped parsley
½ teaspoon sugar
Dash of hot pepper sauce

*Pre-package first 5 ingredients in a large (gallon size) zip lock plastic storage bag.*
• • • • • •

Add chicken parts to plastic bag contining the first 5 ingredients. Shake and massage bag to thoroughly coat chicken.
In Dutch oven, heat oil over medium heat. Add chicken parts and brown. With slotted spoon, remove chicken and set aside.
• • • • • •

Add onion, green pepper, and garlic to Dutch oven. Cook until onion is soft.
• • • • • •

Add remaining ingredients and bring mixture to a boil. Stir until bouillon granules dissolve. Return chicken to Dutch oven and reduce heat. Cover and simmer 35 minutes.
Serve over a bed of white rice.

makes 4 hearty servings

### SWEET SPICED MARINATED ASPARAGUS

6 Tablespoons vegetable oil
¼ cup sugar
¼ cup red wine vinegar
1 garlic clove, minced
⅛ teaspoon paprika
• • • • • •

1 14½-oz. can asparagus spears, drained
3 green onions with tops, chopped
1 celery stalk, finely chopped
½ green pepper, chopped

Pre-package first 5 ingredients in a 8-oz. jar. (Shake after packaging and before using.) Drain asparagus, but DO NOT remove from can. Pour about half the marinade over the asparagus still in the can. Cover with plastic wrap and chill. Add last 3 ingredients to marinade still in the jar. Seal, shake, and chill. To serve: drain asparagus and arrange on individual serving plates. Sprinkle with marinated onions, celery and green pepper mixture.

**Tips:** Prepare marinated asparagus ahead of time. If the canned asparagus falls apart just mash it up and tell the crew it's mashed green potatoes.
Try topping the canned pudding with some whipped topping, chopped nuts and a grape.

# Time Out For Cocktails & Things

*Rafting off can be a lot of fun. But when it's in an over-crowded harbor and you're the boat next to the dock, the boat that everybody else is tied off of, the boat everybody has to cross to get to solid ground, it can be very trying if you don't cop the proper attitude. Just remember one thing: Most of your fellow boaters really feel guilty about having to walk across your boat. So when these trespassers ask for permission to cross, say, "Sure thing. No problem. Be my guest." Then, after they've passed, ask them to stop back for a few cocktails and "hors d'oeuvres".*

*Not only will these folks stop back, but chances are they'll bring a couple of gallons of good hooch and stay for hours, and you'll probably end up being life-long friends.*

## MUSSELS DIJONNAISE

¾ cup vegetable oil
¼ cup red wine vinegar
3 Tablespoons Dijon mustard
½ teaspoon salt
½ teaspoon sugar
• • • • • •
20 mussels, steamed, shelled and rinsed (save half the shells for serving)
• • • • • •
1 Tablespoon chopped parsley
1½ teaspoons chopped pimiento
1½ teaspoons drained capers

In a small bowl, combine first 5 ingredients. Blend well. Place mussels in a small zip lock storage bag. Add mustard mixture. Seal and chill overnight.

In a small bowl, combine remaining ingredients just before serving.

Remove mussels from marinade and place in half shells. Top with parsley mixture.

## NAVY GROG

1 ounce orange juice
1 ounce grapefruit juice
1 ounce white rum
2 ounces 151-proof dark rum
2 ounces lemon juice
2 ounces simple syrup
• • • • • •
Slice of pineapple
Maraschino cherry

In a screw top jar, combine first 6 ingredients. Secure top and shake well. Serve over crushed ice and garnish with pineapple and cherry.

## EMERALD SWIZZLE

1 cup green creme de menthe
2 cups dry vermouth
• • • • • •
32 ounces club soda
Lime slices

Combine first 2 ingredients. Add club soda. Serve over ice and garnish with a slice of lime.

## DOUBLE ORANGE SPRITZER

1½ ounces (1 jigger) Cointreau
3 ounces (2 jiggers) orange juice
6 ounces club soda

Combine all ingredients in a glass over ice. Stir well.

# Group 9
## a three day menu

| | BREAKFAST | LUNCH | DINNER |
|---|---|---|---|
| 1st day | **BAGELS & SHRIMP SPREAD**<br>juice • fruit cocktail<br><br>beverage | **QUARTER HOUR SOUP**<br>crackers<br>cheese & salami platter | **SUNSHINE CHICKEN**<br>salad • stuffing • green beans<br><br>pudding |
| 2nd day | **NEW ORLEANS POACHED EGGS**<br>juice • peaches<br><br>beverage | **FRANKS & PASTA SALAD**<br>melba toast • cheese & crackers | **SMOTHERED BEEF & ONIONS**<br>salad<br>mashed potatoes • marinated asparagus<br>custard sauce ambrosia |
| 3rd day | **POTATO PANCAKES**<br>juice • eggs • sausage<br><br>beverage | **CHINESE CHICKEN SALAD**<br>cheese & crackers<br>fruit platter with creamy orange dip | **CHEESE-STUFFED PORK CHOPS**<br>salad<br>spanish rice • marinated broccoli<br>cantalope compote |

## 1st day BAGELS & SHRIMP SPREAD
Breakfast juice • canned fruit cocktail • beverage

*Yes, this is the same great shrimp and cucumber spread I recommended as an appetizer way back on page 46. "So" you ask, "why is it here once again as a breakfast item?" Because we discovered quite by accident, it's just as great in the morning.*

*It seems there was, at one time, long, long ago, a very hung-over, fuzzy-mouthed sailor, who, in an effort to fill and still an angry, empty stomach, grabbed the first thing he could find in the ice chest. Of course, a shrimp spread wasn't what he expected or wanted. And it wasn't his normal chili, cold pizza, and Coca-Cola remedy, but it would do. Much to his relief, he discovered it was really quite refreshing, delicious, nutritious and soothing.*

*Shrimp and Cucumber Spread: it's not just for happy hour any more.*

¼ **teaspoon garlic powder**
2 **teaspoons dry mustard**
2 **teaspoons minced onion**
• • • • • •

1 **8-oz. package cream cheese, cubed and softened**
4 **Tablespoons mayonnaise**
2 **Tablespoons catsup**
• • • • • •

2 **4½-oz. cans shrimp, drained**
½ **cup finely chopped cucumber**

*Pre-package first 3 ingredients in a plastic zip lock envelope.*
• • • • • •

In a large bowl, blend cream cheese, mayonnaise and catsup. Stir in pre-packaged spices.
• • • • • •

Add remaining ingredients and blend well.
Spread mixture on each half bagel.

makes 4 servings

**Tip:** This spread is definitely better when made ahead of time.

# QUARTER HOUR SOUP
crackers • cheese & salami platter

*I run a small, inexpensive catering service for single, professional people. Each week, I provide them with home-cooked gourmet meals packed in little styrofoam containers that can be popped into the old microwave whenever they wish. It's sort of like fancy leftovers.*

*It's inexpensive because the clients have no choice on what foods they'll be receiving. Each week they get something different. Unless there's a groundswell or an overwhelming demand for a certain dish, the same recipe is never repeated. These individuals are my taste testers; my guinea pigs. Why do I tell you this? Well, besides being a great, quick, delicious little recipe to prepare on the boat, Quarter Hour Soup just happens to be one of the most popular, most requested dishes I deliver.*

| | | | |
|---|---|---|---|
| 2 | Tablespoons vegetable oil | 1 | 6¾-oz. can chunk ham, broken-up |
| 1 | onion, finely chopped | 1 | 6½-oz. can minced clams, undrained |
| | • • • • • • | | |
| 3 | tomatoes, chopped | 1 | 4½-oz. can shrimp, drained |
| ¼ | cup blanched almonds, finely chopped | | • • • • • |
| 6 | cups water | 1 | cup cooked rice |
| 6 | teaspoons instant chicken bouillon granules | 1 | 8-oz. can sweet peas, drained |

In Dutch oven, heat oil over medium-high heat. Add onions and cook until tender, but not browned.

• • • • • •

Add next 7 ingredients and blend well. Bring mixture to a boil.

• • • • • •

Add rice and peas. Reduce heat. Cover and simmer 5 minutes.

makes 4 hearty servings

> **Tips:** Although this is a quick and easy soup to prepare, you might want to make it in the morning and store it in a thermos until lunch.
> You can substitute ½ cup instant rice for the cooked rice.
> Some chopped hard-boiled eggs make an excellent garnish for this soup.

---

# SUNSHINE CHICKEN
salad • instant stuffing • canned green beans • canned pudding

*I have only one thing to say about this recipe... Sunshine brings happiness.*

*The cook is happy because it's so easy to prepare. The crew is happy because it's so easy to clean up the mess the cook makes...oops! Excuse me! I meant to say that the crew is happy because it tastes so good. It's so light and heavenly, it will bring a smile to their faces with every bite. (Is that syrupy enough for you or what?)*

| | | | |
|---|---|---|---|
| 2 | teaspoons brown sugar | | |
| ⅛ | teaspoon mace | 1 | cup water |
| | | 1 | cup orange juice |
| | • • • • • • | 1 | teaspoon instant chicken bouillon granules |
| 1 | Tablespoon butter | | |
| 1 | Tablespoon vegetable oil | | • • • • • |
| 4 | chicken breast halves, skinned and boned | 2 | Tablespoons cornstarch |
| | | 2 | Tablespoons water |

• • • • • •

*Pre-package first 2 ingredients in a plastic zip lock envelope.*

• • • • • •

In a large skillet, heat butter and oil over medium heat. Add chicken breasts and brown on both sides. Discard excess grease.

• • • • • •

In a small bowl, combine the next 3 ingredients and pre-packaged spices. Stir well and pour over chicken. Bring to a boil. Reduce heat. Cover and simmer 30 minutes. Remove chicken from skillet.

• • • • • •

In a cup, blend cornstarch and water. Add to skillet. Stirring constantly, continue to cook until thick and bubbly. Pour sauce over chicken.

makes 4 servings

**Tip:** To heat canned green beans, simply drain and place on a sheet of foil. Form a packet just small enough to fit in a skillet. Place on top of chicken during the last 15 minutes of cooking.
Try topping the canned pudding with some flaked coconut and nuts.
**Note:** Prepare the marinated asparagus for tomorrow night's dinner.

---

2nd day **NEW ORLEANS POACHED EGGS**
Breakfast  juice • canned sliced peaches • beverage

---

*Disaster is the Mother of Creative Cooking.*
*Have you ever tried to poach an egg without using one of those cute little poacher cups?*
*It looked and sounded so easy when I read about it in the cookbook, I figured it was a snap. "Heck, I could do this on the boat." Or so I thought. I was so confident that it would work I never tried doing it until I had five hungry sailors anxiously waiting for their Eggs and Crabmeat New Orleans, sort of a seafood Eggs Benedict. Then it dawned on me that if I used the French method of swirling the water like it said in the cookbook, I could only poach one egg at a time. At that rate it would take 30 or 40 minutes to cook all the eggs. Oh well, I mixed another batch of Mimosas and gave it a try. That's when disaster struck. Everytime I tried to poach an egg it either broke, separated, stuck to the bottom of the pan or turned into floating cobwebs.*
*If I would've had the cookbook with me, I might have been able to figure out what I was doing wrong, but I didn't. So there I was, the crab meat was ready. The sauce was ready. And the crew was definitely ready. But the eggs weren't. And I had no idea of how to poach them. No idea except. . .except, except the same way I poach them for Mexican and Portuguese Poached Eggs. . .on top of the meat and sauce mixture.*

**Cream Sauce**

¼  cup (½ stick) butter

• • • • • •

3   Tablespoons flour
½   teaspoon salt
¼   teaspoon nutmeg

1½ cups milk
3   Tablespoons brandy
⅛   teaspoon hot sauce

• • • • • •

*Pre-package first 3 ingredients in a plastic zip lock envelope.*

• • • • • •

In a large skillet, melt butter over low heat. Add pre-packaged ingredients and stir until smooth. Cook 1 minute, stirring constantly.

• • • • • •

Gradually add milk. Stirring constantly, cook over medium heat until thick and bubbly. Stir in brandy and hot sauce.

131

### Crab Meat & Eggs

½ cup (1 stick) butter
1 cup chopped green onions and tops
2 4-oz. cans sliced mushrooms, drained
• • • • • •

3 6-oz. cans crab meat, drained and flaked
½ cup cream sherry
• • • • • •
4 eggs
4 sliced rye bread

In Dutch oven, melt butter over medium heat. Add onions and mushrooms. Cook until onions are soft.
• • • • • •
Add crab meat and cream sherry. Cook until thoroughly heated.
Break one egg at a time into a cup, then slide it on top of crab meat mixture. Cover and simmer 5 minutes or until eggs are set.
With slotted spoon, remove eggs and crab meat mixture from Dutch oven and serve on a slice of rye bread. Top with cream sauce.

makes 4 servings

> **Tip:** If you don't want to mess around and make the cream sauce from scratch, you can use a can of condensed cream of chicken soup. Just add a little milk, some brandy, a couple drops of hot sauce, and you're all set.
> **Note:** Make sure the eggs and crabmeat are well drained before placing on the bread and plate or the poaching liquid will conflict with the sauce.

---

2nd day **FRANKS & PASTA SALAD**
Lunch melba toast • cheese & crackers

---

*There it was, floating in the cool, undrained water of the ice chest, a forgotten package of hot dogs. After close scrutiny, we determined that it had survived our ten-day voyage without spoiling. I was impressed! This discovery could add a new dimension to our meal-planning. But we couldn't eat just plain old hot dogs all the time. There had to be different ways to utilize this durable delight.*

*Now, I don't recommend eating hotdogs that have been floating around for ten days, but I think if you use some fairly fresh ones, you'll find this dish quite pleasing.*

8 ounces large shell macaroni, cooked
1 16-oz. can cut green beans, drained
½ cup pitted black olives, cut in half
1 celery stalk, sliced
4 to 6 hot dogs, sliced ½-inch thick

½ head lettuce, chopped
½ cup chopped onion
• • • • • •
⅓ cup Italian salad dressing
1 Tablespoon mustard
• • • • • •
2 tomatoes, sliced

In a large bowl, combine first 7 ingredients. Toss to mix.

• • • • • •

In a cup, combine salad dressing and mustard. Pour mixture over salad and toss gently to coat.

Transfer to a large (gallon size) zip lock plastic storage bag. Seal and chill.

Serve on a lettuce-lined plate with sliced tomatoes.

makes 4 servings

> **Tip:** You can use the extra hot dogs to make some Mustard Dogs to snack on. See page 76.
> **Note:** One time I forgot to cook the macaroni ahead of time, so I did it while everybody was waiting for lunch. I also just happened to cook the hot dogs at the same time. When I finally tossed everything together, I ended up with a delightful combination of hot and cold in one salad. You might want to give it a try.
>    Don't you forget to prepare the marinated broccoli for tomorrow night.

---

## SMOTHERED BEEF & ONIONS

2nd day
Dinner
salad • instant mashed potatoes • tangy marinated asparagus
custard sauce ambrosia

---

*I love liver and onions, but I can't find another sailor who also loves it. The mere mention of L&O makes the crew shudder. There's absolutely no way I could ever coax them or trick them into just tasting it, even if it was one of the greatest recipes ever prepared by one of the world's most renowned chefs. So I don't even try. But I can't go without. I happen to love meats smothered in onions and if it can't be liver, it has to be something the crew could fall in love with and at the same time satisfy my craving.*

*Do me one favor! Save yourself a lot of grief and don't ever tell anyone this dish is even vaguely related to my all-time-favorite liver and onions.*

½  **cup butter (1 stick)**
1  **pound cubed steaks (4 to 6 steaks)**

• • • • • •

2  **onions, sliced and separated into rings**
3  **Tablespoons flour**

• • • • • •

1  **10½-oz. can beef consomme, undiluted**
1  **cup dry white wine**
1½ **Tablespoons vinegar**
½  **teaspoon salt**
¼  **teaspoon pepper**

In a large skillet, melt butter over medium heat. Add cube steaks and brown on both sides. Remove steaks from skillet.

• • • • • •

Add onions to skillet and cook until soft.

Sprinkle flour over onions and stir well to blend.

• • • • • •

Stirring constantly, gradually add consomme and wine. Cook until thick and bubbly.

• • • • • •

Stir in vinegar, salt and pepper. Return steaks to skillet. Reduce heat. Cover and simmer 20 minutes.

makes 4 servings

### TANGY MARINATED ASPARAGUS

¼  cup vegetable oil
1   Tablespoon chopped parsley
3   Tablespoons vinegar
1   2-oz. jar sliced pimiento, drained
    and chopped

¾  teaspoon salt
¼  teaspoon pepper
• • • • • •
1   15-oz. can asparagus spears,
    drained

Combine first 6 ingredients in a screw top jar. Cover and shake vigorously. Drain asparagus spears, but DO NOT remove from can. Pour marinade over asparagus in the can. Cover with plastic wrap and chill. Drain marinade and serve.

### CUSTARD SAUCE AMBROSIA

1    16-oz. can egg custard
1½  teaspoons light rum
1    11-oz. can Mandarin oranges,
     drained

2   cups flaked coconut
½  cup chopped pecans

In a large bowl, combine all ingredients. Mix to blend. Serve in bowls or clear plastic cups.

**Tip:** Prepare marinated asparagus ahead of time.
**Note:** Canned asparagus isn't very firm, so it may not come out looking picture perfect.
Make lots and lots of mashed potatoes. Remember, we need the leftovers to make potato pancakes in the morning.
This is one of the few times you don't have to make the dessert ahead of time. But you might consider chilling the can of egg custard first.

---

3rd day
Breakfast

# POTATO PANCAKES
juice • eggs • sausage • beverage

---

*One of our crew members is a major league mashed potato fanatic. Any time a meal calls for mashed potatoes, he insists that only HE (following his family's ancient recipe) is qualified to make them. I have no problem with that, except for the fact that his ancestral secret recipe calls for eleven pounds three-and-one-half ounces of cooked potatoes. This means that out of necessity, we have started our own new tradition: Potato Pancakes for breakfast the next day, and the next day, and the next, and the . . .*

2   eggs, beaten
4   potatoes, peeled and
    shredded
1   cup cooked mashed
    potatoes

½  cup chopped onion
1   teaspoon salt
1   teaspoon sugar
¼  teaspoon pepper

In a large bowl, combine all ingredients. Mix well.
For each pancake, pour or spoon ¼ cup batter onto a hot, lightly greased, griddle. Cook 2 to 3 minutes per side or until golden brown.

makes 12 (4-inch) pancakes

**Tip:** Use the leftover mashed potatoes from last night's dinner.
Cook the sausages first, then push them to the sides of the griddle to keep warm while you cook the pancakes.
Stack pancakes on top of sausages on one side of the griddle and turn that burner off. Cover with aluminum foil to keep warm while frying eggs.
Try adding a little minced garlic, some Parmesan cheese or some chopped parsley to the batter.
**Note:** Prepare the compote for tonight's dessert.

# CHINESE CHICKEN SALAD

cheese & crackers • fruit platter with creamy orange fruit dip

*It used to be that anytime we had any meat left over from dinner, I would use it to make sandwiches the next day for lunch. But usually there wasn't enough for everybody. So in order to keep all the tummies full, I'd end up making a couple different things for lunch instead of just one. Which was a real drag because it meant twice as much work.*

*At first I thought my only alternative was just to toss any left overs over the side. But that was a real waste. Then it was brought to my attention that if I incorporated it with some vegetables and a delightful sauce, a little bit of left over meat could please some pretty big appetites.*

2   **Tablespoons mustard**
3   **Tablespoons vegetable oil**
3   **Tablespoons soy sauce**
   **Dash of hot pepper sauce**
   • • • • • •
2   **6¾-oz. cans chunk chicken, broken-up**

½  **cup sliced onion**
  • • • • • •
1  **14-oz can fancy mixed Chinese vegetables, drained**
  **Lettuce**

In a large bowl, combine first 4 ingredients. Mix well.
  • • • • • •
Add chicken and onions. Stir to blend. Transfer mixture to a large (gallon size) zip lock plastic storage bag. Seal and chill.
  • • • • • •
Just before serving, add Chinese vegetables to mixture. Toss to mix.
Serve on a bed of lettuce.

makes 4 servings

**CREAMY ORANGE FRUIT DIP**

1   **8-oz. container soft cream cheese**
4   **Tablespoons orange marmalade**

In a small bowl, combine both ingredients. Mix well.

**Tip:** For a little variation you can substitute canned turkey or tuna for the chicken.

# CHEESE-STUFFED PORK CHOPS

salad • spanish rice • marinated broccoli • cantaloupe compote

*How come I always have to learn the hard way?*

*One sailing season, I forgot to check our fuel supply for the needs of the alcohol stove before embarking on our cruise. I thought we had enough, but we didn't. So there we were, peacefully anchored in one of the most beautiful harbors in the North Channel, miles away from nowhere. Then it happened! I literally ran out of gas (alcohol). Right in the middle of simmering my chops, the flames went out.*

*I knew this meal would take a little longer to cook, and if I had prepared something that took just, a little less time, we wouldn't have had to eat peanut butter and crackers for dinner that night. But the situation called for something special.*

*Now, I know what you're thinking. But these chops taste soooo good, you've simply got to try them! Just make sure you are in port, the shore power is hooked up and you are using an electric skillet.*

| | |
|---|---|
| 1 4-oz. can sliced mushrooms, drained with liquid reserved and chopped | 4 pork loin chops, ¾ to 1-inch thick |
| 1 cup (4-oz.) shredded Swiss cheese | • • • • • |
| ¼ cup chopped parsley | 1 egg, beaten |
| ½ teaspoon salt | ½ cup bread crumbs |
| • • • • • | ½ teaspoon salt |
| | Dash of pepper |

In a small bowl, combine first 4 ingredients.

• • • • • •

Cut a pocket in each pork chop and stuff with cheese mixture.

• • • • • •

Beat egg in one pie tin and combine bread crumbs, salt and pepper in another.

Dip both sides of pork chops in the beaten egg then the bread crumbs.

• • • • • •

In a large skillet, heat 2 Tablespoons vegetable oil over medium heat. Add chops and brown on both sides. Add reserved mushroom liquid and ½ cup water. Reduce heat. Cover and simmer 45 minutes.

makes 4 servings

### SPANISH RICE

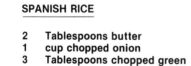

| | |
|---|---|
| 2 Tablespoons butter | 1 11½-oz. can stewed tomatoes |
| 1 cup chopped onion | 2 cups cooked rice |
| 3 Tablespoons chopped green pepper | ¼ cup sliced pimiento-stuffed green olives |
| 2 garlic cloves, minced | 1 8-oz. can sweet peas, drained |
| • • • • • • | |

In Dutch oven, melt butter over medium heat. Cook onion, green pepper and garlic until tender. Stir in remaining ingredients. Mix well. Reduce heat. Simmer uncovered 5 minutes.

## MARINATED BROCCOLI

¾ cup cider vinegar
¼ cup vegetable oil
1 Tablespoon sugar
2 Tablespoons water
1½ teaspoons dill seeds

½ teaspoon salt
¼ teaspoon cayenne pepper
1 garlic clove, minced
• • • • • •
3 cups broccoli flowerets

Pre-package first 8 ingredients in a 12-oz. jar. (Shake jar after pre-packaging and before using.)
• • • • • •
Place flowerets in a large (gallon size) zip lock plastic storage bag. Pour marinade over broccoli. Seal and chill.

## CANTALOUPE COMPOTE

½ cup sugar
¼ cup hot water

¼ cup Cointreau
• • • • • •
4 cups cantaloupe chunks

In a small bowl, combine first 3 ingredients. Mix well. Let cool. Place cantaloupe chunks in a small (quart size) zip lock plastic storage bag. Pour sauce over fruit. Seal and chill.

**Tips:** Rather than cutting the pockets for the stuffing along the outside edge, cut them from the rib (bone) side out, creating a pocket that almost reaches the outer (fat) edge.
Prepare marinated broccoli a couple days ahead of time.
**Note:** You can use the trimmed broccoli leaves, branches and peeled stalks in salads.

# Time Out For Cocktails & Things

*Potato, corn, tortilla, nacho. . .the so-called chips of choice. Although they seem to be the favorite snacks of young and old alike, they fall short on performance aboard the boats I've sailed on.*

*For us, the title of the "PERFECT" junk food is reserved for the "Look mom. No Hands!" pretzel rods. You can trim, tail, perform take downs, pop the chute, plot a course and steer a boat while enjoying the taste and the crunch of a pretzel. Plus, they're a heck of a lot easier to pass to the ape on the foredeck when hard to the wind than it is to pass up a handful of chips. Besides, they don't crumble to pieces when you stick them into a thick dip or spread.*

## SPICY CHEESE SPREAD

8 ounces (2 cups) shredded sharp cheddar cheese
½ cup mayonnaise
½ cup minced onion
¼ cup catsup
1 teaspoon Dijon mustard
1 teaspoon Worcestershire sauce
Salt to taste
Dash of paprika

In a large bowl, combine all ingredients. Mix well. Transfer to a smaller bowl and serve with cocktail breads and crackers.

## BRAUNSCHWEIGER-ONION SPREAD

2 1¾-oz. packages dry onion soup mix
1 16-oz. carton sour cream
2 3-oz. packages cream cheese, cubed and softened
2 teaspoons steak sauce
4 drops hot sauce
2 8-oz. packages braunschweiger, cut into small pieces

Add soup mix to sour cream and mix well. Let stand 15 minutes. In a large bowl, beat cream with a fork until fluffy. Add sour cream mixture and all remaining ingredients. Mix well. Transfer to serving bowls. Great with crackers, chips and pretzel rods.

## KAMIKAZE

⅓  cup tequila
⅓  cup Cointreau
⅓  Rose's lime juice
¾  cup crushed ice

In a screw top jar, combine all ingredients. Secure top and shake well. Strain into glass.

## CLAM DIP

1  6½-oz. can minced clams, drained
1  cup sour cream
1  Tablespoon chopped parsley
2  Tablespoons minced onion
2  teaspoons Worcestershire sauce
   Salt to taste

In a small bowl, combine all ingredients and mix well. Serve with vegetables and chips.

## WINE WELCOMER

2  cups orange juice
1  6-oz. can frozen lemonade concentrate, thawed and undiluted
1  cup Cointreau
1  chilled bottle of Chablis
   • • • • •
32  ounces club soda
   Orange slices

Combine first 4 ingredients. Add club soda. Serve over ice and garnish with orange.

## APPLE JULEP

32  ounces unsweetened apple juice
2  cups unsweetened pineapple juice
1  cup orange juice
¼  cup lemon juice
   • • • • • •
   Lemon slices
   Sprigs of fresh mint

Combine first 4 ingredients. Serve over ice and garnish with a slice of lemon and a sprig of mint.

## PINK LADY

2  cups cranberry juice cocktail
2  cups pineapple juice
¾  cup sugar
4  cups ginger ale

Combine all ingredients. Stir until sugar is dissolved. Serve over ice.

# Chapter 8

## The B-B-Q Option

Instead of slaving over a hot stove, many of us would prefer to practice the delicate culinary art of barbecuing while cruising. Anytime you've got the chance to do some outdoor grilling, forget what _the Two Burner Gourmet's_ meal plan says you're supposed to be doing with that piece of beef or poultry — and follow your heart. Open a couple of cold ones and burn those chunks of meat over a blazing fire. But don't be barbarian about it. Do it in a sophisticated way, with marinades and sauces. After all, we are gourmet cooks.

### LEMONADE CHICKEN

| | |
|---|---|
| 1 | 6-oz. can frozen lemonade concentrate, thawed and undiluted |
| ½ | cup soy sauce |
| 1 | teaspoon seasoned salt |
| ½ | teaspoon celery salt |
| ⅛ | teaspoon garlic powder |

• • • • • •

3 pounds prime chicken parts

Combine first 5 ingredients. Mix well.
• • • • • •
Place chicken parts in a large (gallon size) zip lock plastic storage bag. Pour marinade over chicken. Marinate, chilled, 2 hours.

Reserving marinade for basting, remove chicken and pat dry with paper toweling.

Place chicken, bone side down, 6-inches from medium-hot coals. Turning frequently, grill 20 minutes. Basting and turning, grill for an additional 35 minutes.

makes 4 servings

### SESAME CHICKEN BREAST

| | |
|---|---|
| ¼ | cup soy sauce |
| ¼ | cup Russian salad dressing |
| 1 | Tablespoon sesame seeds |
| 2 | Tablespoon lemon juice |
| ¼ | teaspoon ginger |
| ¼ | teaspoon garlic powder |

• • • • •

4 boned and skinned, chicken breast halves

Combine first 6 ingredients. Mix well.
• • • • •
Place chicken in a large (gallon size) zip lock plastic storage bag. Pour marinade over chicken. Marinate, chilled, 2 hours.

Reserving marinade for basting, remove chicken and place on a grill 6 inches from medium-hot coals. Turning and basting frequently, grill for 20 minutes.

makes 4 servings

## MARINATED PORK CHOPS

½ cup vegetable oil
¼ cup olive oil
¼ cup lemon juice
3 garlic cloves, crushed
1 Tablespoon salt

1 teaspoon paprika
½ teaspoon pepper
6 bay leaves, halved
· · · · · ·
6 1-inch thick loin pork chops

Combine first 8 ingredients. Mix well.
· · · · · ·
Place chops in a large (gallon size) plastic zip lock storage bag. Pour marinade over chops. Marinated, chilled, overnight.
· · · · · ·
Reserving marinade for basting, remove chops and pat dry with paper toweling.

Place chops on grill 4 to 5 inches from medium coals. Turning and basting frequently, grill for 30 to 45 minutes.

makes 6 servings.


## GRILLED PORK CHOPS

½ teaspoon oregano
½ teaspoon garlic salt
¼ cup red wine vinegar
2 tablespoons dry white wine
1 Tablespoon vegetable oil
1 teaspoon Worcestershire sauce

¼ teaspoon basil
· · · · · ·
4 ¾-inch thick, pork chops

Combine first 7 ingredients. Mix well.
· · · · · ·
Place chops in a large (gallon size) zip lock plastic storage bag. Pour marinade over chops. Marinate, chilled, for 2 hours.

Reserving marinated for basting, remove chops and pat dry with paper toweling.

Place chops on grill 4 to 5 inches from medium coals. Turning and basting frequently, grill for 30 to 45 minutes.

makes 4 servings


## SECRET SIRLOIN

¼ cup Worcestershire sauce
2 Tablespoons minced onions
2 Tablespoons lemon juice
2 Tablespoons olive oil

¾ teaspoon salt
½ teaspoon minced garlic
· · · · · ·
1 3-pound sirloin steak

Combine first 6 ingredients. Mix well.
· · · · · ·
Place steak in a large (gallon size) zip lock plastic storage bag. Pour marinade over steak. Marinate, chilled, 4 hours.
· · · · · ·
Remove steak from marinade and place on grill 4 to 5 inches from hot coals. Grill 8 to 12 minutes per-side.

makes 4 to 6 servings.

## ORIENTAL FLANK STEAK

5   green onions, chopped
¾   cup vegetable oil
½   cup soy sauce
1½  teaspoons ginger

1½  teaspoons garlic powder
3   Tablespoons honey
2   Tablespoons vinegar
• • • • • •
1   1½-pound flank steak

Combine first 7 ingredients. Mix well.
• • • • • •
Place steak in a large (gallon size) zip lock plastic storage bag. Pour marinade over steak. Marinate, chilled, overnight.
• • • • • •
Reserving marinade for basting, remove steak and pat dry with paper toweling.

Place steak on grill 4 to 5 inches from hot coals. Grill 5 to 10 minutes per-side, basting occasionally.

makes 4 to 6 servings


## BARBECUED HAM SLICES

½   cup orange marmalade
¼   cup mustard
¼   cup plus 2 Tablespoons water

1   teaspoon Worcestershire sauce
• • • • • •
4   6-oz. slices of fully cooked ham
     (about 1-inch thick)

Combine first 4 ingredients. Mix well. Pour marinade in a large (gallon size) zip lock plastic storage bag. One at a time, add ham slices to marinade. Shake to coat. Chill and marinate 1 hour.

Reserving marinade for basting, remove ham slices and place on a grill 4 to 5 inches from medium coals. Turning and basting frequently, grill 30 minutes.

makes 4 servings


## GOLDEN GRILLED HAM

1   cup ginger ale
1   cup orange juice
½   cup packed brown sugar
3   Tablespoons vegetable oil
1   Tablespoon white wine vinegar

2   teaspoons dry mustard
¾   ginger
½   teaspoon ground cloves
• • • • • •
4   6-oz. slices of fully cooked ham
     (about 1-inch thick)

Combine first 8 ingredients. Mix well.

Pour marinade in a large (gallon size) zip lock plastic storage bag. One at a time, add ham slices to marinade. Shake to coat. Chill and marinate overnight.

Reserving marinade for basting, remove ham slices and place on a grill 4 to 5 inches from medium heat. Turning and basting frequently, grill 30 minutes.

makes 4 servings.

## GRILLED SALMON STEAKS

⅓ cup orange juice
⅓ cup soy sauce
2 Tablespoons snipped parsley
2 Tablespoons vegetable oil

1 clove garlic, minced
½ teaspoon basil
• • • • • •
4 salmon steaks (about 1-inch thick)

Combine first 6 ingredients. Mix well.
• • • • • •
Place salmon steaks in a large (gallon size) zip lock plastic storage bag. Pour marinade over salmon. Marinate at room or cabin temperature for 2 hours.

Reserving marinade for basting, remove salmon and place on a grill 5 inches from medium-hot coals. Basting frequently, grill 8 minutes before turning. Continue to cook and baste another 8 minutes.

makes 4 servings

## DILL-GRILLED TROUT

1 cup mayonnaise
2 Tablespoons finely chopped green onion
4½ teaspoons lemon juice
1 teaspoon dried dillweed
¼ teaspoon salt

2 drops hot pepper sauce
• • • • • •
4 dressed whole rainbow trout
• • • • • •
¼ cup finely chopped, peeled cucumber

Combine first 6 ingredients. Mix well.
• • • • • •
Cut 3 diagonal slashes on each side of the fish. One at a time pour a little of the marinade over fish, rubbing mixture into slashes and over body. Spoon about 1 to 2 Tablespoons into the body cavity. Place in a large (gallon size) zip lock plastic storage bag. Add cucumber to remaining marinade and pour over fish. Marinate at room or cabin temperature for 1 hour.

Reserving marinade for basting, remove fish and place on a grill 5 inches from medium coals. Basting often, grill 5 to 7 minutes before carefully turning. Continue to cook and baste another 5 to 7 minutes.

makes 4 servings

## STEAK & VEGETABLE KABOBS

¼ cup orange marmalade
¼ cup Dijon mustard
2 Tablespoons dry sherry
1 Tablespoon olive oil
1¼ teaspoon salt
• • • • • •
1 pound top round steak
• • • • • •

½ teaspoon rosemary
¼ cup olive oil
• • • • • •
6 green onions, roots and green stems removed, then cut in half
8 cherry tomatoes
8 large mushrooms
1 orange, cut in wedges then cut in half

Combine first 5 ingredients. Mix well.
• • • • • •
With knife slanted, almost parallel to cutting board, slice steak into thin slices.
Place meat in a large (gallon size) zip lock plastic storage bag. Add marinade. Chill and marinate 2 hours.
Reserving marinade for basting, remove steak. Using metal skewers with handles, thread meat accordion-style.
• • • • • •
In a cup, combine rosemary and oil.
• • • • • •
Thread onions, tomatoes, oranges and mushrooms on separate skewers.
Using marinade for the meat and rosemary oil for the vegetables, baste and grill skewers over medium coals for 8 to 10 minutes.

makes 4 servings

## SPICY PORK KABOBS

| | | | | |
|---|---|---|---|---|
| 3 | onions minced | ½ | teaspoon red pepper |
| 1 | garlic clove, minced | ½ | teaspoon pepper |
| ¼ | cup creamy peanut butter | | • • • • • • |
| 3 | Tablespoons soy sauce | 2 | pounds lean pork, cut into |
| 1½ | Tablespoons lemon juice | | 1½-inch cubes |
| 1 | Tablespoon brown sugar | | • • • • • • |
| 1½ | teaspoon ground coriander | 3 | zucchini, cut into ¾-inch pieces |
| 1½ | teaspoon salt | 2 | onions, cut into eighths |
| 1 | teaspoon cumin | 12 | cherry tomatoes |

Combine first 10 ingredients. Mix well.

• • • • • •

Place pork in a large (gallon size) zip lock plastic storage bag. Pour marinade over pork. Marinated, chilled 4 hours.

Reserving marinade for basting, remove pork.
Alternate pork and vegetables on metal skewers. Over medium coals, grill 30 minutes.

makes 6 servings


## NUTTY BURGER

| | | | | |
|---|---|---|---|---|
| 1 | pound ground chuck | 1 | egg, beaten |
| ½ | cup finely chopped walnuts | 2 | Tablespoons soy sauce |
| 2 | Tablespoons finely chopped green onions | ¼ | teaspoon pepper |

Combine all ingredients. Mix well.

Shape into 4 patties. Place on grill 3 to 5 inches from medium coals. Turning once, grill for 15 minutes.

makes 4 servings


## MEX-TEX BURGER

| | | | | |
|---|---|---|---|---|
| | | ½ | teaspoon cumin |
| 1 | pound ground chuck | ½ | teaspoon salt |
| 1 | jalapeno pepper, seeded and finely chopped | ⅛ | teaspoon pepper |
| | | | Dash of cayenne |

Combine all ingredients. Mix well.

Shape into 4 patties. Place on grill 3 to 5 inches from medium coals. Turning once, grill for 15 minutes.

Top with a salsa sauce.

makes 4 servings

## BEER BARBECUE SAUCE

1 cup beer
1 cup catsup
⅓ cup vinegar
⅓ cup packed brown sugar
3 Tablespoons Worcestershire
  sauce

1 teaspoon paprika
1 teaspoon dry mustard
½ teaspoon chili powder
½ teaspoon salt
• • • • • •
1 onion, thinly sliced
1 lemon, thinly sliced

Combine first ingredients in a saucepan and bring to a boil. Reduce heat. Stirring occasionally, cook, uncover, 5 minutes.

Remove from heat. Stir in onion and lemon. Let cool.

makes 3 cups
great on ribs and chicken


## BOURBON BARBECUE SAUCE

1 cup catsup
⅓ cup bourbon
¼ cup vinegar
¼ cup molasses
2 garlic cloves, crushed

1 Tablespoon Worcestershire sauce
1 Tablespoon lemon juice
2 teaspoons soy sauce
½ teaspoon dry mustard
¼ teaspoon pepper

Combine all ingredients. Mix well.

makes 2½ cups
great on beef and pork


## COLA BARBECUE SAUCE

1 onion, finely chopped
2 garlic cloves, finely chopped
2 Tablespoon butter
• • • • • •
7 ounces Coca-Cola

1 Tablespoon Worcestershire sauce
2 teaspoons white wine vinegar
1 teaspoon mustard
1 bay leaf, crumbled
¼ teaspoon pepper

In a saucepan, melt butter over medium heat. Add onions and garlic and cook 5 minutes, but don't brown.
• • • • • •
Add remaining ingredients. Mix well. Bring to a boil. Reduce heat. Stirring occasionally, simmer, uncover, 1 hours.

makes 2½ cups
fantastic on ribs

# Chapter 9

## The Dock Side Bakery

I don't like to bake. I don't bake at home. I don't bake on the boat. I don't bake period! So whenever I have a craving for donuts, breakfast rolls, coffee cake or whatever else is sweet, gooey and comes from the oven, I'll leave it to the professionals at the bakery. And I advise others to do the same. That is, I used to, until I discovered that a friend of mines wife love to bake. Not just bake, but bake on the boat. "There's nothing like the cool crisp morning air, laced with the aroma of cinnamon. A hot cup of coffee. Warm sweet rolls fresh from the oven. It's the only way to greet the morning."

Now I don't know the first thing about baking, especially aboard the boat, but for those of you who do or would like to try, I thought you might enjoy trying a few of Linda's favorite recipes.

### BANANA DONUTS

| | | | |
|---|---|---|---|
| 5 | cups all-purpose flour | 1 | cup sugar |
| 1 | Tablespoon plus 1 teaspoon baking powder | 3 | eggs, beaten |
| 2 | teaspoons salt | • • • • • • | |
| 1 | teaspoon baking soda | ¾ | cup mashed ripe banana |
| 1 | teaspoon nutmeg | ½ | cup butter milk |
| • • • • • • | | 1½ | teaspoons vanilla extract |
| ¼ | cup shortening | • • • • • • | |
| | | | Vegetable oil |
| | | | Powdered sugar |

Pre-package first 5 ingredients in a large (gallon size) zip lock plastic storage bag.
• • • • • •
In a large bowl, cream shortening and sugar. Add eggs and beat well.
• • • • • •
In a small bowl, combine next 3 ingredients.
• • • • • •
Alternating between pre-packaged ingredients and banana mixture, add to shortening, sugar and egg mixture (start and end with dry ingredients). Mix well.
• • • • • •
On a lightly floured surface, roll dough out to ½-inch thickness. Cut with floured donut cutter.

In Dutch oven, heat 3 to 4 inches of oil to 375°; add donuts and cook 1 minute per side or until golden brown. Remove and drain on paper toweling.

Place in paper bag with powdered sugar and shake gently.

makes 2½ dozen
hope you're hungry

## POTATO DONUTS

| | | | |
|---|---|---|---|
| | | 1 | cup sugar |
| 3 | cups all-purpose flour | 1 | egg, beaten |
| 1½ | Tablespoons baking powder | | • • • • • • |
| ½ | teaspoon salt | ¼ | cup milk |
| 1 | teaspoon nutmeg | 1 | cup cooked mashed potatoes |
| ¼ | teaspoon ground cinnamon | | • • • • • • |
| | • • • • • • | 1 | cup sugar |
| 3 | Tablespoons shortening | 1½ | teaspoons ground cinnamon |

Pre-package first 5 ingredients in a large (gallon size) zip lock plastic storage bag.
• • • • • •
In a large bowl, cream shortening and sugar. Add egg and beat well.
• • • • • •
Stir in milk and mashed potatoes.
• • • • • •
Add pre-packaged ingredients. Mix well.
• • • • • •
On a lightly floured surface, roll dough out to ½-inch thickness. Cut with floured donut cutter.
In Dutch oven, heat 3 to 4 inches of oil to 375°; add donuts and cook 1 minute per side or until golden brown. Remove and drain on paper toweling.
Combine sugar and cinnamon and sprinkle over donuts.

makes 2 dozen
hope you're hungry


## ANY-FRUIT COFFEE CAKE

| | | | |
|---|---|---|---|
| 1½ | cups all-purpose flour | 3 | Tablespoons cornstarch |
| ½ | cup sugar | | • • • • • • |
| 1½ | teaspoons baking powder | ½ | cup butter |
| ½ | teaspoon cinnamon | | • • • • • • |
| ⅛ | teaspoon mace | 1 | egg, beaten |
| | • • • • • • | ½ | cup milk |
| 2 | cups raspberries or 2 cups | ½ | teaspoon vanilla |
| | chopped, peeled apples, apricots, | | • • • • • • |
| | peaches, or pineapple | ¼ | cup sugar |
| ½ | cup water | ¼ | cup all-purpose flour |
| 1 | Tablespoon lemon juice | 2 | Tablespoons butter |
| ½ | cup sugar | ¼ | cup chopped walnuts |

Pre-package first 5 ingredients in a large (gallon size) zip lock plastic storage bag.
• • • • • •
Heat water in a saucepan. Add fruit. Cover and simmer 5 minutes. Stir in lemon juice.
• • • • • •
Combine sugar and cornstarch. Add to fruit. Cook and stir until mixture thickens. Cool.
Place pre-packaged ingredients in a large bowl. With a fork, cut in butter until mixture is crumbly.
• • • • • •
Add milk, egg and vanilla. Mix well.
Pour half into a greased 9x9-inch baking pan. Spread cooled fruit over batter. Add remaining batter.
• • • • • •
In a small bowl, combine sugar and flour. Cut in butter until mixture is crumbly. Stir in nuts. Sprinkle on top of batter. Bake in a 350° oven for 40 minutes.

makes 12 servings

## PEANUT BRITTLE COFFEE CAKE

| | | | |
|---|---|---|---|
| 2 | cups packaged biscuit mix | 2 | Tablespoons butter |
| 1 | cup finely crushed peanut brittle (about 5 ounces) | | • • • • • • |
| ¼ | cup packed brown sugar | ⅔ | cup butter milk |
| ¼ | teaspoon cinnamon | 1 | egg, beaten |
| ¼ | teaspoon nutmeg | 1 | teaspoon vanilla |
| | • • • • • • | | |

Pre-package first 5 ingredients in a large (gallon size) zip lock plastic storage bag.
• • • • • •
Place pre-packaged ingredients in a large bowl. With a fork, cut in butter until mixture is crumbly. Reserve ⅔ cup for topping.
• • • • • •
Add milk, egg and vanilla. Mix well.
Pour into a greased 9-inch round cake pan. Sprinkle reserved mixture on top. Bake in a 350° oven for 30 minutes.

makes 6 to 8 servings, so invite a few people over for breakfast


## CRESCENT COFFEE CAKE

| | | | |
|---|---|---|---|
| | | 2 | 8-oz. cans refrigerated crescent dinner rolls |
| ¼ | cup butter | 1 | Tablespoon butter melted |
| ¾ | cup pineapple preserves | | • • • • • • |
| ½ | cup flaked coconut | | Powdered sugar |
| | • • • • • • | | |

In a small bowl, combine first 3 ingredients. Mix well.
• • • • • •
Separate rolls into triangles.

Place a heaping Tablespoon of pineapple mixture on the wide end of each and roll up. Place rolls, seam side down, in two rows, in a greased 9x9-inch baking pan. Brush with melted butter.

Bake at 375° for 30 minutes. Let cool.

Turn up side down to remove from pan. Sprinkle with powdered sugar.

makes 8 servings


## CREAMY SWEET ROLLS

| | | | |
|---|---|---|---|
| ⅓ | cup raisins | 1 | package (8) refrigerated breadsticks, separated but not uncoiled |
| | • • • • • • | | |
| ⅓ | cup sugar | | • • • • • • |
| 1 | Tablespoon cinnamon | ⅓ | cup light cream |
| ½ | cup melted butter | | |

Spread raisins on the bottom of a greased 9-inch round baking pan.
• • • • • •
Combine sugar and cinnamon in one aluminum pie tin and the melted butter in another. Dip coils in butter then roll in sugar mixture. Place coils, coil side down in pan.
• • • • • •
Pour cream over the top and bake at 350° for 25 minutes.

## EASY CINNAMON ROLLS

½  cup sugar
½  cup packed brown sugar
1  Tablespoon cinnamon
¾  cup chopped pecans
½  cup raisins
• • • • • •
3  cups self-rising flour

¼  cup plus 1½ teaspoons
   shortening
1  cup milk
• • • • • •
½  cup butter, softened
• • • • • •
1¼  cups powdered sugar
3  Tablespoons milk

Pre-package first 5 ingredients in a large (gallon size) zip lock plastic storage bag.
• • • • • •
Place flour in a large bowl. With a fork, cut shortening into flour until crumbly.

Add milk and stir until dry ingredients are moist.

Turn dough out onto a floured surface. Knead lightly.

With a floured rolling pin or wine bottle, roll dough into a 20x14-inch rectangle.

Spread butter over surface to within ½-inch of edges.

Sprinkle pre-packaged ingredients evenly over buttered surface.

Starting along the edge, roll up jellyroll fashion. Press edges to seal edges and ends.
Cut into 1-inch pieces.

Place on a greased 13x9-inch baking pan. Bake at 375° for 20 minutes
• • • • • •
In a small bowl, combine powdered sugar and milk. Drizzle over warm rolls.

## A Cup of Joe For Josephine

There's nothing like a good strong cup of black coffee to get an ornery crew going in the morning. Unfortunately, our crew has to suffer the indignity of drinking instant coffee because I don't carry a coffee pot aboard the boat.

I realize that instant can't replace the flavor of fresh brewed coffee, so in an effort to redeem myself of this terrible transgression, I also like to take along a few "Designer" type hot drink mixes for those special after dinner occasions. I know these won't tame the savage beast, but they'll sure mellow one out.

### CAFE VIENNSES

1  cup instant coffee granules
1  cup sugar
⅔  cup nonfat dry milk powder
½  teaspoon ground cinnamon

In an airtight container, combine all ingredients. Mix well. To serve, add 1 cup hot water to 2½ to 3 Tablespoons dry mix, and stir.

### CAFE CAPPUCCINO

½  cup instant coffee granules
¾  cup sugar
1  cup nonfat dry milk powder
½  teaspoon dried orange peel, crushed

In an airtight container, combine all ingredients. Mix well. To serve, add 1 cup hot water to 2½ to 3 Tablespoons dry mix, and stir.

## HOT MOCHA-COCOA

3 cups nonfat dry milk powder
1 cup sugar
1 cup cocoa
½ cup instant coffee granules
1 teaspoon ground cinnamon
1 teaspoon ground nutmeg
⅛ teaspoon ground cloves

In an airtight container, combine all ingredients. Mix well. To serve, add 1 cup hot water to 2 Tablespoons dry mix, and stir.

## SPICED TEA MIX

2 26-oz. jars Tang
1 3-oz. jar instant tea
2 8½-oz. packages red cinnamon candies
1 6-oz. package pre-sweetened lemonade mix
1 cup sugar
2 teaspoons ground cinnamon
2 teaspoons ground nutmeg
2 teaspoons ground allspice
2 teaspoons ground cloves

In an airtight container, combine all ingredients. Mix well. To serve, add 1 cup hot water to 1½ Tablespoons dry mix, and stir.

## ITALIAN MOCHA ESPRESSO

1 cup instant coffee granules
1 cup sugar
4½ cups nonfat dry milk powder
½ cup cocoa

In an airtight container, combine all ingredients. Mix well. To serve, add 1 cup hot water to 6 Tablespoons dry mix, and stir.

## LEMON SPICED TEA

⅔ cup orange Pekoe tea leaves
3 Tablespoons minced crystallized ginger
3 Tablespoons sugar
2 Tablespoons ground lemon peel
1½ teaspoons ground cardamon
⅛ teaspoon ground cloves

In an airtight container, combine all ingredients. Mix well. Store for up to one month. To serve, add 1 cup boiling hot water to 1 heaping Tablespoon dry mix. Steep 5 minutes.

## FRIENDSHIP TEA

1 18-oz. jar Tang
1 cup sugar
½ cup pre-sweetened lemonade mix
½ cup instant tea
1 3-oz. package apricot-flavored gelatin
2½ teaspoons ground cinnamon
1 teaspoon ground cloves

In an airtight container, combine all ingredients. Mix well. To serve, add 1 cup hot water to 1 heaping Tablespoon dry mix, and stir.

# A Look At The Shopping List

Some people will call it Italian bread, other will call it French bread. Do you know which one is which?

Can you tell the difference between fresh sausage, breakfast sausage and fully-cooked smoked sausage?

In one part of the country, they're known as garbanzo beans; in another, they're chick-peas. Which are they?

Just so there's no misunderstanding, I thought I'd go through the shopping list and show you just what I'm talking about. I hope it helps.

Note: The weight of canned and packaged goods may vary with different manufacturers. As long as there's no big discrepancy between the two, don't worry, everything will work out fine.

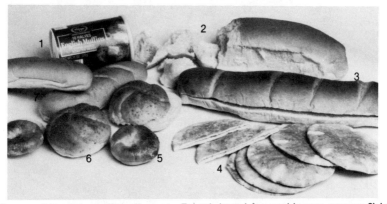

1) canned English muffins 2) crusty French bread for soaking up sauces 3) long light Italian bread for making sub-sandwiches 4) pocket breads (pita) 5) bagels 6) Kaiser rolls 7) French rolls . . . Remember, if any of these aren't available, plain white bread makes a great substitute.

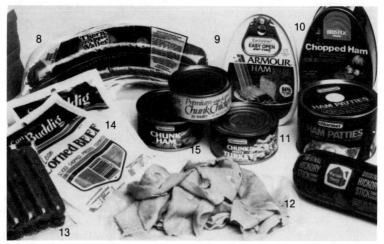

8) fully cooked smoked sausage 9) canned ham that needs refrigeration 10) canned ham that doesn't need refirgeration 11) canned meat patties, keep in cooler 12) Hickory stick sausage for snacking / fresh shaved meat 13) fully cooked link sausage 14) chipped meats 15) canned chunk meats

**16)** whipped topping **17)** condensed milk **18)** carton of milk, quart size **19)** processed cheese spreads that don't need refrigeration **20)** cheese spreads that need refrigeration **21)** package of sliced cheese **22)** 8-oz. and 3-oz. packages cream cheese **23)** different bricks of cheese, including Cracker Barrel, if you need shredded just grate one of these **24)** butter or margarine in tubs and sticks

The most important thing here are the small packages up front. **25)** these are the condiments from dinners I refer to on page 16 **26)** are the individual serving packages of soup, oatmeal, cocoa ...see you don't need the big boxes **27)** 4-pack of apple sauce, also available in puddings and various fruit cups **28)** canned green chilies **29)** 6-pack raisins **30)** jar of bouillon **31)** hot pepper rings **32)** small jar mayo **33)** pickled vegetables **34)** fancy Chinese mixed vegetables **35)** chow mein vegetables **36)** boxed noodle mixes **37)** French fried onion rings **38)** croutons **39)** 6-packs of vegetable juice **40)** instant soup **41)** instant hot cereal **42)** instant cocoa **43)** cereal

A few close friends brought up a couple of interesting questions about shopping and the shopping list that I hadn't addressed earlier. So in closing I'd like to share them with you.

You won't find bacon on any of the shopping lists because none of the meal plans call for it. I realize it's a breakfast tradition, but I prefer and encourage other boaters to use fully cooked link sausages instead. Not only will they survive longer in the cooler, but they're easier to cook than bacon and you don't have all that extra grease. Plus you don't have to worry about pan flare ups or the spitting and spattering of hot grease associated with cooking bacon.

Some people love thick slices of meat for their sandwiches. Not I. I prefer shaved. Shaved meat gives a sandwich texture and character. You get the same flavor sensation with less, which lets you make more. Besides, what's more impressive; 4 ounces of shaved ham piled 2½-inches high and cascading aimlessly over the edges of the bread, or a half pound of ham, sliced ¾-inch thick, and placed neatly within the confines of a slice of bread?

One recipe will call for shaved meat, another for chipped meat. What's the difference? One is freshly sliced and comes from the butcher. The other is chopped, pressed, packaged in plastic and comes from a processing plant. Those sealed in plastic will endure the hardships of a cruise and last longer than those wrapped in butcher brown paper.

The term "Prime Chicken Parts" simply means chicken without all the extra garbage. No backs attached to breast or leg quarters. No necks. No livers, hearts and giblets stuffed in little packages. No excess skin or fat hanging around. Just the prime meat of the chicken.

I know...sticker shock!, it's more expensive than just chicken parts or a whole chicken. Not really. We're on a vacation cruise, we won't be using all that other stuff to make stocks, soups, chicken salads and pates, so we'd just be throwing it away. Where's the savings if you don't use it.

Sliced cheese sold in those packages where every single slice is individually wrapped are very nice, but once the package is broken, the unused slices seem to develop a mind of their own and will slide and hide all over the place. Have the deli man or the butcher cut a few slices from a good block of real cheese. This way you purchase only what you need and there's no extra slices floating around the cooler.

*"Heavy cream. The recipe calls for it but I can't find it. I can find light cream, coffee creamer, half-and-half but no heavy cream. What is it? Can I substitute any of the others?"* No! Heavy cream has a higher butterfat content than the others, so it's used to give soups and chowders a thick velvety texture and to make rich creamy sauces. No other will do. Oh yes, it has another use. If you take an electric beater to it, you'll end up with whipped cream. So if you can't find a small 8 ounce milk-like carton of heavy cream, look for one that says "whipping cream".

While looking over the shopping lists, you'll discover there are a few more fruits and vegetables listed than are called for in the recipes. In fact, there are a few more dried and canned goods that may seem necessary. All these extras, radishes, french fried onion rings, cookies, bacon bits, etc., are meant to give you a little more latitude when creating snacks, appetizers, side dishes and salads.

Fruits will continue to ripen during your trip. So don't be afraid of buying some green bananas. They'll be a ripe sun shiny yellow in a few days. In fact, if you purchase your fruit at various stages of ripeness you'll find that as the days go by, they'll be ripe and ready when you are (kinda like your own on time delivery system).

All the ingredients for the *"pre-packaged"* seasoning, batters, marinades and sauces are on the shopping list according to their recipe, **not** as individual ingredients. In some instances, the same ingredient may appear more than once, first, under the heading of Cooking Supplies and later, as an ingredient in one or two of the *"pre-packaged"* listings. Just because something will be carried aboard anyhow, **DO NOT** over look pre-packing it. Later on you may forget about it (or better yet, you might get lucky and someone else will do the cooking, but they won't know about the missing ingredient).

Backpacks aren't just for camping anymore. I take one along on the boat just in case the grocery store or markets are a few miles from the dock. It's a lot easier walking back to the boat with a full pack on your back than it is trying to carry a bunch of bags.

# Index

## Side Dishes:

Carrots in Brandy Sauce, 120
Creole-Style Tomatoes & Corn, 88
Cucumber Cooler, 103
Deviled Eggs with Smoked Oysters, 61
Eight-Vegetable Marinated Salad, 80
Green Beans in Tomato Garlic Sauce, 85
Green Beans with Mushrooms, 70
Ham Deviled Eggs, 40
Marinated Broccoli, 138
Marinated Mushrooms & Vegetables, 98
Mushroom Salad with Mustard Vinaigrette, 75
Nippy Deviled Eggs, 75
Saucy Beans & Noodles, 41
Spanish Rice, 136
St. Louis Cocktail Sandwiches, 89
Sweet Spice Marinated Asparagus, 127
Sunshine Carrots, 54
Tangy Marinated Asparagus, 134

## Desserts:

Banana Supreme, 123
Black Forest Trifle, 68
Cantaloupe Compote, 138
Cherry Salad with Honey Lime Dressing, 120
Custard Sauce Ambrosia, 134
Fruit Fans, 72
Fruited Pudding, 35
Fruit with Sweet Sauced Sauce, 100
Honeydew Cups, 114
Honeydew Salad wth Apricot Cream Sauce, 90
Lost Wafers, 56
Lovin'Trifle, 103
Melon-Mint Julep, 82
Melon Wedges with Blueberry Sauce, 110
Peach Ambrosia, 97
Pineapple Compote, 117
Strawberries & Orange Marsala, 58
Stuffed Pears, 43
Watermelon Sparkle, 88

## Fruit Dips:

Coconut-Honey, 60
Creamy Orange, 135
Peanut Butter, 67
Tangy Coconut, 106

## hors d' oeuvres

Beef Roll-Ups, 46
Beer Cheese Spread, 61
Braunschweiger-Onion Spread, 138
Caviar Ball, 93
Cheese & Beef Ball, 46
Clam Dip, 139
Crabmeat Spread, 93
Deviled Cheese Dunk, 121
Jalapeno Mexican Dip, 76
Liver Pops, 61
Marinated Shrimp, 111
Mussels Dijonnaise, 128
Mustard Dogs, 76
Nordic Dip, 46
Pecan Cheese Spread, 76
Pineapple Cheese Ball, 104
Salmon Party Ball, 76
Seafood Dip, 104
Shrimp & Cheese Log, 121
Shrimp & Cucumber Spread, 46
Smoked Oyster Cheese Ball, 61
Spicy Cheese Spread, 138
Spinach Dip, 61

Stuffed Nuts, 94
Zippy Vegetable Dip, 94

## Cocktails:

Apple Julep, 139
Bowl Weevil, 62
Carmel Fog, 62
Cherry Blizzard 121
Cherry Bomb 121
Different Drummer, 77
Double Orange Spritzer, 128
Emerald Swizzle, 128
Fogcutter, 77
French 125, 177
Honolulu Fizz, 77
Hot Buttered Rum, 48
Iguana, 111
India Cup, 94
Irish Coffee, 105
Kamikaze, 139
Mai Tai, 105
Mimosa Hawaiian, 94
Mint Juleps, 94
Navy Grog, 128
Orange-Cranberry Refresher, 62
Pineapple Rum Spritzer, 48
Pink Landy, 139
Rangoon Racquet Club Punch, 48
Sea Breeze Cocktail, 111
Surber's Revenge, 48
Tequila Sunrise, 62
Wine Welcomer, 139

## Barbecue Recipes:

Barbecued Ham Slices, 142
Beer Barbecue Sauce for Chicken, 145
Bourbon Barbecue Sauce for Beef, 145
Cola Barbecue Sauce for Ribs, 145
Dill-Grilled Trout, 143
Golden Grilled Ham, 142
Grilled Pork Chops, 141
Grilled Salmon Steaks, 143
Lemonade Chicken, 140
Marinated Pork Chops, 141
Mex-Tex Burger, 144
Nutty Burger, 144
Oriental Flank Steak, 142
Secret Sirloin, 141
Sesame Chicken Breast, 140
Spicy Pork Kabobs, 144
Steak & Vegetable Kabobs, 143

## Baked Goods:

Any-Fruit Coffee Cake, 147
Banana Donuts, 146
Creamy Sweet Rolls, 148
Crescent Coffee Cake, 148
Easy Cinnamon Rolls, 149
Peanut Brittle Coffee Cake, 148
Potato Donuts, 147

## Powder Drink Mixes:

Cafe Cappuccino, 149
Cafe Viennse, 149
Friendship Tea, 150
Hot Mocha-Cocoa, 150
Italian Mocha Espresso, 150
Lemon Spiced Tea, 150
Spiced Tea Mix, 150

# Shopping List for Group #1
## a 5 day meal plan ... pages 33 - 48

cut alone dotted line or make photocopies

## Meats

- [ ] 1 pound shaved ham
- [ ] 1½ pounds boneless chicken breast
- [ ] 1 pound ground beef
- [ ] 2 pounds pork steaks
- [ ] 1 pound boneless round steak, ½-inch thick
- [ ] 12 thin slices salami
- [ ] 1 16-oz. pkg. fully cooked smoked sausage
- [ ] 1 10-oz. pkg. fully cooked link sausage
- [ ] 1 pound hickory stick salami

## Vegetables

- [ ] 1 cucumber
- [ ] 4 tomatoes
- [ ] 11 onions
- [ ] 5 green peppers
- [ ] 2 heads of garlic
- [ ] 2 heads of lettuce
- [ ] 1 bunch of parsley
- [ ] 1 bunch of broccoli
- [ ] 1 bunch of radishes
- [ ] 1 stalk of celery
- [ ] 1 bag of carrots

## Dairy

- [ ] milk
- [ ] butter
- [ ] 1 dozen eggs
- [ ] ½ pound shaved Swiss cheese
- [ ] 1 10-oz. brick sharp cheddar cheese
- [ ] 2 10-oz. bricks cheddar cheese
- [ ] 1 10-oz. brick Monterey Jack cheese
- [ ] 1 10-oz. brick colby cheese
- [ ] 1 4-oz. pkg. blue cheese
- [ ] 1 8-oz. pkg. cream cheese
- [ ] 1 5-oz. jar processed cheese
- [ ] 2 5-oz. jars of your favorite process cheese spreads
- [ ] 1 8-oz. carton plain yogurt
- [ ] 1 8-oz. carton sour cream

## Bakery

- [ ] an assortment of donuts
- [ ] bread sticks
- [ ] 1 loaf white bread
- [ ] 1 loaf Italian bread
- [ ] 4 bagels

## Fresh Fruit

- [ ] apples
- [ ] avacados
- [ ] bananas
- [ ] cantaloupe
- [ ] grapefruit
- [ ] grapes
- [ ] honeydew melon
- [ ] kiwi
- [ ] lemon
- [ ] lime
- [ ] oranges

## Canned Vegetables & Sauces

- [ ] 1 4-oz. can chopped green chilies
- [ ] 4 4-oz. cans sliced mushrooms
- [ ] 1 10-oz. can cut okra
- [ ] 1 16-oz. can whole kernal corn
- [ ] 2 16-oz. cans whole tomatoes
- [ ] 2 16-oz. cans refried beans
- [ ] 2 16-oz. cans 3-bean salad
- [ ] 1 16-oz. jar spaghetti sauce

## Canned Fruit & Juices

- [ ] 3 (6-oz. can) 6-packs of your favorite fruit juices
- [ ] 1 8-oz. can crushed pineapple
- [ ] 1 16-oz. can sliced peaches
- [ ] 1 16-oz. can pear halves
- [ ] 1 16-oz. can pineapple slices
- [ ] 1 16-oz. can fruit cocktail

## Canned & Dry Soup Mixes

- [ ] 1 4-oz. jar instant beef bouillon granules
- [ ] 1 4-oz. jar instant chicken bouillon granules
- [ ] 1 10½-oz. can cream of mushroom soup
- [ ] 2 1.6-oz. boxes of your favorite cup-a-soups

## Canned Meat

- [ ] 1 2½-oz. can Deviled Ham
- [ ] 2 4½-oz. cans crab meat
- [ ] 2 6¾-oz. cans chunk chicken
- [ ] 4 6¾-oz. cans chunk ham
- [ ] 4 6½-oz. cans tuna

## Dry & Packaged Goods

- [ ] a selection of your favorite cereals
- [ ] 4 ounces egg noodles
- [ ] 6 ounces elbow macaroni
- [ ] 8 ounces spaghetti
- [ ] 1 14-oz. box instant rice

## Condiments

- [ ] 2 8-oz. jars mayonnaise
- [ ] 1 8-oz. jar mustard
- [ ] 1 8-oz. jar Dijon-style mustard
- [ ] 1 5-oz. jar horseradish
- [ ] 1 5-oz. bottle Worcestershire sauce
- [ ] 1 10-oz. bottle taco sauce
- [ ] 1 2-oz. bottle hot pepper sauce

## Accents

- [ ] 1 jar dill pickles
- [ ] 1 jar sweet pickles
- [ ] 1 jar hot or mild peppers rings
- [ ] 1 jar pimiento-stuffed green olives
- [ ] 1 can pitted black olives
- [ ] 1 jar maraschino cherries
- [ ] 1 pkg. of 6 (1½-oz.) boxes of raisins
- [ ] 1 pkg. chopped walnuts
- [ ] 1 can mixed nuts
- [ ] 1 can french fried onion rings
- [ ] seasoned croutons
- [ ] your favorite salad dressings
- [ ] Bac-O's

## Snack & Desserts

- [ ] 1 (4½-oz. can) 4-pack of your favorite pudding
- [ ] 1 (4-oz. can) 4-pack apple sauce
- [ ] 1 16-oz. can tapioca pudding
- [ ] saltine crackers
- [ ] club crackers
- [ ] tortilla chips
- [ ] potato chips
- [ ] sugar cookies

## Cooking Supplies

- [ ] vegetable oil
- [ ] salt & pepper
- [ ] seasoned salt
- [ ] sugar
- [ ] flour
- [ ] cornstarch
- [ ] white vinegar
- [ ] lemon juice
- [ ] dry sherry

## Beverages

- [ ] coffee
- [ ] tea
- [ ] hot chocolate mix
- [ ] lemonade mix
- [ ] soft drink mixes
- [ ]

## Pre-packaged Ingredients

dinner, 1st day
CHICKEN INDIENNE

- [ ] ¼ cup flour
- [ ] ¼ teaspoon cayenne
- [ ] 1 teaspoon turmeric
- [ ] 1½ teaspoons paprika
- [ ] 2 teaspoons cumin
- [ ] 2 Tablespoons curry powder

lunch, 2nd day
SUPER NACHOS

- [ ] 1 teaspoon seasoned salt
- [ ] 1 teaspoon chili powder
- [ ] ½ teaspoon cumin
- [ ] ¼ teaspoon paprika
- [ ] ¼ teaspoon salt
- [ ] Dash of turmeric
- [ ] Pinch of cayenne

dinner, 2nd day
CHINESE HONEY PORK

- [ ] ½ cup honey
- [ ] ½ cup soy sauce
- [ ] ¼ cup red wine vinegar
- [ ] 1 teaspoon garlic salt
- [ ] 2 teaspoons ginger
- [ ] 2 ¼-oz. pkgs. brown gravy mix

dinner, 3rd day
SKILLET ROUND STEAK

- [ ] ¼ cup flour
- [ ] ¼ teaspoon pepper
- [ ] 1 teaspoon salt

lunch, 4th day
MULLIGATAWNY SOUP

- [ ] ½ teaspoon dried parsley flakes
- [ ] 1 teaspoon curry powder
- [ ] 2 whole cloves
- [ ] Dash of nutmeg

breakfast, 5th day
CORN FRITTERS

- [ ] 1 cup flour
- [ ] 1 teaspoon salt
- [ ] 1 Tablespoon sugar

dinner, 5th day
TUNA GUMBO

- [ ] ¼ teaspoon thyme
- [ ] ½ teaspoon salt
- [ ] 1 Tablespoon flour
- [ ] 1 bay leaf
- [ ] Dash of cayenne

# Shopping List for Group #2
## a 5 day meal plan ... pages 49 - 62

## Meats

- [ ] 2 pounds pork steaks
- [ ] 4 ounces shaved ham
- [ ] 4 ounces shaved cooked turkey
- [ ] 3 pounds prime chicken parts
- [ ] 1 pound shaved roast beef
- [ ] 1 pound boneless round steak
- [ ] 1 pound hickory stick salami
- [ ] 1 10-oz. pkg. fully cooked link sausage
- [ ] 1 12-oz. can ham patties

## Vegetables

- [ ] 1 zucchini
- [ ] 3 green peppers
- [ ] 6 onions
- [ ] 4 tomatoes
- [ ] 1 head of garlic
- [ ] 2 heads of lettuce
- [ ] 1 bunch of parsley
- [ ] 1 bunch of green onions
- [ ] 1 bunch of broccoli
- [ ] 2 stalks of celery
- [ ] 1 bag of carrots

## Dairy

- [ ] milk
- [ ] butter
- [ ] 2½ dozen eggs
- [ ] 4 slices Swiss cheese
- [ ] 4 slices cheddar cheese
- [ ] 1 10-oz. brick sharp cheddar cheese
- [ ] 1 10-oz. brick Monterey Jack cheese
- [ ] 1 10-oz. brick colby cheese
- [ ] 1 8-oz. package cheddar cheese
- [ ] 1 8-oz. carton sour cream
- [ ] 1 8-oz. carton plain yogurt
- [ ] 1 16-oz. carton creamy-style cottage cheese
- [ ] 1 7-oz. can whipped topping
- [ ] 1 5-oz. can condensed milk

## Bakery

- [ ] coffee cake
- [ ] bread sticks
- [ ] 4 French rolls
- [ ] 1 loaf white bread

## Fresh Fruit

- [ ] apples
- [ ] bananas
- [ ] cantaloupe
- [ ] grapes
- [ ] kiwi
- [ ] lemons
- [ ] limes
- [ ] oranges
- [ ] strawberries

## Canned Vegetables & Sauces

- [ ] 1 4-oz. jar sliced pimiento
- [ ] 1 4-oz. jar diced pimiento
- [ ] 1 4-oz. can chopped green chilies
- [ ] 5 4-oz. cans sliced mushrooms
- [ ] 1 8-oz. can tomato paste
- [ ] 1 8-oz. can sliced water chestnuts
- [ ] 2 16-oz. cans tomatoes
- [ ] 2 16-oz. cans small whole carrots
- [ ] 1 16-oz. French cut green beans
- [ ] 1 16-oz. can 3-bean salad

## Canned Fruit & Juices

- [ ] 3 (6-oz. can) 6-packs of your favorite fruit juices
- [ ] 1 8-oz. can crushed pineapple
- [ ] 3 8-oz. cans pineapple chunks
- [ ] 1 10-oz. bottle orange juice
- [ ] 1 11-oz. can Mandarin orange segments
- [ ] 1 16-oz. can sliced peaches

## Canned & Dry Soup Mixes

- [ ] 1 4-oz. jar instant beef bouillon granules
- [ ] 1 4-oz. jar instant chicken bouillon granules
- [ ] 1 16-oz. can chili with beans
- [ ] 1 25-oz. can chili with beans
- [ ] 3 1.6-oz. boxes of your favorite cup-a-soups
- [ ] 3 10½-oz. cans of your favorite soup

## Canned Meat

- [ ] 2 6¾-oz. cans chunk ham
- [ ] 2 6¾-oz. cans chunk chicken
- [ ] 1 10-oz. can whole baby clams
- [ ] 2 6½-oz. cans crab meat
- [ ] 1 3½-oz. can smoked oysters

## Dry & Packaged Goods

- [ ] your favorite instant hot cereal
- [ ] 6 ounces linguine
- [ ] 8 ouncs small shell macaroni
- [ ] 6 ounces egg noodles
- [ ] 1 5½-oz. box instant scalloped potato mix
- [ ] 1 14-oz. box instant rice

159

## Condiments

- [ ] 2 8-oz. jars mayonnaise
- [ ] 1 8-oz. jar mustard
- [ ] 1 8-oz. jar Dijon-style mustard
- [ ] 1 5-oz. jar horseradish
- [ ] 1 5-oz. bottle Worcestershire sauce
- [ ] 1 10-oz. bottle soy sauce
- [ ] 1 12-oz. bottle chili sauce
- [ ] 1 2-oz. bottle hot pepper sauce
- [ ] 1 small bottle pancake syrup

## Accents

- [ ] 1 jar dill pickles
- [ ] 1 jar sweet pickles
- [ ] 1 jar hot or mild pepper rings
- [ ] 1 jar pimiento-stuffed green olives
- [ ] 2 cans pitted black olives
- [ ] 1 jar honey
- [ ] 1 jar orange marmalade
- [ ] 1 pkg. of 6 (1½-oz.) boxes of raisins
- [ ] 1 pkg. chopped walnuts
- [ ] 1 pkg. chopped pecans
- [ ] 1 pkg. flaked coconut
- [ ] 1 can french fried onion rings
- [ ] seasoned croutons
- [ ] your favorite salad dressings
- [ ] Bac-O's

## Snacks & Desserts

- [ ] 2 (4½-oz. can) 4-packs of your favorite pudding
- [ ] 1 (4-oz. can) 4-packs apple sauce
- [ ] 1 16-oz. can lemon pudding
- [ ] saltine crackers
- [ ] club crackers
- [ ] potato chips
- [ ] vanilla wafers
- [ ] sugar cookies

## Cooking Supplies

- [ ] vegetable oil
- [ ] salt & pepper
- [ ] sugar
- [ ] flour
- [ ] cornstarch
- [ ] white wine vinegar
- [ ] lemon juice
- [ ] beer
- [ ] garlic powder
- [ ] cayenne pepper

## Beverages

- [ ] coffee
- [ ] tea
- [ ] hot chocolate mix
- [ ] lemonade mix
- [ ] soft drink mix

## Pre-packaged Ingredients

breakfast, 2nd day
BEER PANCAKES

- [ ] 2 cups packaged biscuit mix
- [ ] 2 Tablespoons sugar
- [ ] ½ teaspoon cinnamon
- [ ] Dash of nutmeg

dinner, 2nd day
CHICKEN CONTINENTAL

- [ ] ¼ cup flour
- [ ] ¼ teaspoon pepper
- [ ] ¼ teaspoon thyme
- [ ] ½ teaspoon paprika
- [ ] 1 teaspoon salt

dinner, 3rd day
MEXICAN BEEF STROGANOFF

- [ ] 1 teaspoon seasoned salt
- [ ] 2 teaspoons paprika
- [ ] 2 teaspoons chili powder

breakfast, 4th day
POLYNESIAN BREAKFAST CAKES

- [ ] ⅔ cup flour
- [ ] 1 teaspoon baking soda
- [ ] ¼ teaspoon dry mustard

dinner, 4th day
STRAWBERRIES & ORANGES MARSALA

- [ ] ½ cup sugar
- [ ] ½ cup water
- [ ] ½ cup Marsala
- [ ] ½ teaspoon anise seeds

dinner, 5th day
HAM & POTATO SKILLET

- [ ] ⅛ teaspoon pepper
- [ ] ¼ teaspoon garlic salt
- [ ] ½ teaspoon basil

# Shopping List for Group #3
## a 5 day meal plan ... pages 63 - 78

### Meats

- [ ] 1 pound shaved corned beef
- [ ] 1 pound ground beef
- [ ] ½ pound ground beef
- [ ] 8 pork chops, ½-inch thick
- [ ] 1 pound bulk pork sausage
- [ ] 1 pound shaved roast beef
- [ ] 3 pounds prime chicken parts
- [ ] 1 3-oz. pkg. thinly sliced (chipped) corned beef
- [ ] 1 10-oz. pkg. fully cooked link sausage
- [ ] 1 16-oz. pkg. hot dogs
- [ ] 1 16-oz. pkg. fully cooked smoked sausage
- [ ] 1 pound hickory stick salami

### Vegetables

- [ ] 1 cucumber
- [ ] 1 jalapeno pepper
- [ ] 3 tomatoes
- [ ] 10 onions
- [ ] 3 green peppers
- [ ] 6 potatoes
- [ ] 1 head of garlic
- [ ] 2 heads of lettuce
- [ ] 1 bunch of parsley
- [ ] 1 bunch of green onions
- [ ] 1 bunch of broccoli
- [ ] 1 bunch of radishes
- [ ] 1 stalk of celery
- [ ] 1 bag of carrots

### Dairy

- [ ] milk
- [ ] butter
- [ ] 1½ dozen eggs
- [ ] 4 slices of cheddar cheese
- [ ] 8 slices of Swiss cheese
- [ ] 2 10-oz. bricks sharp cheddar cheese
- [ ] 1 10-oz. brick Swiss cheese
- [ ] 10-oz. brick colby cheese
- [ ] 1 3-oz. pkg. cream cheese
- [ ] 1 8-oz. pkg. cream cheese
- [ ] 1 16-oz. carton sour cream
- [ ] 1 8-oz. carton heavy cream
- [ ] 1 7-oz. can whipped topping
- [ ] 1 5-oz. can condensed milk

### Bakery

- [ ] breakfast rolls
- [ ] English muffins
- [ ] hot dog buns
- [ ] 4 Kaiser rolls
- [ ] 1 loaf rye bread
- [ ] 2 loaves French bread
- [ ] 1 pkg. short cakes
- [ ] 1 small chocolate cake

### Fresh Fruit

- [ ] apples
- [ ] avacados
- [ ] bananas
- [ ] blueberries
- [ ] cantaloupe
- [ ] grapes
- [ ] kiwi
- [ ] lemons
- [ ] limes
- [ ] oranges
- [ ] strawberries

### Canned Vegetables & Sauces

- [ ] 1 2-oz. jar sliced pimiento
- [ ] 1 8-oz. can sauerkraut
- [ ] 7 4-oz. cans sliced mushrooms
- [ ] 1 4-oz. can chopped green chilies
- [ ] 4 8-oz. cans tomato sauce
- [ ] 1 16-oz. can mixed vegetables
- [ ] 1 16-oz. can stewed tomatoes
- [ ] 1 14-oz. can artichoke hearts
- [ ] 1 16-oz. can 3-bean salad
- [ ] 1 16-oz. can whole kernel corn
- [ ] 1 16-oz. can potato salad
- [ ] 1 16 oz. can cut green beans

### Canned Fruit & Juices

- [ ] 3 (6-oz. can) 6-packs of your favorite fruit juices
- [ ] 1 8-oz. can pineapple slices
- [ ] 1 10-oz. bottle orange juice
- [ ] 1 16-oz. can fruit cocktail
- [ ] 1 16-oz. can cherry pie filling
- [ ] 1 6-oz. can frozen orange juice concentrate

### Canned & Dry Soup Mixes

- [ ] 2 15-oz. cans Beefaroni
- [ ] 2 10-oz. cans cream of mushroom soup
- [ ] 2 16-oz. cans chili with beans
- [ ] 2 1.6-oz. boxes of your favorite cup-a-soups
- [ ] 1 1.9-oz. box onion soup mix

### Canned Meat

- [ ] 1 6¾-oz. can chunk ham
- [ ] 2 6-oz. cans shrimp
- [ ] 1 10-oz. can baby clams

## Dry & Packaged Goods

- [ ] your favorite breakfast cereal
- [ ] 12 ounces spinach noodles
- [ ] 6 ounces shell macaroni
- [ ] 1 14-oz. box instant rice

## Condiments

- [ ] 1 8-oz. jars mayonnaise
- [ ] 1 8-oz. jar Dijon-style mustard
- [ ] 1 5-oz. jar horseradish
- [ ] 1 10-oz. bottle taco sauce
- [ ] 1 12-oz. bottle chili sauce

## Accents

- [ ] 1 jar dill pickles
- [ ] 1 jar sweet pickles
- [ ] 1 jar hot or mild peppers rings
- [ ] 1 jar pimiento-stuffed green olives
- [ ] 1 can pitted black olives
- [ ] 1 jar apricot preserves
- [ ] 1 jar maraschino cherries
- [ ] 1 jar peanut butter
- [ ] 1 pkg. of 6 (1½-oz.) boxes of raisins
- [ ] 1 pkg. chopped walnuts
- [ ] 1 can french fried onion rings
- [ ] seasoned croutons
- [ ] your favorite salad dressings
- [ ] Bac-O's

## Snack & Desserts

- [ ] 2 (4½-oz. can) 4-packs of your favorite pudding
- [ ] 1 16-oz. can chocolate pudding
- [ ] saltine crackers
- [ ] club crackers
- [ ] tortilla chips
- [ ] potato chips
- [ ] corn chips
- [ ] sugar cookies

## Cooking Supplies

- [ ] vegetable oil
- [ ] salt & pepper
- [ ] sugar
- [ ] flour
- [ ] cornstarch
- [ ] white wine vinegar
- [ ] dry white wine
- [ ] light rum
- [ ] brandy
- [ ] Kahlua
- [ ] vanilla extract
- [ ] cream sherry
- [ ] nutmeg
- [ ] garlic powder

## Beverages

- [ ] coffee
- [ ] tea
- [ ] hot chocolate mix
- [ ] lemonade mix
- [ ] soft drink mixes

## Pre-packaged Ingredients

dinner, 1st day
PICADILLO

- [ ] ¾ teaspoon salt
- [ ] ¼ teaspoon pepper
- [ ] ¼ teaspoon cinnamon
- [ ] ¼ teaspoons ground cloves

lunch, 2nd day
BEEFARONI TOSTADA

- [ ] ¼ teaspoon garlic powder
- [ ] 1 Tablespoon chili powder

dinner, 3rd day
DRUNKEN CHICKEN

- [ ] 1/8 teaspoon marjoram
- [ ] 1/8 teaspoon thyme
- [ ] ¼ teaspoon oregano
- [ ] ½ teaspoon chili powder
- [ ] ½ teaspoon salt
- [ ] 1 bay leaf
- [ ] Dash of pepper

dinner, 4th day
PASTA with SEAFOOD-ARTICHOKE SAUCE

- [ ] 3 Tablespoons flour
- [ ] ½ teaspoon salt
- [ ] ¼ grated lemon peel
- [ ] 1/8 teaspoon white pepper

dinner, 5th day
SAUSAGE SKILLET DINNER

- [ ] 1/8 teaspoon oregano
- [ ] ¼ teaspoon paprika
- [ ] ¼ teaspoon pepper
- [ ] 1 teaspoon chili powder

dinner, 5th day
MUSHROON SALAD with MUSTARD VINAIGRETTE

- [ ] ½ teaspoon oregano
- [ ] ½ teaspoon tarragon
- [ ] 1 teaspoon salt
- [ ] 1/8 teaspoon cayenne pepper
- [ ] ¼ cup Dijon mustard
- [ ] ¼ cup white wine vinegar
- [ ] ½ cup vegetable oil

# Shopping List for Group #4
## a 5 day meal plan ... pages 79 - 94

## Meats

- [ ] 3 pounds prime chicken parts
- [ ] 1 pound frozen shrimp
- [ ] 1 pound ground beef
- [ ] 1 pound boneless beef
- [ ] ½ pound shaved cooked turkey
- [ ] ½ pound shaved ham
- [ ] ½ pound thinly sliced hard salami
- [ ] 4 pork loin chops, ¾ to 1-inch thick
- [ ] 1½ pounds pork steaks
- [ ] 1 pound fully cooked smoked sausage
- [ ] 1 16-oz. pkg. hot dogs
- [ ] 1 10-oz. pkg. fully cooked link sausage

## Vegetables

- [ ] 9 green peppers
- [ ] 6 tomatoes
- [ ] 1 red onion
- [ ] 11 onions
- [ ] 2 cucumbers
- [ ] 2 red peppers
- [ ] 2 heads of garlic
- [ ] 2 heads of lettuce
- [ ] 1 bunch of parsley
- [ ] 3 bunches green onions
- [ ] 1 bunch of radishes
- [ ] 2 stalks of celery
- [ ] 1 bag of carrots

## Dairy

- [ ] milk
- [ ] butter
- [ ] 2 dozen eggs
- [ ] 4 slices Provolone cheese
- [ ] 4 slices cheddar cheese
- [ ] ¼ pound thinly sliced Swiss cheese
- [ ] ¼ pound thinly sliced cheddar cheese
- [ ] 1 10-oz. brick sharp cheddar cheese
- [ ] 1 10-oz. brick Monterey Jack cheese
- [ ] 1 3-oz. pkg. cream cheese
- [ ] 2 5-oz. jars of your favorite process cheese spreads
- [ ] 1 8-oz. carton sour cream

## Bakery

- [ ] coffee cake
- [ ] 1 loaf white bread
- [ ] 1 loaf Italian bread
- [ ] 4 6-inch pocket bread rounds (pita)

## Fresh Fruit

- [ ] apples
- [ ] bananas
- [ ] cantaloupe
- [ ] grapes
- [ ] honeydew melon
- [ ] lemons
- [ ] limes
- [ ] oranges
- [ ] watermelon

## Canned Vegetables & Sauces

- [ ] 1 2-oz. jar chopped pimiento
- [ ] 3 4-oz. cans sliced mushrooms
- [ ] 1 8-oz. can sliced water chestnuts
- [ ] 1 8-oz. can bamboo shoots
- [ ] 1 8-oz. can sweet peas
- [ ] 1 8-oz. can lima beans
- [ ] 1 8-oz. can whole kernel corn
- [ ] 2 8-oz. cans tomatoes
- [ ] 1 14-oz. can tomatoes
- [ ] 1 16-oz. can stewed tomatoes
- [ ] 1 16-oz. can chow mein vegetables
- [ ] 2 16-oz. cans cut green beans
- [ ] 1 16-oz. can cut wax beans
- [ ] 1 15½-oz. can kidney beans
- [ ] 1 16-oz. can whole kernel corn
- [ ] 1 17-oz. can sweet potatoes (or yams)
- [ ] 1 16-oz. can potato salad

## Canned Fruit & Juices

- [ ] 3 (6-oz. can) 6-packs of your favorite fruit juices
- [ ] 1 6-oz. can orange juice
- [ ] 1 6-oz. can unsweetened orange juice
- [ ] 3 6-oz. cans tomato juice
- [ ] 1 20-oz. can unsweetened pineapple chunks
- [ ] 2 16-oz. cans fruit cocktail
- [ ] 1 16-oz. can pear halves

## Canned & Dry Soup Mixes

- [ ] 1 4-oz. jar instant beef bouillon granules
- [ ] 1 4-oz. jar instant chicken bouillon granules
- [ ] 3 1.6-oz. boxes of your favorite cup-a-soups

## Canned Meat

- [ ] 1 6¾-oz. can chunk ham
- [ ] 1 6¾-oz. can chunk chicken
- [ ] 1 6½-oz. can minced clams
- [ ] 1 15½-oz. can pink salmon
- [ ] 1 16-oz. can cooked boneless ham

## Dry & Packaged Goods

- [ ] your favorite instant hot cereal
- [ ] 8 ounces spaghetti
- [ ] 8 ounces large shell macaroni
- [ ] 6 ounces egg noodles
- [ ] 1 6-oz. box hash brown potato mix
- [ ] 1 14-oz. box instant rice

## Condiments

- [ ] 2 8-oz. jars mayonnaise
- [ ] 1 8-oz. jar mustard
- [ ] 1 8-oz. jar Dijon-style mustard
- [ ] 1 5-oz. jar horseradish
- [ ] 1 5-oz. bottle Worcestershire sauce
- [ ] 1 10-oz. bottle soy sauce
- [ ] 1 2-oz. bottle hot pepper sauce
- [ ] 1 small bottle pancake syrup

## Accents

- [ ] 1 jar dill pickles
- [ ] 1 jar sweet pickles
- [ ] 1 jar hot or mild pepper rings
- [ ] 1 jar pimiento-stuffed green olives
- [ ] 1 can pitted black olives
- [ ] 1 jar peanut butter
- [ ] 1 jar honey
- [ ] 1 jar apricot preserves
- [ ] 1 pkg. chopped pecans
- [ ] 1 pkg. flaked coconut
- [ ] 1 bottle Italian salad dressing
- [ ] 1 can french fried onion rings
- [ ] seasoned croutons
- [ ] your favorite salad dressings
- [ ] Bac-O's

## Snacks & Desserts

- [ ] 1 (4½-oz. can) 4-pack of your favorite pudding
- [ ] 1 (4-oz. can) 4-packs apple sauce
- [ ] saltine crackers
- [ ] club crackers
- [ ] melba toast
- [ ] potato chips
- [ ] corn chips

## Cooking Supplies

- [ ] vegetable oil
- [ ] salt & pepper
- [ ] sugar
- [ ] brown sugar
- [ ] cornstarch
- [ ] lemon juice
- [ ] lime juice
- [ ] white vinegar
- [ ] red wine vinegar
- [ ] light rum
- [ ] vanilla extract
- [ ] ground cinnamon
- [ ] fresh mint

## Beverages

- [ ] coffee
- [ ] tea
- [ ] hot chocolate mix
- [ ] lemonade mix
- [ ] soft drink mix

## Pre-packaged Ingredients

dinner, 1st day
JAMBALAYA

- [ ] ¼ teaspoon pepper
- [ ] 1 teaspoon salt
- [ ] 1 teaspoon thyme
- [ ] 1 Tablespoon paprika

dinner, 2nd day
GREEN BEANS in GARLIC TOMATO SAUCE

- [ ] 1 Tablespoon flour
- [ ] 1¼ teaspoon paprika

dinner, 3rd day
PORK in ADOBO SAUCE

- [ ] ¼ cup vinegar
- [ ] 1 8-oz. can tomato sauce
- [ ] ¼ teaspoon cumin
- [ ] ½ teaspoon oregano
- [ ] 1 teaspoon salt
- [ ] 2 Tablespoons chili powder
- [ ] 2 Tablespoons flour
- [ ] 1 Tablespoon vegetable oil
- [ ] 1 medium onion, finely chopped
- [ ] 2 garlic cloves, minced

dinner, 4th day
CHINESE SPAGHETTI

- [ ] 1 Tablespoon sugar
- [ ] 1 Tablespoon flour
- [ ] 3 Tablespoons shredded gingerroot
- [ ] ¼ cup soy sauce
- [ ] ¼ cup sherry
- [ ] 4 garlic cloves, minced

# Shopping List for Group #5
## a 3 day meal plan ... pages 95 - 104

## Meats

- ☐ ½ pound shaved ham
- ☐ ½ pound thinly slices salami
- ☐ 4 pork steaks
- ☐ 1 pound Italian sausage
- ☐ 2 pounds boneless chicken breasts
- ☐ 1 pound fully cooked smoked sausage
- ☐ 1 10-oz. pkg. fully cooked link sausage

## Vegetables

- ☐ 2 cucumbers
- ☐ 1 zucchini
- ☐ 5 onions
- ☐ 2 tomatoes
- ☐ 3 green peppers
- ☐ 2 heads of garlic
- ☐ 2 heads of lettuce
- ☐ 1 bunch of parsley
- ☐ 1 bunch of green onions
- ☐ 2 bunches of broccoli
- ☐ 2 stalks of celery
- ☐ 1 bag of carrots
- ☐ cherry tomatoes
- ☐ chives

## Dairy

- ☐ milk
- ☐ butter
- ☐ 1 dozen eggs
- ☐ ½ pound thinly sliced Provolone cheese
- ☐ 4 slices Swiss cheese
- ☐ 1 10-oz. brick sharp cheddar cheese
- ☐ 1 10-oz. brick Monterey Jack cheese
- ☐ 1 12-oz. carton cottage cheese
- ☐ 1 8-oz. carton sour cream
- ☐ 1 7-oz. can whipped topping

## Bakery

- ☐ breakfast rolls
- ☐ bread sticks
- ☐ 4 hard rolls
- ☐ 1 loaf Italian bread
- ☐ 1 loaf French bread
- ☐ 4 6-inch pocket bread rounds (pita)
- ☐ small angel food cake

## Fresh Fruit

- ☐ apples
- ☐ bananas
- ☐ grapes
- ☐ lemon
- ☐ lime
- ☐ oranges
- ☐ strawberries

## Canned Vegetables & Sauces

- ☐ 1 2-oz. jar sliced pimiento
- ☐ 4 4-oz. cans sliced mushrooms
- ☐ 1 8-oz. can tomato sauce
- ☐ 1 16-oz. can sweet peas
- ☐ 1 16-oz. can small whole carrots
- ☐ 1 14-oz. can artichoke hearts
- ☐ 1 16-oz. can mixed vegetables

## Canned Fruit & Juices

- ☐ 2 (6-oz. can) 6-packs of your favorite fruit juices
- ☐ 1 8-oz. can pineapple tidbits
- ☐ 1 16-oz. can blueberry pie filling
- ☐ 1 16-oz. can pitted tart red cherries
- ☐ 1 11-oz. can Mandarin orange segments
- ☐ 1 16-oz. can peach halves
- ☐ 1 10-oz. bottle orange juice

## Canned & Dry Soup Mixes

- ☐ 1 4-oz. jar instant beef bouillon granules
- ☐ 2 1.6-oz. boxes of your favorite cup-a-soups

## Canned Meat

- ☐ 2 6½-oz. cans white tuna
- ☐ 2 15½-oz. can pink salmon

## Dry & Packaged Goods

- ☐ 1 5-oz. box stroganoff noodle mix
- ☐ 6 ounces wide egg noodles
- ☐ 1 14-oz. box instant rice

## Condiments

- ☐ 1 8-oz. jar mayonnaise
- ☐ 1 8-oz. jar mustard
- ☐ 1 2-oz. jar hot pepper sauce
- ☐ 1 small bottle pancake syrup

## Accents

- ☐ 1 jar dill pickles
- ☐ 1 jar sweet pickles
- ☐ 1 jar hot or mild pepper rings
- ☐ 1 jar mixed vegetables (pickled or marinated)
- ☐ 1 jar pimiento stuffed green olives
- ☐ 1 jar pitted black olives
- ☐ 1 jar honey
- ☐ 1 jar orange marmalade
- ☐ 1 pkg. of 6 (1½-oz.) boxes of raisins
- ☐ 1 pkg. chopped walnuts
- ☐ 1 pkg. flaked coconut
- ☐ 1 pkg. miniature marshmallows
- ☐ seasoned croutons
- ☐ your favorite salad dressings
- ☐ Bac-O's

## Snacks & Desserts

- ☐ 1 16-oz. can vanilla pudding
- ☐ saltine crackers
- ☐ club crackers
- ☐ potato chips
- ☐ corn chips

## Cooking Supplies

- ☐ vegetable oil
- ☐ salt & pepper
- ☐ sugar
- ☐ brown sugar
- ☐ cornstarch
- ☐ lemon juice
- ☐ white wine
- ☐ rum
- ☐ Irish whiskey

## Beverages

- ☐ coffee
- ☐ tea
- ☐ hot chocolate mix
- ☐ soft drink mix

## Pre-packaged Ingredients

lunch, 2nd day
Marinated MUSHROOMS & VEGETABLES

- ☐ *1 teaspoon sugar*
- ☐ *1 teaspoon basil*
- ☐ *1 teaspoon oregano*
- ☐ *1 teaspoon salt*
- ☐ *¼ teaspoon pepper*

dinner, 2nd day
CHICKEN & CHERRIES

- ☐ *¼ teaspoon ginger*
- ☐ *½ teaspoon instant chicken bouillon granules*
- ☐ *¼ cup honey*
- ☐ *¼ cup red wine vinegar*
- ☐ *½ cup water*
- ☐ *3 Tablespoons soy sauce*

breakfast, 3rd day
NUTTY ORANGE PANCAKES

- ☐ *1¾ cups pkg. biscuit mix*
- ☐ *½ cup ground walnuts*

dinner, 3rd day
PASTA with SAUSAGE & VEGETABLES

- ☐ *¼ teaspoon garlic powder*
- ☐ *2 teaspoon oregano*

# Shopping List for Group #6
## a 2 day meal plan ... pages 105 - 111

## Meats

- ☐ 1 pound bulk pork sausage
- ☐ 1 pound boneless pork loin
- ☐ 1 pound boneless chicken breasts
- ☐ 1 16-oz. pkg. hot dogs
- ☐ 2 pounds frozen cod or perch fillets

## Vegetables

- ☐ 3 onions
- ☐ 4 green peppers
- ☐ 1 zucchini
- ☐ 1 sweet potato
- ☐ 2 heads of lettuce
- ☐ 1 head of garlic
- ☐ 1 bunch of parsley
- ☐ 1 bunch of radishes
- ☐ 1 stalk of celery
- ☐ cherry tomatoes

## Dairy

- ☐ milk
- ☐ butter
- ☐ 1 dozen eggs
- ☐ 1 4-oz. brick Swiss cheese
- ☐ 1 10-oz. brick cheddar cheese
- ☐ 1 10-oz. brick Monterey Jack cheese

## Bakery

- ☐ a variety of donuts
- ☐ 1 loaf rye bread
- ☐ 1 loaf French bread

## Fresh Fruit

- ☐ apples
- ☐ bananas
- ☐ blueberries
- ☐ cantaloupe
- ☐ grapes
- ☐ honeydew melon
- ☐ lemon
- ☐ lime
- ☐ strawberries

## Canned Vegetables & Sauces

- ☐ 1 2-oz. jar diced pimiento
- ☐ 1 4-oz. can green chili peppers
- ☐ 1 7-oz. can tomatoes
- ☐ 2 8-oz. cans tomato sauce
- ☐ 1 15-oz. can garbanzo beans
- ☐ 2 16-oz. cans tomatoes
- ☐ 1 16-oz. can cut okra
- ☐ 1 16-oz. can 3-bean salad

## Canned Fruit & Juices

- ☐ 2 (6-oz. can) 6-packs of your favorite fruit juices
- ☐ 1 8-oz. can pineapple chunks
- ☐ 1 16-oz. can sliced peaches
- ☐ 1 10-oz. bottle orange juice
- ☐ 1 15-oz. can cream of coconut
- ☐ 1 6-oz. can frozen lemonade concentrate

## Canned & Dry Soup Mixes

- ☐ 1 4-oz. jar instant chicken bouillon granules
- ☐ 1 10¾-oz. can condensed manhattan-style clam chowder
- ☐ 2 1.6-oz. boxes of your favorite cup-a-soups

## Canned Meat

- ☐ 2 6¾-oz. cans chunk ham

## Dry & Packaged Goods

- ☐ 1 14-oz. box instant rice

## Condiments

- ☐ 1 8-oz. jar mayonnaise
- ☐ 1 8-oz. jar mustard
- ☐ 1 8-oz. jar Dijon-style mustard

## Accents

- ☐ 1 jar dill pickles
- ☐ 1 jar pimiento-stuffed green olives
- ☐ 1 can pitted black olives
- ☐ 1 pkg. chopped walnuts
- ☐ seasoned croutons
- ☐ your favorite salad dressings
- ☐ Bac-O's

## Snacks & Desserts

- [ ] 1 (4½-oz. can) 4-pack of your favorite pudding
- [ ] potato chips
- [ ] tortilla chips
- [ ] sugar cookies

## Cooking Supplies

- [ ] vegetable oil
- [ ] salt & pepper
- [ ] sugar
- [ ] flour

## Beverages

- [ ] coffee
- [ ] tea
- [ ] hot chocolate mix
- [ ] soft drink mix

## Pre-packaged Ingredients

lunch, 1st day
MEX-TEX SALAD

- [ ] *2 teaspoons chili powder*
- [ ] *1 Tablespoon flour*

dinner, 1st day
CHICKEN & PORK
TABLECLOTH STAINER

- [ ] *¼ teaspoon ground cloves*
- [ ] *¼ teaspoon cinnamon*
- [ ] *2 teaspoons chili powder*
- [ ] *2 teaspoons salt*

# Shopping List for Group #7
## a 3 day meal plan ... pages 112 - 120

## Meats

- ☐ 4 pork loin chops, ¾ to 1-inch thick
- ☐ 2 1-pound boneless sirloin strip steaks
- ☐ 4 chicken breast halves, boned and skinned

## Vegetables

- ☐ 1 cucumber
- ☐ 1 zucchini
- ☐ 3 green peppers
- ☐ 2 tomatoes
- ☐ 4 onions
- ☐ 1 head of garlic
- ☐ 2 heads of lettuce
- ☐ 1 stalk of celery
- ☐ 1 bunch of parsley
- ☐ 1 bunch of green onions
- ☐ 1 bunch of radishes
- ☐ 1 bunch of broccoli

## Dairy

- ☐ milk
- ☐ butter
- ☐ 1½ dozen eggs
- ☐ 1 4-oz. pkg. blue cheese
- ☐ 1 8-oz. carton plain yogurt
- ☐ 2 5-oz. jars of favorite process cheese spreads
- ☐ 1 10-oz. brick cheddar cheese
- ☐ 1 10-oz. brick Monterey Jack cheese

## Bakery

- ☐ 1 loaf white bread

## Fresh Fruit

- ☐ apples
- ☐ bananas
- ☐ grapes
- ☐ honeydew melon
- ☐ lemons
- ☐ limes
- ☐ strawberries

## Canned Vegetables & Sauces

- ☐ 1 2-oz. jar sliced pimiento
- ☐ 5 4-oz. cans sliced mushrooms
- ☐ 1 4-oz. jar diced pimiento
- ☐ 1 8-oz. can sliced water chestnuts
- ☐ 1 8-oz. can sweet peas
- ☐ 1 16-oz. can show mein vegetables
- ☐ 2 16-oz. cans sweet potatoes (or yams)
- ☐ 1 16-oz. can potato salad
- ☐ 1 16-oz. can 3-bean salad
- ☐ 1 16-oz. can whole baby carrots

## Canned Fruit & Juices

- ☐ 2 (6-oz. can) 6-packs of your favorite fruit juices
- ☐ 2 8-oz. cans sliced peaches
- ☐ 1 10-oz. bottle pineapple juice
- ☐ 3 8-oz. cans pineapple chunks
- ☐ 2 16-oz. cans pineapple chunks
- ☐ 1 16-oz. can sweet cherries
- ☐ 1 16-oz. can pears
- ☐ 1 17-oz. jar pitted dark sweet cherries

## Canned & Dry Soup Mixes

- ☐ 1 4-oz. jar instant chicken bouillon granules
- ☐ 2 1.6-oz. boxes of your favorite cup-a-soups

## Canned Meat

- ☐ 1 8-oz. can whole oysters
- ☐ 1 7¾-oz. can red salmon
- ☐ 1 6½-oz. can crab meat
- ☐ 3 4½-oz. cans shrimp
- ☐ 2 6¾-oz. cans chunk ham
- ☐ 1 6¾-oz. can chunk turkey
- ☐ 1 6¾-oz. can chunk chicken
- ☐ 2 6½-oz. cans tuna

## Dry & Packaged Goods

- ☐ your favorite breakfast cereal
- ☐ dry pina colada cocktail mix
- ☐ 1 14-oz. box instant rice

## Condiments

- [ ] 1 8-oz. jars mayonnaise
- [ ] 1 8-oz. jar mustard
- [ ] 1 14-oz. bottle catsup
- [ ] 1 5-oz. jar horseradish
- [ ] 1 10-oz. bottle soy sauce
- [ ] 1 12-oz. bottle chili sauce
- [ ] 1 2-oz. bottle hot pepper sauce
- [ ] 1 12-oz. bottle seafood cocktail sauce

## Accents

- [ ] 1 jar dill pickles
- [ ] 1 jar hot or mild pepper rings
- [ ] 1 jar pimiento-stuffed green olives
- [ ] 1 jar honey
- [ ] 1 jar pineapple preserves
- [ ] 1 pkg. flaked coconut
- [ ] seasoned croutons
- [ ] your favorite salad dressings
- [ ] Bac-O's

## Snacks & Desserts

- [ ] saltine crackers
- [ ] melba toast
- [ ] sugar cookies
- [ ] potato chips
- [ ] corn chips

## Cooking Supplies

- [ ] vegetable oil
- [ ] salt & pepper
- [ ] sugar
- [ ] cornstarch
- [ ] lemon juice
- [ ] lime juice
- [ ] cherry brandy
- [ ] dry white wine
- [ ] brandy

## Beverages

- [ ] coffee
- [ ] tea
- [ ] hot chocolate mix
- [ ] soft drink mix

## Pre-packaged Ingredients

lunch, 2nd day
CALYPSO SALAD

- [ ] ½ teaspoon ginger
- [ ] 1 Tablespoon curry powder

dinner, 3rd day
CHICKEN in LEMON & WINE SAUCE

- [ ] ¼ teaspoon sage
- [ ] ¼ teaspoon thyme
- [ ] ½ teaspoon ginger
- [ ] ½ teaspoon dry mustard

# Shopping List for Group #8
## a 2 day meal plan ... pages 121- 128

## Meats

- ☐ 2 pounds pork steaks
- ☐ ½ pound sweet Italian sausage
- ☐ ½ pound shaved pastrami
- ☐ ½ pound shaved cooked turkey
- ☐ ½ pound shaved roast beef
- ☐ 3 pounds prime chicken parts
- ☐ 1 16-oz. pkg. frozen cod or perch fillets

## Vegetables

- ☐ 3 onions
- ☐ 4 green peppers
- ☐ 4 tomatoes
- ☐ 1 head of garlic
- ☐ 2 heads of lettuce
- ☐ 1 bunch of parsley
- ☐ 1 bunch of broccoli
- ☐ 1 bunch of green onions
- ☐ 1 bunch of radishes
- ☐ 1 stalk of celery
- ☐ 1 bag of carrots

## Dairy

- ☐ milk
- ☐ butter
- ☐ 1½ dozen eggs
- ☐ 4 ounces thinly sliced Swiss cheese
- ☐ 1 4-oz. brick Swiss cheese
- ☐ 1 10-oz. brick cheddar cheese
- ☐ 1 10-oz. brick colby cheese
- ☐ 2 5-oz. jars of your favorite process cheese spreads
- ☐ 1 7-oz. can whipped topping

## Bakery

- ☐ coffee cake
- ☐ 1 loaf French bread
- ☐ 1 8-inch round loaf rye bread

## Fresh Fruit

- ☐ apples
- ☐ bananas
- ☐ grapes
- ☐ lemon
- ☐ lime
- ☐ oranges
- ☐ strawberries

## Canned Vegetables & Sauces

- ☐ 1 4-oz. can sliced mushrooms
- ☐ 1 8-oz. can tomato sauce
- ☐ 2 11-oz. cans tomatoes
- ☐ 1 14½-oz. can asparagus spears
- ☐ 1 16-oz. can tomatoes
- ☐ 1 16-oz. can potato salad

## Canned Fruit & Juices

- ☐ 2 (6-oz. can) 6-packs of your favorite fruit juices
- ☐ 1 10-oz. bottle of orange juice
- ☐ 1 16-oz. can fruit cocktail

## Canned & Dry Soup Mixes

- ☐ 1 4-oz. jar instant chicken bouillon granules
- ☐ 2 1.6-oz. boxes of your favorite cup-a-soups

## Canned Meat

- ☐ 1 4½-oz. can shrimp
- ☐ 1 6½-oz. can minced clams

## Dry & Packaged Goods

- ☐ 1 14-oz. box instant rice

## Condiments

- ☐ 1 8-oz. jar mayonnaise
- ☐ 1 8-oz. jar Dijon-style mustard
- ☐ 1 5-oz. jar horseradish
- ☐ 1 10-oz. bottle soy sauce
- ☐ 1 2-oz. bottle hot pepper sauce

## Accents

- ☐ 1 jar dill pickles
- ☐ 1 jar pimiento-stuffed green olives
- ☐ 1 pkg. of 6 (1½-oz.) boxes of raisins
- ☐ 1 pkg. chopped cashews
- ☐ 1 pkg. chopped pecans
- ☐ 1 pkg. flaked coconut
- ☐ 1 can french fried onion rings
- ☐ seasoned croutons
- ☐ your favorite salad dressings
- ☐ Bac-O's

## Snacks & Desserts

- ☐ 1 (4½-oz. can) 4-pack of your favorite pudding
- ☐ potato chips

## Cooking Supplies

- ☐ vegetable oil
- ☐ salt & pepper
- ☐ sugar
- ☐ spiced rum

## Beverages

- ☐ coffee
- ☐ tea
- ☐ hot chocolate mix
- ☐ soft drink mix

## Pre-packaged Ingredients

lunch, 1st day
SEAFOOD STEW

- ☐ *1 teaspoon salt*
- ☐ *½ teaspoon oregano*
- ☐ *½ teaspoon basil*
- ☐ *¼ teaspoon paprika*
- ☐ *Dash of cayenne pepper*
- ☐ *Dash of pepper*

dinner, 1st day
PORK in ORANGE SAUCE

- ☐ *1 teaspoon sugar*
- ☐ *2 teaspoons cornstarch*
- ☐ *⅛ teaspoon ginger*

dinner, 2nd day
COUNTRY CAPTAIN

- ☐ *⅛ teaspoon pepper*
- ☐ *½ teaspoon salt*
- ☐ *½ teaspoon thyme*
- ☐ *1 Tablespoon curry powder*
- ☐ *⅓ cup flour*

dinner, 2nd day
SWEET SPICED ASPARAGUS

- ☐ *₆ Tablespoons vegetable oil*
- ☐ *¼ cup sugar*
- ☐ *¼ cup red wine vinegar*
- ☐ *1 garlic clove, minced*
- ☐ *⅛ teaspoon paprika*

# Shopping List for Group #9
## a 3 day meal plan ... pages 129 - 139

## Meats

- ☐ 4 chicken breast halves, boned and skinned
- ☐ 1 16-oz. pkg. hot dogs
- ☐ 1 pound cubed steaks (4 to 6 steaks)
- ☐ 4 pork loin chops, ¾ to 1-inch thick
- ☐ 1 pound hickory stick salami
- ☐ 1 10-oz. pkg. fully cooked link sausage

## Vegetables

- ☐ 3 cucumbers
- ☐ 7 onions
- ☐ 5 tomatoes
- ☐ 4 potatoes
- ☐ 2 green peppers
- ☐ 1 head of garlic
- ☐ 2 heads of lettuce
- ☐ 1 stalk of celery
- ☐ 1 bunch of parsley
- ☐ 1 bunch of green onions
- ☐ 1 bunch of broccoli

## Dairy

- ☐ milk
- ☐ butter
- ☐ 1 dozen eggs
- ☐ 1 4-oz. brick sharp cheddar cheese
- ☐ 1 10-oz. brick Monterey Jack cheese
- ☐ 2 5-oz. jars of your favorite process cheese spreads
- ☐ 1 8-oz. pkg. cream cheese
- ☐ 1 8-oz. container soft cream cheese

## Bakery

- ☐ 4 bagels
- ☐ 1 loaf rye bread
- ☐ 1 loaf white bread

## Fresh Fruit

- ☐ apples
- ☐ bananas
- ☐ cantaloupe
- ☐ grapes
- ☐ lemons
- ☐ limes
- ☐ oranges

## Canned Vegetables & Sauces

- ☐ 1 2-oz. jar sliced pimiento
- ☐ 3 4-oz. cans sliced mushrooms
- ☐ 2 8-oz. cans sweet peas
- ☐ 1 14-oz. can mixed Chinese vegetables
- ☐ 2 16-oz. cans cut green beans
- ☐ 1 14½-oz. can asparagus spears
- ☐ 1 11½-oz. can stewed tomatoes

## Canned Fruit & Juices

- ☐ 2 (6-oz. can) 6-packs of your favorite fruit juices
- ☐ 1 10-oz. bottle orange juice
- ☐ 1 11-oz. can Mandarin orange segments
- ☐ 1 16-oz. can fruit cocktail
- ☐ 1 16-oz. can sliced peaches

## Canned & Dry Soup Mixes

- ☐ 1 4-oz. jar instant chicken bouillon granules
- ☐ 1 10½-oz. can beef consomme
- ☐ 3 1.6-oz. boxes of your favorite cup-a-soups

## Canned Meat

- ☐ 1 6½-oz. can minced clams
- ☐ 1 6¾-oz. can chunk ham
- ☐ 2 6¾-oz. cans chunk chicken
- ☐ 3 6-oz. cans crab meat
- ☐ 3 4½-oz. cans shrimp

## Dry & Packaged Goods

- ☐ 8 ounces large shell macaroni
- ☐ 1 14-oz. box instant rice
- ☐ 1 6-oz. box instant stuffing
- ☐ 2 2-oz. pkgs. instant mash potatoes

## Condiments

- ☐ 1 8-oz. jars mayonnaise
- ☐ 1 8-oz. jar mustard
- ☐ 1 14-oz. bottle catsup
- ☐ 1 10-oz. bottle soy sauce
- ☐ 1 2-oz. bottle hot pepper sauce
- ☐ 1 small bottle pancake syrup

## Accents

- [ ] 1 jar hot or mild pepper rings
- [ ] 1 jar pimiento-stuffed green olives
- [ ] 1 can pitted black olives
- [ ] 1 jar orange marmalade
- [ ] 1 pkg. chopped pecans
- [ ] 1 pkg. chopped almonds
- [ ] 1 pkg. flaked coconut
- [ ] seasoned croutons
- [ ] your favorite salad dressings
- [ ] 1 bottle Italian salad dressing
- [ ] Bac-O's

## Snacks & Desserts

- [ ] 1 (4½-oz. can) 4-pack of your favorite pudding
- [ ] 1 16-oz. can egg custard
- [ ] saltine crackers
- [ ] melba toast

## Cooking Supplies

- [ ] vegetable oil
- [ ] salt & pepper
- [ ] sugar
- [ ] flour
- [ ] cornstarch
- [ ] white vinegar
- [ ] dry white wine
- [ ] rum
- [ ] brandy
- [ ] cointreau
- [ ] cream sherry

## Beverages

- [ ] coffee
- [ ] tea
- [ ] hot chocolate mix
- [ ] soft drink mix

## Pre-packaged Ingredients

breakfast, 1st day
SHRIMP SPREAD

- [ ] ¼ teaspoon garlic powder
- [ ] 2 teaspoons dry mustard
- [ ] 2 teaspoons minced onion

dinner, 1st day
SUNSHINE CHICKEN

- [ ] 2 teaspoons brown sugar
- [ ] ⅛ teaspoon mace

breakfast, 2nd day
NEW ORLEANS POACHED EGGS

- [ ] 3 Tablespoons flour
- [ ] ½ teaspoon salt
- [ ] ¼ teaspoon nutmeg

dinner, 3rd day
MARINATED BROCCOLI

- [ ] ¾ cup cider vinegar
- [ ] ¼ cup vegetable oil
- [ ] 1 Tablespoon sugar
- [ ] 2 Tablespoons water
- [ ] 1½ teaspoons dillseeds
- [ ] ½ teaspoon salt
- [ ] ¼ teaspoon cayenne pepper
- [ ] 1 garlic clove, minced

# Check List
(things you might want to take along)

## Cooking Equipment

☐ Dutch oven
☐ fry pan
☐ skillet
☐ large sauce pan
☐ lids & covers
☐ griddle
☐ electric tea kettle
☐ electric fry pan
☐ electric toaster
☐ knives & cutting board
☐ vegetable peeler
☐ cheese grater
☐ can opener
☐ slotted spoon
☐ wooden spoon utensils
☐ spatula
☐ tongs
☐ pie tins
☐ bowls
☐ measuring tools
☐ apron
☐ hot pads
☐ long nose lighter
☐ plastic zip lock envelopes
(sold in office supply stores)
☐ zip lock plastic storage bags
☐ garbage bags
☐ plastic wrap
☐ aluminum foil

## Tableware

☐ tablecloth
☐ place mats
☐ napkins
☐ plates
☐ soup or salad bowls
☐ eating utensils
☐ cups, mugs or glasses
☐ salt & pepper shakers
☐ tooth picks
☐ silk flowers
☐ candles
☐ matches

## Clean Up Supplies

☐ paper toweling
☐ sponge
☐ scrub pads
☐ dish towels
☐ dish cloth
☐ dish detergent (bio-degradable)
☐ a soft abrasive cleaner
☐ baking soda
☐ large bucket
☐ mesh bag
(to dip utensils in boiling water,
not to drag behind the boat)

## Head Supplies

☐ hand towels
☐ wash cloth
☐ bar of soap
☐ toilet paper
☐ tissues
☐ spray air deodorant
☐ head chemicals

## Necessities & Niceties

☐ fan
☐ pump thermos
☐ beverage jug
☐ metal grills
☐ back pack
☐ first aid kit
☐ sun screen & lotion
☐ aspirin
☐ reading material
☐ note book
☐ pencils & pens
☐ playing cards
☐ board games
☐ music
☐ camera & film
☐ TV & VCR
☐ blender
☐ microwave
☐ food processor

# Things to do and Don't Forget!!!

# Ahoy Mates

I'd like to welcome you aboard for what I hope you'll find to be an enjoyable adventure in cooking whether you're on your boat, camping, cruising the highways in your RV, or simply enjoying some good home cooking.

If at any time you have any questions about anything in this book, feel free to give me a call. If you have any questions about cooking, feel free to give me a call. If you have any comments, notice any mistakes, or have any criticism about the book, feel free to call me. If you just need someone to talk to, feel free to call me. But if you need additional copies of the book, the call is free but the book will cost you a few bucks. But I will autograph them for you. (they make nice presents)

Thank you for buying my book and helping me pay my bar bills. I hope this book brings you many years of good eating.

**1-800-8-GALLEY**
(1-800-842-5539)

# EXTRA BONUS !!!

Since you have read or are about to read all about me and my wacky friends, how about telling me a little bit about you. I'm not asking you to spill your guts and tell me about all the stupid stuff you have done or all about your goofy friends, I just want to know who and where you are, so we can keep in touch. I've got a few more books to write and I thought you might want to know when their published.

If you give me a call or drop me a line, I'll be glade to send you a FREE packet of spices for one of my most favorite barbecue recipes.

**the Two Burner Gourmet**
**1800 Wilson Avenue**
**Saginaw, MI   48603**
**1-800-8-GALLEY**
(1-800-842-5539)